Equality at work:
Tackling the challenges

REPORT OF THE DIRECTOR-GENERAL

Equality at work: Tackling the challenges

Global Report under the follow-up to the ILO Declaration
on Fundamental Principles and Rights at Work

INTERNATIONAL LABOUR CONFERENCE
96th Session 2007

Report I (B)

INTERNATIONAL LABOUR OFFICE   GENEVA

This Report may also be consulted on the ILO web site (www.ilo.org/declaration).

ISBN 978-92-2-118130-9
ISSN 0074-6681

First published 2007

Photocomposed in Switzerland
Printed in Switzerland

WEI
SRO

Contents

Executive summary

The second Global Report on discrimination under the follow-up to the ILO Declaration on Fundamental Principles and Rights at Work[1] examines emerging issues in patterns of workplace discrimination and inequalities and recent policy responses, and outlines the ILO's experience and achievements to date and the challenges it faces.

It points to the need for better enforcement of legislation against discrimination, as well as non-regulatory initiatives by governments and enterprises, and equipping the social partners to be more effective in making equality a reality at the workplace. The Report puts forward other proposals for future action, including making equality a mainstream objective of the ILO's Decent Work Country Programmes.

The Global Report describes major advances in the struggle against discrimination, including progress in ratification of related ILO Conventions, as well as improvements on the national legal and institutional fronts, and action plans and programmes to combat inequalities stemming from discrimination. It also identifies challenges such as weak law enforcement, lack of resources among bodies set up to fight discrimination, plans that are too narrow in scope and programmes too short in duration, and the informal economy as one area where equality-enhancing policies face particular difficulties in making an impact.

New approaches

One approach recommended by the Report in achieving equality at the workplace is to complement conventional anti-discrimination policy measures, such as coherent and comprehensive laws, effective enforcement mechanisms and specialized bodies, with other policy instruments, such as active labour market policies. While improving the functioning of labour markets, these can counter discrimination with comprehensive policies that enhance the job placement function in both the public and private employment services, and increase the employability of those who are vulnerable to discrimination.

New policies are also required to close the gender gap in employment and pay. Despite advances, in particular the considerable progress in women's educational attainments, women continue to earn less than men everywhere, and the unequal burden of family responsibilities places them at a disadvantage in finding full-time employment.

The Report underscores the fact that further inclusion of fundamental principles and rights in regional economic integration and free trade agreements can play a major role in reducing discrimination at work. Where the parties to such agreements make commitments on non-discrimination and equality issues, attention needs to be paid to effective follow-up mechanisms. Development finance institutions have in recent years begun to require their private borrowers to respect the principles and rights laid down in the fundamental international labour standards. This will lead to the obligation for employers to institute equality-enhancing labour practices at the workplace.

The need for better data

National political commitment to combat discrimination and promote equal treatment and opportunities at the workplace is widespread, as shown by the almost universal ratification of the two main ILO instruments in this area, the Equal Remuneration

---

1. The first Global Report on this subject, *Time for equality at work*, was published in 2003.

Convention, 1951 (No. 100), and the Discrimination (Employment and Occupation) Convention, 1958 (No. 111). Only a handful of member States have yet to ratify these Conventions.

However, discrimination is an insidious and shifting phenomenon that can be difficult to quantify and therefore to address meaningfully. No single indicator can capture progress in its elimination, although the available data clearly show that the gaps between those in the mainstream and groups vulnerable to discrimination are significant and slow to narrow. Privacy protection considerations and ideological and political barriers often prevent the collection of data on certain groups. In addition, many countries do not seek to quantify the gaps in equality for fear of exacerbating tensions. This raises the important question of how to reconcile the protection of personal data and an individual's right to privacy with the need to monitor discrimination through statistical means. Some progress has been made, however, in the quality of data on gender inequalities, although further efforts are required in regard to certain key indicators, such as the gender pay gap.

New forms of discrimination

The problem of data collection is exacerbated by the fact that newer forms of discrimination are being added to long-recognized patterns such as those based on sex, race and religion. There is increasing awareness of unfair treatment of both young and older persons, people with disabilities and those with HIV/AIDS. An additional challenge is the emergence of practices that penalize those with a genetic predisposition to developing certain diseases or who have lifestyles that are considered unhealthy. Virtually every lifestyle choice has some health-related consequence; the question therefore is where to draw the line between what an employer can regulate and the freedom of an employee to lead the life of his or her choice.

Trends in institutional and policy responses

Since the publication of the first Global Report on the subject, there has been a worldwide trend towards ensuring that the four sets of ILO fundamental principles and rights at work are covered by labour law. In addition to greater acceptance of the need for specific legal provisions on non-discrimination and equality

at the workplace, national governmental and non-governmental specialized bodies have been set up or restructured to assist individuals in taking legal action, promote reform and design and oversee national anti-discrimination action plans. These bodies reflect a broader focus on equal treatment and opportunities at work. One example is the National Council for the Prevention of Discrimination set up in Mexico in 2003, which launched the first national public policy to combat discrimination in 2006.

In Europe, the racial equality Directive[2] requires European Union (EU) Member States to designate a national body responsible for combating discrimination. To date, 19 countries have changed their institutions either by extending the mandate of existing bodies or by creating new ones. In Latin America, the elimination of racial and ethnic inequalities features prominently on the public agendas of several countries, including Brazil, where a Special Secretariat for Policies to Promote Racial Equality has been set up, with ministerial rank.

Making laws work

In many countries, victims of employment discrimination cannot always bring their case to court, for reasons often related to their disadvantaged social position, lack of access to legal assistance, fear of reprisal or distrust of the judicial system.

One example of how the courts can be made more accessible is the Roma Anti-Discrimination Customer Service Network in Hungary, a joint initiative by several ministries, which helps complainants in eliminating discrimination and obtaining reinstatement.

Keenly aware of difficulties faced by victims in speaking out and obtaining redress in the courts, the ILO has provided training for judges and lawyers on international labour standards through courses organized by the International Training Centre of the ILO in Turin, and these have shown positive results.

The potential for labour inspection to deal with issues of discrimination is often underutilized. Labour inspection services can monitor and enforce legal compliance, obviating the need for victims to take legal action through the courts or even to give evidence. They also have power to inspect workplaces and determine whether discrimination has occurred without it having necessarily been reported. Examples in several countries show that governments are assigning greater importance and committing more

---

2. Council Directive 2000/43/EC of 29 June 2000 implementing the principle of equal treatment between persons irrespective of racial or ethnic origin.

funds to the enforcement and advisory services provided by labour inspectors. In Brazil, a programme instituted with ILO assistance, entitled "Brazil, Gender and Race – United for Equal Opportunities", in cooperation with the units for promoting equal opportunities and fighting discrimination in employment and occupation, has provided awareness-raising and mediation services. This led to the setting up, in 2006, of a Special Advisory Unit on discrimination and equality in the Brazilian Ministry of Labour. In the Czech Republic, the Ministry of Labour and Social Affairs issued an instruction to labour inspectors in 2003 regarding equal opportunities for women and men, providing concrete guidance on how to carry out gender equality inspections. Several other countries, including Belgium, Cyprus and Poland, have placed greater stress on the importance of labour inspection in resolving discrimination issues.

However, more effort is required in collecting and assessing information on the number, nature and outcomes of cases involving discrimination in order to provide an indicator for the practical effect and impact of anti-discrimination legislation.

Changing labour demand

Affirmative action measures that are integrated in human resource policies can help employers create more inclusive workplaces. The Global Report provides information on programmes in Canada, India, Malaysia, Namibia, South Africa, the United Kingdom and the United States, which have adopted laws aimed at eliminating or compensating employment discrimination through the introduction of numerical targets or quotas to be met within given timeframes. Results show that where employers' commitment has been high and law enforcement effective, affirmative action has improved the representation of groups affected by discrimination, even though impact has varied depending on the group and the terms of the legislation itself. To have an impact, however, affirmative action must be accompanied by investment in quality education for disadvantaged groups.

Procurement policy – does it work against discrimination?

Public procurement policies embodying racial or sex equality clauses are increasingly viewed as an effective tool to combat discrimination. The scale and economic importance of public tenders provide considerable potential for eliminating discrimination. In South Africa, for instance, the State and state-owned enterprises spent over US$123 billion in 2004 on purchasing goods and services. However, the question still remains as to the conditions under which they can help to create more diverse workforces, while ensuring quality standards and achieving "value for money".

The Global Report presents examples of promoting racial equality through public procurement policies in Europe, South Africa and the United States, illustrating the significant potential of such measures. However, certain conditions have to be met, the most important of which is political commitment. Rules must be clear and transparent; information on how to link procurement and equality must be widely distributed; and know-how must be disseminated. The long-term financial benefits to business must also be seen to be worth the effort involved in achieving equality goals.

Active labour market policies

Active labour market policies comprise many measures: job search, recruitment and placement; training; hiring subsidies; job-creation programmes; and various support services. They are used in many countries in different ways and with varying results. They can clearly offer significant opportunities for narrowing inequalities. However, evidence shows that members of discriminated groups often fail to achieve success in job placement and training schemes. The Report reviews experience to date in mainstreaming gender and promoting gender equality within the European Employment Strategy (EES), a unique instrument that requires EU Member States to develop annual National Action Plans on employment based on common agreed targets.

Examples of job placement services for disadvantaged groups in Peru and Spain, among others, are provided to illustrate how private and public employment agencies can have a positive impact on employment opportunities. The Report also describes employment and training programmes to develop employability, run by both public and private services in Brazil, Cambodia, India and Peru.

Policies to close the gender gap

Opportunities for women in employment have increased, and they have taken up careers once considered the exclusive prerogative of men. Despite this, and despite advances in women's educational achievements, their earnings are still on average less than men's. It is also difficult for women to reconcile family duties with paid work without affecting their chances of promotion or skill enhancement. However, even where they manage to overcome these obstacles, they earn less than men.

One method of establishing pay equity is through job evaluation methods that are free from gender bias. A number of methods have been developed in recent years in countries such as Spain, Sweden and Switzerland. Pay equity commissions also play a major role, particularly for small and medium-sized enterprises, in Portugal, Sweden and the United Kingdom.

However, job evaluation does not always correct pay gaps, as countries have different understandings of pay equity and different models to promote it. The complexities of analytical job evaluation remain a challenge for many, and although a number of recent laws and regulations have begun to refer to "identical" work, they do not include the notion of "work of equal value". Nevertheless, some countries, such as Lebanon, Mauritius and Nigeria, have sought ILO assistance in this area.

Encouraging results have been recorded by the global union federation Public Services International (PSI), which has run a campaign to show that pay equity programmes contribute to broader goals such as poverty reduction, social inclusion and increased quality of public services.

Workplace family policies are required for both men and women in order to help overcome the problems of workers with family responsibilities in better balancing work–family issues in a world of longer working hours and work patterns that disadvantage women and affect their careers. This Report shows that the fertility rate improved where better childcare availability and easier access to part-time work were introduced.

The growth of part-time work has been significant in the past ten years and resulted in greater female participation and employment rates. However, opportunities for women are often concentrated in low-status jobs. One exception is the Netherlands, which, through greater labour market regulation, has managed to introduce part-time work throughout all sectors and occupations to achieve a more even distribution of part-time work between women and men.

Childcare arrangements, especially for children under three years old, are still limited and have not been a priority in many parts of the world. There is a special need for childcare in the informal sector and, in this respect, initiatives in India and South Africa have shown positive results.

At the same time, there has been significant change in policies encouraging fathers to take care-related leave. Both developed and developing countries around the world have made it easier for men to take parental leave, although take-up rates are still low in most countries.

Anti-discrimination lending policies

In recent years, development finance institutions have begun to examine the environmental and social impact of their lending, including respect of international labour standards in employment. The International Finance Corporation (IFC) has adopted Performance Standards under which it undertakes to abide by commitments based on ILO core labour standards, as well as standards on safety and health and retrenchment, in its lending policies. These Performance Standards were developed in consultation with a broad range of actors, including the ILO and the International Confederation of Free Trade Unions (ICFTU). More than 40 national development banks (the "Equator Banks"), representing about 85 per cent of global lending for development projects, have committed themselves to applying the IFC Performance Standards to projects with a budget of at least US$10 million. The IFC has also issued a Good Practice Note on non-discrimination and equal opportunity. In June 2006, the Inter-American Development Bank issued even more comprehensive requirements for applying international labour standards to infrastructure projects, while the European Investment Bank adopted a similar standard. The Asian Development Bank published a *Core Labour Standards Handbook* in 2006, developed in close cooperation with the ILO. The President of the World Bank has expressed his willingness to ensure that all World Bank-financed infrastructure projects respect ILO core labour standards.

Regional economic integration and free trade agreements – a mixed picture

Free trade agreements have proliferated in recent years; however, they vary in their approach to discrimination. While several refer explicitly to non-discrimination and equal pay, others do not, although they include non-discrimination and equality as subjects for technical cooperation. Other agreements fail to address workplace discrimination altogether; this is the case of the economic partnership agreements (EPA) being negotiated between the EU and 77 African, Caribbean and Pacific countries, due to come into force in 2008.

Some analysts consider that non-discrimination and equality are treated as a secondary right as regards enforcement in the North American Agreement on Labor Cooperation (NAALC) and the Canada-Chile Agreement on Labor Cooperation (CCALC). Differing national legal contexts lead to discrepancies in the way discrimination is addressed across regions, as evidenced by the treatment of gender issues under the North American Free Trade Agreement (NAFTA) and the Southern Common Market (MERCOSUR). In the case of NAFTA, women's groups in the United States and Mexico appeared largely uninterested in shaping the Agreement, and this is reflected in the lack of substantive provisions. In the case of MERCOSUR, the women's rights agenda was not firmly established, although tripartite national commissions operating under the agreement are evaluating their capacity to mainstream gender through national labour ministries.

One example of a positive impact on discrimination under the NAALC involved Mexican and US non-governmental organizations (NGOs) introducing a complaint about mandatory pregnancy testing and resulting dismissal, which led to the Mexican Government discontinuing the practice for public sector employees.

Some benefits have also been gained through capacity building under these regional agreements.

The social partners on the move

Workers' and employers' organizations have developed initiatives to eliminate discrimination at the workplace, as well as making equality a focal point of collective bargaining.

Private and public sector employers in New Zealand, for instance, have launched a joint initiative, the Equal Employment Opportunities Trust, since 1992 and, together with the Recruitment and Consulting Services Association, have developed a publication targeting recruitment agencies and aimed at removing discriminatory practices. The Employers' Forum on Disability in the United Kingdom issued the Disability Standard 2005 and 2007, a benchmarking tool that assesses the performance of employers and service providers in respect of disability. Employers in Kenya and Sri Lanka have developed policies on equality and sexual harassment, while the Employers Confederation of the Philippines launched several initiatives on good practices, designed to persuade member organizations of the benefits to be gained from the adoption of work–family reconciliation measures. The International Organisation of Employers has published a guide that identifies the barriers faced by women entrepreneurs and demonstrates how employers' organizations can provide better support and representation.

Within trade unions, a tendency for increased female membership is apparent in some countries and sectors. To capitalize on these gains, unions will need to address the specific circumstances of women workers, such as the gender bias in wages. The five-year campaign (2002–07) launched by PSI has shown that pay equity can be an effective organizing strategy for female workers and a positive development for a union as a whole.

A significant development in 2006 was the affiliation to the ICFTU of the Self Employed Women's Association (SEWA), now a founder member of the new International Trade Union Confederation (ITUC). The participation of ethnic and racial minorities has made great strides in the United Kingdom and the United States, while in France, trade unions have been working to raise the representation of ethnic minorities in their structure in order to improve their position at the workplace.

In the field of collective bargaining, trade unions, especially in the industrialized countries, are putting work–family reconciliation high on their agenda, partly as a way of increasing membership. In some countries, collective bargaining has achieved benefits beyond what is required by law, especially in regard to work–family reconciliation measures. However, issues such as family care provisions are still absent from collective agreements in other countries, including new EU Member States. Incorporation of pay equity in collective agreements is another trend in industrialized nations. France, for instance, has set 2010 as the target date for eliminating the remuneration gap between women and men through collective agreements.

The Global Report also demonstrates that enterprises can adapt their human resource management practices and policies through non-regulatory measures, ranging from government purchasing policies to corporate social responsibility (CSR) initiatives. Increased interest in CSR programmes can be viewed as a response to the challenges posed by an emerging global labour market. These programmes are a voluntary means of affirming principles and have helped raise awareness of the importance of non-discrimination. A World Bank review of some 100 multinational enterprises, published in 2003–04, showed that some form of non-discriminatory clause or equality guarantee had been incorporated in four out of the five industrial and service sector codes examined.

The ILO intends to document promising practices, produce policy briefs and set up knowledge sharing forums at national and regional levels in order to achieve non-discrimination and equality goals.

ILO achievements

The Global Report details progress made by a series of ILO interventions under the follow-up action plan regarding the elimination of discrimination in employment and occupation for the years 2004–07.

The plan focused on two priorities: the gender pay gap and racial/ethnic equality and its gender dimension, while consolidating ongoing activity regarding HIV/AIDS and disability. Technical cooperation was extended to several countries for the design of employment policies and job evaluation methods, for example. The Report is rich in examples of ILO cooperation work throughout the world. The Gender Equality Partnership Fund, launched in 2003, has been a further means to give practical effect to gender equality at work. The ILO is committed to strengthening legislative provisions and has assisted a very wide range of countries in this respect both in the North and in the South. In the area of gender mainstreaming, the Gender Network in the Office connects focal points and facilitates the sharing of experience and practices. Between 2001 and 2005, gender audits were carried out in 25 headquarters units and field offices of the ILO – a first for the UN system.

The Global Report notes that "equal pay for work of equal value" is one of the least understood concepts in the field of action against discrimination: it is often given a narrow interpretation in laws and regulations, and the lack of reliable sex-disaggregated data on wages makes it difficult to monitor trends. The action plan therefore focused on generating knowledge on the costs and benefits of promoting pay equity; the trends in the gender pay gap and underlying causes; networking and cooperating with global union federations; and providing technical assistance at country level. Country fact sheets covering Africa, Europe and Latin America were prepared to provide an overview of: trends in the gender pay gap over the previous 15 years by sector and occupation; relevant national institutional and regulatory frameworks; and related comments by the Committee of Experts on the Application of Conventions and Recommendations over the previous 15 years. Similar work has also begun in East Asia. A paper assessing the costs and benefits of pay equity partly makes up for the lack of studies that have addressed the subject.

As employment policies and programmes are often gender-blind, the ILO has sought to provide advice to ministries of labour in the design and implementation of national employment policies. An example is the Belgian-funded project entitled "Promoting Equal Opportunities for Women and Men in the Country Employment Reviews of the Stability Pact Countries". The ILO has also provided assistance to Bolivia, Colombia, Ecuador and Peru on improving the way employment policies address gender discrimination.

Technical assistance has been offered to governments in their efforts to promote racial equality, for example to Brazil under the National Policy for Racial Equality Project. An ethnic audit of Poverty Reduction Strategy Papers (PRSPs) in 14 countries concluded that recognition of the rights of indigenous and tribal peoples, as articulated in the ILO Indigenous and Tribal Peoples Convention, 1989 (No. 169), was an essential requirement for addressing their poverty and social exclusion, and recommended capacity building for indigenous organizations and local authorities for the implementation of inclusive local development plans.

Ongoing ILO commitments

The action plan recognized the need to consolidate traditional ILO action such as supervising the application of Conventions. Guidelines were produced on how to promote equal employment opportunities for people with disabilities through legislation, and impact studies carried out in selected countries shed light on the variety of forms and objectives of non-discrimination law. In Bosnia and Herzegovina, for example, following discussion at the Conference Committee on the Application of Standards in 2005 of the country's failure to provide reports on ratified Conventions, the ILO assisted in the formulation in 2006 of a strategy outlining the priorities of the public authorities and the social partners for the effective implementation of the Gender Equality Law. A project was launched in Mauritius to develop measures to redress gender inequalities within the framework of the National Gender Policy and National Gender Action Plan.

One indicator to measure the effectiveness of law is the number of discrimination cases brought before the courts and adequately handled, and the training of judges and lawyers is essential in this respect. The International Training Centre of the ILO in Turin (the Turin Centre) has played an active role in the training of judges, lawyers and law professors on international labour law. As a result, long-term cooperation is now in place with judicial training centres and universities in Albania, Argentina, Brazil, Madagascar, Morocco and Senegal. The Turin Centre has also assisted the European Commission in placing gender equality at the heart of its aid delivery agenda.

In March 2005, the Governing Body of the International Labour Office adopted a decision requiring all ILO technical cooperation projects to give due consideration to gender equality. Framework agreements have been signed with six donor countries in this respect, some even setting aside contributions to the Gender Equality Partnership Fund launched in 2003 to enhance the capacity of constituents to take positive steps to promote equal opportunities. Under the auspices of the Fund, 13 projects are under way in 25 countries. Since 2006, a key criterion in the screening of new technical cooperation proposals is the inclusion of a strategy to mainstream gender equality.

The Global Report provides details on the technical support given to government or employer-led initiatives aimed at developing equal employment opportunity policies at the enterprise level in Chile, Cambodia, Indonesia and Sri Lanka. "Better Factories Cambodia", a unique ILO programme, is an example of how tripartism, together with an integrated strategy, can improve working conditions in global production systems.

The ILO code of practice on HIV/AIDS and the world of work now provides guidance in around 40 countries and is used as a reference tool by policy-makers and the social partners in over 60 countries. The ILO programme "Strategic HIV/AIDS Responses by Enterprises" (SHARE) has reached out to 300,000 formal and informal workers in 23 countries and has been instrumental in the adoption of enabling legislative frameworks. Since 2000, over 2,500 people, including representatives of trade unions and employers' organizations, labour inspectors, judges and NGOs, have been trained under the SHARE programme.

Using the ILO code of practice on managing disability at the workplace, "AbilityAP", the ILO's disability programme in Asia and the Pacific, has created a comprehensive database on laws and policies and provided advice on policies and programmes. Action in Africa has aimed at enhancing disabled workers' skills and developing entrepreneurship among women with disabilities.

The ILO Multilateral Framework on Labour Migration, adopted in 2005, places special emphasis on the discrimination faced by migrants and calls for promotion of their rights. The ILO has created a database of 150 good practices on the integration of migrant workers and in 2004 launched a programme to strengthen the capacity of African States in the management of labour migration.

Decent Work Country Programmes (DWCPs) are the main means for the ILO to assist Members in their efforts to make decent work a national reality. Recent developments include the launching of the Asian Decent Work Decade and the Decade for Promoting Decent Work in the Americas in 2006. Specific commitments and targets have been set in both regions to curb decent work gaps between mainstream groups and groups vulnerable to discrimination.

Future focus

ILO follow-up action under the second Global Report on discrimination will draw on experience gained in the four years since the first Report and will be aligned with the Organization's strategic planning, in particular the DWCPs, as the main framework for work at the national level. This means that the forms of discrimination warranting priority focus will be determined on a case-by-case basis in response to the needs and demands of constituents and the comments of the ILO's supervisory bodies. In all cases, however, gender equality will be a universal strategic goal, to be pursued with determination. The approach to gender equality has been gradually shifting towards mainstreaming a gender perspective in ILO technical cooperation and policy areas.

In order to ensure better enforcement of equality legislation, the ILO will produce and widely disseminate materials on the legal requirements of Convention Nos. 100 and 111, as well as other relevant Conventions. The importance of strong and effective labour inspection and labour administration will be promoted and national and international networking encouraged, in order to improve the professional competence and experience of labour inspectors.

The promotion of non-regulatory measures will also be a focus of ILO advocacy with governments and business to influence policies and practices in investment and trade, as well as CSR initiatives or codes of conduct that refer to fundamental principles and rights at work.

The critical role of the social partners will be highlighted in key areas such as collective bargaining to bring about concrete change in the working lives of those subject to discrimination. Information will be compiled under the action plan on the experiences of employers' and workers' organizations in this field in order to provide model codes of conduct or guidelines for promoting equal treatment and opportunities for all. Through these different actions, the ILO will continue to address the challenges of discrimination in the world of work.

Introduction

1. Four years ago the first Global Report on discrimination, *Time for equality at work*, stressed that the workplace – be it a factory, an office, a farm or the street – was a strategic entry point to free society from discrimination.[1] Like any other social institutions, the labour market and its institutions are both a cause of and a solution to discrimination. In the workplace, however, discrimination can be tackled more readily and effectively. *Time for equality at work* also highlighted the high economic, social and political costs of tolerating discrimination at work, and argued that the benefits stemming from more inclusive workplaces surpassed the cost of dealing with discrimination.

2. Four years later these same messages remain valid, but the need to combat discrimination at work is even more urgent in the face of a world that appears increasingly unequal, insecure and unsafe. Discrimination bars people from some occupations, denies them a job altogether or does not reward them according to their merit because of the colour of their skin or their sex or social background. This generates social and economic disadvantages that, in turn, lead into inefficiency and unequal outcomes. At the same time, significant and persistent inequalities in income, assets and opportunities dilute the effectiveness of any action aimed at combating discrimination. This may lead to political instability and social upheaval, which upset investment and economic growth.

3. The global picture of the struggle to overcome discrimination shows a mixture of major advances and failures. The condemnation of discrimination in employment and occupation is today almost universal, as is the political commitment to tackle it. Nine out of ten ILO member States have ratified the Equal Remuneration Convention, 1951 (No. 100), and the Discrimination (Employment and Occupation) Convention, 1958 (No. 111), the two fundamental international labour standards on the subject (Part I, Chapter 1). With the ratification of Convention No. 111 by China in 2006, the number of people covered worldwide by this Convention has expanded considerably.

4. Progress on the legal and institutional fronts in many countries has also been remarkable. Non-discrimination and equality provisions feature in labour codes that have recently been reformed; many countries, especially in sub-Saharan Africa, have adopted laws protecting workers living with HIV/AIDS from discrimination; and sexual harassment is prohibited in many jurisdictions. Countries have expanded the number of grounds on which discrimination is forbidden beyond those explicitly mentioned in Convention No. 111. These include, among others, the European Union (EU) Member States that in the past few years have transposed the 2000 Directives regulating discrimination in employment throughout the EU,[2] thus making unlawful discrimination based on race, religion or belief, age, disability or sexual orientation.

5. Although this trend has been more marked in some regions than others, overall there has been a tendency towards greater institutional commitment to

---

1. ILO: *Time for equality at work*, Global Report under the follow-up to the ILO Declaration on Fundamental Principles and Rights at Work, Report I(B), International Labour Conference, 91st Session, Geneva, 2003, para. 11.
2. Council Directive 2000/43/EC of 29 June 2000 implementing the principle of equal treatment between persons irrespective of racial or ethnic origin, which requires all Member States to designate a body to promote racial or ethnic equality; and Council Directive 2000/78/EC of 27 November 2000 establishing a general framework for equal treatment in employment and occupation, which is aimed at prohibiting discrimination based on religion or belief, age, disability or sexual orientation.

non-discrimination and equality. Specialized bodies or commissions responsible for providing legal assistance to victims of discrimination or supplying information and guidance to employers on how to make their wage systems more transparent and gender neutral have been set up or restructured in the past four years. For example, in Brazil, where 46 per cent of the population is black, a Special Secretariat for Policies to Promote Racial Equality (SEPPIR), with ministerial rank, was established for the first time in 2003.

6. There has been no shortage of action plans, special programmes or active labour market policies aimed at enhancing the status and employment prospects of groups vulnerable to discrimination. These range from low-income women or mothers of small children to people with disabilities and older workers. Tripartite commissions, such as the Tripartite Commission on Gender and Racial Equality at Work in Brazil, have been established to draw up employment policies aimed at eliminating the decent work deficits affecting particular segments of the population. Collective agreements granting fathers family-related leave have been signed in a growing number of countries in Europe and Latin America, thus encouraging a more equitable share of paid and unpaid work between men and women.

7. These are all encouraging developments, but many shortcomings persist. Enforcement is often weak, especially but not only in developing and transition economies, as illustrated by the relatively small number of discrimination complaints and even fewer convictions in many countries. Specialized bodies or commissions operate under serious staffing and resource constraints. Action plans and special programmes have often been narrow in scope, not sustained over time, and subject to political changes. Millions of workers in the informal economy, where social norms maintain social barriers and divisions,[3] do not benefit from equality-enhancing policies that are usually designed for formal workplaces and employees. Set against these constraints, the new measures do not appear to have yielded a net reduction in discrimination.

8. If we are to move forward it is essential to understand the reasons why the achievement of equality is so challenging.

9. First, discrimination is entrenched both in human nature and in the way institutions operate. It has always been a part of the community everywhere and at all times. This makes it more difficult to challenge it until the situation becomes unmanageable.

10. Second, discrimination is an evolving phenomenon: long-recognized forms of discrimination, such as racial, religious, class or sex discrimination, do not easily die out; they may acquire more subtle manifestations or may even be legitimized with more sophisticated arguments. For instance, terrorism and security policies since 11 September 2001 have contributed to reinforcing suspicion in regard to Muslim and Arab people, raising serious issues of discrimination in the workplace. Expressions of hostility and racism towards actual or perceived foreign workers are common in both industrialized and developing regions. These sentiments are rooted in feelings of anxiety and insecurity in the host countries, which have been exacerbated by the profound socio-economic changes brought about by globalization. Earlier justifications of racism in terms of the alleged superiority of one culture over another are now joined by arguments based on the need to preserve national identities and cultures from values and institutions of a different culture. Meanwhile, new forms of discrimination are emerging as a result of both structural economic changes and societal and cultural transformations. A person's age or perceived lifestyle may become a serious disadvantage at work, especially in industrialized countries.

11. Third, while there is consensus that discrimination is both wrong and inefficient, opinions diverge about how to eliminate it and about what promoting equal opportunities means in practice. The ongoing heated debate on the desirability, legitimacy and effectiveness of affirmative action in favour of underrepresented groups is indicative of these divergent views.

12. Fourth, the eradication of discrimination is felt to be too costly and its benefits hard to measure, with the costs perceived as outweighing potential benefits, especially in the short and medium term. This explains why, often in periods of economic recession or stagnation, policies that increase equality face backlash, lose legitimacy and may be discontinued.

13. Lastly, trade and financial liberalization, and tight monetary and fiscal policies that were meant to create a more level playing field for healthy market competition, have not always resulted in more equal social outcomes or greater solidarity among individuals and groups of workers. At the same time, the global spread of democracy and the growing power of the media have helped disadvantaged groups to have their voices heard, thus generating strong pressures for more effective mechanisms of social solidarity.

---

3. B. Harriss-White: "Inequality at work in the informal economy: Key issues and illustrations", in *International Labour Review*, Vol. 142 (2003), No. 4, pp. 459–469.

14. Why then is the lower level of achievement of certain social groups perceived as reflecting only their lack of abilities and not the result of denied opportunities due to systemic past and present discrimination? While it is undisputable that discrimination, and the inequalities it entrenches, are a structural problem for which quick fixes do not work, robust evidence shows that the economic, social and political costs of tolerating discrimination are high.[4]

15. This Report builds on the first Global Report on the elimination of discrimination in employment and occupation under the follow-up to the ILO Declaration on Fundamental Principles and Rights at Work.[5] Its main message is that, to effectively continue to tackle discrimination at work, the creation of more equal societies must become a central goal of development paradigms and policies, and the promotion of equal opportunities for decent work for all women and men, irrespective of race, religion, disability, age or sexual orientation, one of the means to advance in this direction. The endorsement of decent work as a global goal by the high-level segment of the United Nations Economic and Social Council in July 2006, and the adoption, six months later, by the Council of the European Union of a set of conclusions on the promotion of decent work in the EU and the world[6] provide new support to efforts aimed at making equality at work a global reality.

16. This second Global Report on discrimination is divided into four parts. Part I briefly defines the concepts of discrimination and equality of treatment and opportunities and discusses the advances and challenges in measuring discrimination and assessing progress in the promotion of equality in the world of work on a global scale.

17. Part II describes patterns of discrimination in employment and occupation worldwide, building upon the first Global Report on the subject. This part assesses the global situation in respect of the more traditional forms of discrimination, especially on grounds of sex or race, which the first Global Report on discrimination had identified as priority areas for ILO action in the period 2004–07. It then reviews recent trends in respect of forms of discrimination already examined by the earlier Global Report, but recognized in more recent times as intolerable, namely discrimination based on disability, perceived or actual HIV/AIDS status or age. The novelty of this Global Report lies in its review of discrimination based on sexual orientation, of increasing concern in a growing,

though still limited, number of countries. Another new element is the examination of emerging practices in advanced economies that appear to penalize individuals with a genetic predisposition to particular diseases or who pursue a certain lifestyle. All these trends warrant careful monitoring.

18. Part III gives an overview of the scope and impact of laws, policies and practical action by a range of actors – the State, the social partners and other relevant institutions – to combat discrimination and promote equality at the national, international and global levels. The national initiatives covered concern mainly high-income and middle-income countries, owing to the larger number of anti-discrimination measures and availability of related data in those countries. This allows a better grasp of the actual effects of national action, and yields some useful conclusions to assist future policy-making, but it also mirrors the low profile of discrimination at work in the public agendas of low-income countries, suggesting that these matters either are difficult to address or are not considered as warranting priority attention. On the other hand, the international and global review points to increasing references in corporate social responsibility (CSR) instruments to non-discrimination and equality matters, as well as the implications of regional economic integration processes and trade negotiations for the advancement of an equality agenda.

19. Part IV reviews the ILO's assistance to member States for the elimination of discrimination and the promotion of equal opportunities. This yields a picture of both achievements and challenges. The ILO has continued to provide assistance in drafting or revising legislation on equality and in mainstreaming non-discrimination and equality concerns into labour code reforms. Through its supervisory machinery, it has highlighted both traditional and new problems, while encouraging positive developments. Action geared towards guaranteeing equal opportunities for people with disabilities or people living with actual or perceived HIV/AIDS has continued apace, as has work focusing on certain aspects of gender equality. There have been some efforts, though not on a consistent basis, to mainstream non-discrimination and equality concerns in Decent Work Country Programmes (DWCPs) as well as in employment-driven Poverty Reduction Strategies (PRSs) and programmes. Progress has also been slow on pay equity issues and on the fight against

---

4. World Bank: *World Development Report 2006: Equity and development* (Washington DC, 2005).
5. ILO: *Time for equality at work*, op. cit.
6. Council of the European Union: Council Conclusions on decent work for all, at www.consilium.europa.eu.

racial discrimination, two areas in which the earlier Global Report had identified important needs and gaps. This is perhaps not surprising, given the persistence of these problems worldwide as shown by the global picture, but it raises important questions about the way forward.

20.   Part IV discusses these and other matters and puts forward proposals for the future. It advocates mainstreaming equal opportunities at work in the next stages of ILO's Decent Work Agenda, namely the DWCPs and the quest for policy coherence at the global level.

21.   While the elimination of discrimination and the promotion of equality is a constant challenge requiring renewed political and policy commitment, it is nonetheless a goal towards which the ILO and its constituents and international partners can progress if there is a sustained effort by all the parties involved.

PART I

Defining and measuring discrimination

22. There is consensus that discrimination at work is a violation of a human right that entails a waste of human talents, with detrimental effects on productivity and economic growth, and generates socio-economic inequalities that undermine social cohesion and solidarity and act as a brake on the reduction of poverty. There is also agreement that promoting equality of opportunity and equality of treatment is necessary in order to move towards the elimination of discrimination in law and in practice.[1]

23. Political commitment to combating discrimination and promoting equal treatment and opportunities at the workplace is almost universal. This is reflected in the high and steadily increasing number of ratifications of the Equal Remuneration Convention, 1951 (No. 100), and the Discrimination (Employment and Occupation) Convention, 1958 (No. 111), in the past years (figure 1.1 and table 1.1).

24. Against this background the main question is to assess progress in making equality a reality for everyone, and in distilling lessons to guide future action by the State, the social partners and other relevant actors. This part of the Global Report briefly defines the concepts of discrimination and equality of treatment and opportunities in employment and occupation. This is necessary given the misunderstandings and lack of clarity that often surround these notions.

---

1. See ILO: *Time for equality at work*, Global Report under the follow-up to the ILO Declaration on Fundamental Principles and Rights at Work, Report I(B), International Labour Conference, 91st Session, Geneva, 2003.

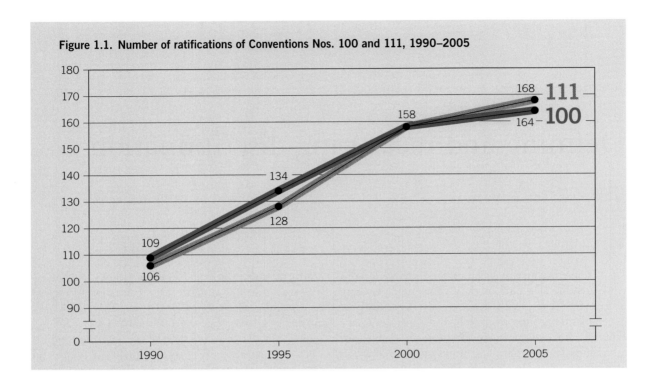

Figure 1.1. Number of ratifications of Conventions Nos. 100 and 111, 1990–2005

Table 1.1. Countries which have not yet ratified Convention No. 100 and Convention No. 111

Countries which have not yet ratified Convention No. 100 (16)	Countries which have not yet ratified Convention No. 111 (14)
Bahrain, Kiribati, Kuwait, Lao People's Democratic Republic, Liberia, Montenegro, Myanmar, Namibia, Oman, Qatar, Samoa, Solomon Islands, Somalia, Suriname, Timor-Leste and United States	Japan, Kiribati, Lao People's Democratic Republic, Malaysia, Montenegro, Myanmar, Oman, Samoa, Singapore, Solomon Islands, Suriname, Thailand, Timor-Leste and United States

1. Discrimination and equality: Defining the concepts

25. Convention No. 111 defines discrimination as "any distinction, exclusion or preference made on the basis of race, colour, sex, religion, political opinion, national extraction or social origin, which has the effect of nullifying or impairing equality of opportunity or treatment in employment or occupation", and allows additional criteria to be included after consultation by the governments concerned with employers' and workers' organizations. Based on the information gathered from member States, the Committee of Experts on the Application of Conventions and Recommendations (CEACR) has noted that in many countries grounds for discrimination in addition to those mentioned in Convention No. 111 have been recognized, and both the previous and the present Global Report on the subject have confirmed this. In a growing number of countries the list has expanded in recent years to include disability, age, state of health (including actual or perceived HIV/AIDS status), trade union membership and family status, among other grounds.

26. Discrimination may occur when looking for a job, while on the job or upon leaving. Discrimination is a differential and less favourable treatment of certain individuals because of any of the abovementioned characteristics, regardless of their ability to fulfil the requirements of the job. Discrimination occurs when a qualified member of a minority religious group is denied a job, or when competent workers are mobbed because of their religion or trade union affiliation. Discrimination also arises when, for the same job, a migrant worker receives lower pay than a national worker, or when payment is systematically delayed for low-caste or indigenous agricultural workers compared to their higher-caste or non-indigenous peers. Similarly, a female nurse or radiologist who does work of equal value to that of a paramedical technician, but is paid less is subject to discrimination.

27. Discrimination is not an exceptional or aberrant occurrence, but a systemic phenomenon, frequently embedded in the way in which workplaces operate and rooted in prevalent cultural and social values and norms. Discrimination does not distinguish between formal and informal workplaces, although in the latter it may acquire more overt forms, as they fall outside the scope or outreach of labour laws and enforcement mechanisms.

28. Discrimination can be direct or indirect. It is direct when rules, practices and policies exclude or give preference to certain individuals just because they belong to a particular group. Forms of direct discrimination include job advertisements stating that persons above a certain age need not apply, or human resource practices that require regular pregnancy tests of female employees with a view to refusing to hire or even dismissing those who happen to be pregnant. Discrimination based on pregnancy appears to be on the increase, even in countries that have long combated it and are facing plummeting fertility rates. In the United Kingdom, for example, a recent report by the Equal Opportunities Commission states that 30,000 women each year lose their jobs because of their pregnancy, and only 3 per cent of those who experience a problem lodge a claim at an employment tribunal.[2] Discrimination also occurs when enterprises recruiting female workers require them to work for a certain period in the enterprise before being allowed to become pregnant.[3]

29. Discrimination is indirect when apparently neutral norms and practices have a disproportionate effect on one or more identifiable groups, without justification. Organizing training courses outside working hours, for instance, over the weekends or late in the day may exclude workers who may be interested in attending them but cannot do so because of their family responsibilities, thus compromising their career prospects.

30. The differential treatment of particular categories of workers, in the form of inferior social benefits or pay, may also amount to indirect discrimination. The lower legal protection granted everywhere to domestic workers, most of whom are low-income women belonging to racial or ethnic minorities, and who are often foreigners, has been recognized as a form of indirect discrimination based on class, sex, race or migrant status.

31. Structural discrimination is inherent or institutionalized in social patterns, institutional structures and legal constructs that reflect and reproduce discriminatory practices and outcomes. These may include, for example, differential or inferior conditions of training available to ethnic minorities, or shortcomings in educational, transport and other services

---

2. Equal Opportunities Commission: "Pregnancy discrimination: EOC investigation", at www.eoc.org.uk.
3. Research Centre for Female Labour and Gender, Institute of Labour Science and Social Affairs, Ministry of Labour, Invalids and Social Affairs; F. Howell: *Equality, labour and social protection for women and men in the formal and informal economy in Viet Nam: Issues for advocacy and policy development* (Hanoi, ILO, 2003), p. 90.

in neighbourhoods or ghettoes in which there is a large proportion of ethnic minorities or immigrants.

32. All discrimination produces unequal effects that place the victims of discrimination in a situation of disadvantage, impairing their access to opportunities for employment, let alone equality of treatment at the workplace. It also translates into lower motivation for work and performance, leading to lower labour productivity and tensions at the workplace, with negative results for the enterprise's overall performance and welfare. Human resource management practices and policies that prevent discrimination at work and promote equal treatment and opportunities without arbitrary distinctions are not only beneficial to the individual but also good for business.

33. Severe and persistent discrimination at work contributes to poverty and social exclusion. Prejudices based on people's social and family backgrounds often prevail over their actual skills and aspirations, thus condemning them to social immobility. Deprivation is especially severe for people who face multiple discriminations, such as those who not only happen to be poor but also belong to a religious or racial minority, in addition to being older.

34. This is why the incidence of discrimination is so high among the poor and why poverty prevents people from escaping discrimination. It is clear from the above that only deliberate policy interventions by the State, the social partners and other stakeholders can effectively overcome structural discrimination, along with direct and indirect discrimination.

35. Not all differences in treatment, however, are unlawful. For instance, those that are based on the actual exigencies of a job are not. Being male or female may be a legitimate requirement for jobs involving close physical contact or for the performing arts. Distinctions based on skills or effort are just and legitimate: disparities in remuneration that reflect differences in years of education or the number of hours worked are in order.

36. Similarly, special measures that entail non-identical treatment of individuals with particular needs, owing to reasons such as their sex, mental, sensory or physical impairment or social origin, do not constitute discrimination. Giving effect to the principle of equal treatment and opportunities means more than treating persons in the same way; it also requires special measures and the accommodation of differences. Building ramps in the workplace for workers with physical impairments is one such measure; guaranteeing pregnancy and maternity protection to women workers is essential to ensure genuine equality with men in the world of work.

37. Special temporary measures, also known as affirmative action policies, may be also used to accelerate the pace of improvement of the situation of groups that are at a serious disadvantage because of past or present discrimination. They consist of a range of interventions that are temporary (although this does not necessarily mean short-term), may target different groups and may be justified by different rationales (see section on affirmative or positive action in Part III, Chapter 1). They cover different stages and aspects of the employment relationship and can be associated with the achievement of goals in hiring, training or promotion, or quotas, whereby a certain share of positions are allocated to members of underrepresented groups. Irrespective of these variations, affirmative action measures are based on recognition of the fact that the mere act of ending discrimination will never level the playing field once deep-seated and long-standing deprivation has occurred.

38. These measures have generated considerable debate and controversy, including in more recent times in the context of labour law reforms. Critics contend that they unduly penalize members of non-beneficiary groups, further stigmatize beneficiary groups and lead to a decline in overall efficiency and productivity. Experience shows that these policies can attain the intended goals, provided that certain conditions are respected.

39. Equality at work therefore is not just about prohibiting discrimination; it is about changing the status quo and transforming the workplace to make it more inclusive. How much change is desirable, in what respects and by when, must be determined at the national level according to each country's possibilities and bearing in mind cultural and social sensitivities.

40. Sensitivity towards discrimination and willingness to tackle it vary over time and by ground of discrimination: in the EU Member States, for instance, sexual orientation is the ground on which the least progress has been achieved up to now, compared to the other recently recognized grounds of discrimination. In some instances, gender equality may conflict with customary norms, and promoting it may be perceived as a strategy to weaken societies, such as indigenous peoples, that may already face considerable pressure to abandon their cultural identity.

41. While flexibility is necessary, what ultimately counts is the results achieved in practice. This in turn requires constant monitoring, assessment and adjustment of the measures in place to promote equality, the impact of these measures on the situation of protected groups and the incidence of discrimination.

2. Measuring discrimination: Where do we stand?

42. Gathering statistics on discrimination on a regular basis is crucial to making it visible and developing cost-effective measures to tackle it. Measuring discrimination is also important because it helps reduce the stigma affecting certain groups. If the members of these groups are shown that their disadvantage is the result of wrongdoing, they may claim their rights and ask redress.

43. Measuring and monitoring discrimination at both the global and national levels is not simple, although some progress has been made in the past years. Problems relate to both what should be measured and how. One obvious way of capturing discrimination at work is by compiling and processing data on the number of discrimination complaints, the number of cases settled and the number of convictions handed down. The advantage of compiling this kind of data is that it helps identify the population vulnerable to discrimination and illustrate changes in policies and practices, and their impact.[4]

44. These data, however, capture only a small fraction of actual discrimination occurrences. This is especially so in countries where the knowledge of rights and legal remedies is limited, law enforcement weak, litigation burdensome and costly, and informal work prevalent. Paradoxically, the number of discrimination complaints, if high and on the rise, is usually an indicator of progress: it reflects a better understanding of what discrimination is and mirrors trust in the impartiality and efficiency of the judiciary or other redress systems. Hence this type of data constitutes a useful, though insufficient, indicator of the extent of discrimination in a country.

45. Another way to measure discrimination consists of gathering statistics on inequalities in labour market outcomes between mainstream groups and groups defined by grounds of discrimination, at the national level. Although, as stated earlier, not all disparities can be attributed to discrimination, discrimination generates inequalities. When these are significant and persistent, it is plausible to conclude that discrimination may be at work. The regular measurement of inequalities across groups may therefore help place some pressure on policy-makers to adopt public policies aimed at levelling such inequalities. Regression analyses make it possible to determine which part of the gap is due to discrimination, and which part depends on objective factors such as education, years of work experience or occupational sector, thus providing guidance for better targeted policy interventions.

46. In some countries, eligible enterprises are required by law to gather statistics on the sex or racial composition of their workforce to determine whether discrimination is being practised and, if so, to take corrective action. These results are then contrasted with the data provided by national official statistics on the sex or racial composition of the national or local working-age populations. In the event of discrepancies, enterprises are asked to redress the situation with a view to improving the representation of under-represented groups in terms of employment levels and across occupations (Part III, Chapter 1, section on changing labour demand). The number of countries where proactive anti-discrimination law is in force is small, albeit increasing.

47. The challenge of measuring inequalities across groups is that relevant data are available nationally only for a few grounds (although these vary considerably by country) and, globally, for even fewer grounds. Data on the religion or sexual orientation of the working-age population, for instance, are scarce because national law often prohibits data reporting on these grounds. This raises the important question of how to reconcile the protection of personal data and an individual's right to privacy with the need to monitor discrimination through statistical means. A European Commission study reports on a number of countries that have been able to solve this dilemma. A key factor appears to be trust in national statistical institutions and in their ability to respect confidentiality and operational security when using "sensitive" information.[5]

48. Statistical information has considerably improved in recent years for grounds such as disability, although comparability across countries and over time within countries remains problematic. The ILO issued a compendium in 2004 reviewing the

4. S. Bruyère: "The measurement of discrimination and inequalities: Conceptualization and methodological issues", paper prepared for this Global Report.
5. European Commission: *Comparative study on the collection of data to measure the extent and impact of discrimination within the United States, Canada, Australia, the United Kingdom and the Netherlands* (Luxembourg, Office for Official Publications of the European Communities, 2004), p. 83.

Table 1.2. Census questions relating to race or ethnicity, selected countries

Country	Questions
Australia	Citizenship, indigenous identity, ancestry, country of birth, parents overseas-born or Australian-born, language
Brazil	Race and colour
Canada	Race, language, ancestry, and specific questions for Aboriginal or First Nation, Inuit and Métis people
Fiji	Ethnic group, place of birth
Germany	Nationality/citizenship
Mauritius	Community, citizenship, linguistic group
New Zealand	Ethnic group, Maori descent, country of birth, language(s) in which respondent is able to hold a conversation
South Africa	Population group, citizenship, country of birth, language spoken at home
United States	Race, ethnicity for Hispanics, place of birth, citizenship, ancestry, language spoken at home

Source: J. Allan: *International concepts and classifications: Review of the measurement of ethnicity* (Wellington, Statistics New Zealand, 2001).

methodologies used in 95 countries that collect or plan to collect disability statistics in employment.[6] The ILO has prepared guidelines entitled *The employment situation of people with disabilities: Towards improved statistical information*, which should be finalized for publication in early 2007.

49. The statistical definition of grounds such as race or ethnic origin has been resolved in a considerable number of countries. In the past few years, countries such as Bolivia, Ecuador and Guatemala have made important efforts to obtain data on their indigenous peoples.[7] An international comparison, however, is not possible because countries use different classification categories (table 1.2). Concepts such as "race" or "ethnic origin" acquire distinct and different meanings in different national contexts, as they are the product of different historical, socio-economic and legal processes. It is important, however, not to use variables such as "nationality" or "country of birth" of respondents or their parents as proxies to measure the racial or ethnic composition of a society. "Country of birth" is not a reliable indication of "colour" or other features associated with ethnic origin. Moreover, it

gives the wrong impression that racism is a phenomenon limited to the results of immigration.[8]

50. Other countries, such as France, hesitate to collect statistics on the ethnic composition of their societies. Following the social unrest in the French *banlieues* or suburbs at the end of 2005, the Government has intensified its action against racial discrimination. The issue of whether or not statistics should be gathered to gauge the extent and nature of the problem of racism has generated a lively national debate.[9] Critics contend that quantifying the disadvantages associated with ethnic origin would lead to greater social fragmentation, while supporters claim that a failure to do so may worsen the situation further.[10]

51. Sex is the ground of discrimination for which the most – though still unsatisfactory – progress has been made (box 1.1) both in terms of data gathering and reporting at the country level, and development of gender equality indicators at regional and international levels. The European Commission has come up with a comprehensive set of gender equality indicators in the areas of access to employment, segregation, pay and family/work reconciliation measures.[11]

---

6. ILO: *Statistics on the employment situation of people with disabilities: A compendium of national methodologies*, Working Paper No. 40, Policy Integration Department, Bureau of Statistics (Geneva, 2004). Most of these use household surveys (40 per cent) or the population census (30 per cent), while only 10 per cent have special household surveys on disability.

7. See J. Renshaw; N. Wray: "Indicadores de pobreza indígena" (unpublished document, Jan. 2004).

8. See European Commission: *Comparative study* ..., op. cit., p. 85.

9. See R. Fauroux: *La lutte contre les discriminations ethniques dans le domaine de l'emploi* (Paris, Ministry of Employment, Social Cohesion and Housing, 2005).

10. See J-B. de Montvalon ; L. Van Eeckhout: "La France résiste au comptage ethnique", in *Le Monde*, 3 July 2006.

11. J. Rubery; D. Grimshaw; C. Fagan; H. Figueiredo; M. Smith: "Gender equality still on the European agenda – but for how long?", in *Industrial Relations Journal*, Vol. 34, No. 5, pp. 484–486.

Box 1.1.
How much progress has been made on measuring gender inequalities?

A United Nations report, *The world's women 2005: Progress in statistics*, examines official national data for 1995–2003 in 204 countries or areas. The report concludes that the limited availability of data on gender equality indicators is a reflection of poor national statistical capacity, lack of gender mainstreaming in public policies and inadequate concepts and methods. Progress in data collection on gender labour market indicators has been very unequal by indicator and across regions. The economically active population (EAP) is the indicator on which the highest number of countries or areas provided data disaggregated by sex, but this number has steadily declined since 1975. The highest frequency of reporting was noted in Europe and the lowest in Africa. Out of the 50 Asian countries, 34 reported data on this indicator by sex and age, but China and India were not among them. In Oceania, only six out of the 17 countries supplied data on the EAP by sex and age, but they account for 95 per cent of the total population. The number of countries reporting data on their unemployed population by sex was slightly lower. In the period under review, 87 countries reported unemployment data by both sex and educational level at least once, but only 72 were able to do so more frequently. It is important to note, however, that the largest improvement in data reporting was in the area of unemployment statistics. Data collection regarding occupational divisions across gender lines continues to lag behind. Out of 204 countries or areas, 105 were able to provide this kind of information – with only 68 countries providing the information frequently. More than half of reporting countries were in the Americas, Europe and Asia. The indicator for which the least progress has been made is statistics on wages by major industry group and by sex. Only 52 countries reported data for this indicator. Although this represents a dramatic increase since 1995, Europe and Asia account for almost three-quarters of the available data. While the informal economy is an important source of employment for women in many countries, only about 60 countries have produced related statistics since 1995.

Source: United Nations: *The world's women 2005: Progress in statistics* (New York, 2006).

52. Numerous countries have begun collecting statistics on important gender indicators, such as violence against women, including at the workplace, or how women and men divide their time between paid and unpaid work and leisure. Efforts in this domain are still at an incipient stage, especially in developing countries, but by providing a picture of the workload of men and women, they offer useful pointers for policy choices to policy-makers who may be interested, for instance, in increasing women's employment rates.

53. The Organisation for Economic Co-operation and Development (OECD) has set up the Gender, Institutions and Development Data Base (GID), which combines existing indicators of gender (in)equality in education, health, employment or political representation with indicators measuring biases in institutions which influence the extent and forms in which women participate in the economy.[12] The GID encompasses a total of 50 indicators for 162 countries. Indicators are grouped into four categories: family codes (including information on marriage customs, parental authority, repudiation); physical integrity (female genital mutilation, rape, assault, etc.); civil liberties (the extent to which women can run for political office or move freely outside the home); and ownership rights (right to hold property or other material assets). Although the GID covers a broad set of parameters that include and go beyond employment and the workplace, some of them, such as marriage customs, women's freedom of movement and women's property rights, have a direct bearing on women's opportunities and choices in the labour market.

54. There is not one single indicator that can meaningfully capture progress or lack thereof in the elimination of discrimination and promotion of equality at work. Several indicators are needed, each measuring different but interrelated aspects, such as inequalities in labour market outcomes, which point to policy failures and discrimination. The availability of relevant data is uneven, depending on both the ground and the variables concerned, but efforts are under way to remedy this.

55. In any event, and despite these shortcomings, data consistently show that, everywhere, disparities in occupational achievements between mainstream groups and those vulnerable to discrimination are important and slow to narrow. This confirms the need for and importance of an enabling environment that combines anti-discrimination laws with supportive equality institutions and coherent policy packages promoting equality at the workplace and beyond.

12. The database is accessible at www.oecd.org/dev/institutions/GID database.

PART II

Patterns of discrimination at work: Recent developments

56. *Time for equality at work* showed that discrimination at work is a moving target: while long-recognized patterns of discrimination based on sex, race and religion persist, often acquiring new expressions, newer forms are emerging such as discrimination on account of actual or perceived HIV/AIDS status or against workers at both ends of the age spectrum. At the same time, other practices, such as those that penalize individuals with habits regarded as unhealthy, have begun to surface in several countries.

57. The "vitality" of discrimination at work is closely associated with the transformations in the structures and dynamics of labour markets everywhere induced by broader economic and political processes. Such transformations redefine the patterns of social mobility and stratification, altering societal views about the work ethics or attitudes that are considered to lead to success at the workplace. These attitudes, in turn, are commonly associated with particular social groups, while other groups are perceived as not possessing them and, as a result, are deprived of equal opportunities regardless of merit. A striking feature of this global picture is how certain groups, irrespective of the socio-economic development of a country and its economic openness and dynamism, consistently occupy the lowest rungs of the occupational and pay ladder.

58. Part II provides an overview of the most recent developments in respect of the patterns of discrimination in employment and occupation across the world: it reviews continuity and change in the long-recognized forms of discrimination (those explicitly mentioned in Convention No. 111), highlights the persistence of the more recently recognized forms, and advocates a close scrutiny of emerging workplace practices that give rise to concern.

1. Long-recognized forms of discrimination

Gender equality in the world of work: A mixed picture

59. A key prerequisite for effectively addressing sex-based discrimination in employment and occupation is to understand both its significance and its progression over time. In the absence of global data on sex discrimination, inequalities between men and women in labour market outcomes are taken as valid proxies for sex discrimination (Part I, Chapter 2). Although gender inequality coexists and interacts with other forms of inequality, such as age-based or racial inequalities, data on a global scale are more readily available for sex than for other personal attributes. This section therefore focuses on inequalities between men and women in respect of a number of labour market variables.

60. Eight indicators were chosen to examine women's relative status in the labour market: the labour force participation rate; the employment and unemployment rates by sex; the female share in both non-agricultural and total paid employment; the percentage distribution of women workers by status (unpaid, self-employed and employee); the female shares in legislative and managerial positions; and the gender pay gap (see methodological note in the appendix).

Women's entry into the labour market continues

61. Data for 1995–2004 confirm that women's participation in the labour force and in paid employment has maintained an upward trend in almost all regions of the world (table 2.1). Female labour force participation rates continued to rise significantly, thus narrowing the worldwide gender gap in labour participation rates by 3.5 percentage points. Table 2.1 shows that this increase was strongest in Latin America and the Caribbean, followed by the European Union (EU), South Asia and, from very low levels, the Middle East and North Africa. This indicator registered moderate increases in East Asia and the Pacific but remained almost unchanged in the transition economies and sub-Saharan Africa.

62. Women's employment rates also increased in most regions (with significant variations from one region to another). North America still displays the highest women's employment rates, while the Middle East and North Africa continue to show the lowest rate (table 2.2). Moreover, while women's employment rates have been increasing, men's employment rates have registered a slight decline in five out of eight regions, especially in Europe (non-EU) and Central Asia and South Asia.

Table 2.1. Female labour force participation (LFP) rates and share of female as a percentage of male rates, by region, 1995–2004 (percentages)

	Number of countries or areas	Female LFP rates			Female as % of male rates	
		1995	2000	2004	1995	2004
World	**173**	**54.8**	**55.7**	**56.6**	**66.2**	**69.6**
East Asia and the Pacific	24	59.5	60.3	61.2	71.6	74.3
Europe (non-EU) and Central Asia	23	62.2	60.6	60.9	79.3	80.3
European Union	25	57.9	60.4	62.0	74.3	80.8
Latin America and the Caribbean	28	48.1	51.5	53.9	58.0	65.3
Middle East and North Africa	19	27.5	29.8	32.0	34.0	39.5
North America	2	68.6	70.4	71.2	83.0	86.7
South Asia	8	39.5	41.3	43.5	46.8	52.6
Sub-Saharan Africa	44	64.6	63.7	63.0	73.6	73.0

All values shown are medians.
Sources: ILO: *Key Indicators of the Labour Market (KILM), Fourth edition* (Geneva, 2006), table 1a; ILO: Global Employment Trends Model.

Table 2.2. Employment-to-population ratios by sex and by region, 1995–2004 (percentages)

	Female employment rates		Male employment rates	
	1995	2004	1995	2004
World	**51.2**	**53.0**	**78.4**	**77.5**
East Asia and the Pacific	58.1	59.3	81.7	80.6
Europe (non-EU) and Central Asia	57.3	56.7	71.8	69.6
European Union	52.5	56.9	72.3	72.1
Latin America and the Caribbean	43.3	49.2	79.3	80.0
Middle East and North Africa	23.3	26.8	74.3	74.5
North America	64.8	68.6	78.2	78.7
South Asia	37.5	40.7	84.2	82.1
Sub-Saharan Africa	62.6	60.6	83.6	81.6

Sources: *KILM, Fourth edition*, table 1a; ILO: Global Employment Trends Model.

Table 2.3. Unemployment rates by sex and by region, 1995–2004

	Female unemployment rates		Male unemployment rates	
	1995	2004	1995	2004
World	**9.8**	**9.3**	**8.4**	**8.2**
East Asia and the Pacific	4.7	5.0	4.6	5.0
Europe (non-EU) and Central Asia	11.2	11.1	11.4	11.2
European Union	11.1	9.3	9.0	7.8
Latin America and the Caribbean	11.8	10.4	8.1	6.8
Middle East and North Africa	16.9	16.1	10.7	10.6
North America	7.4	6.1	7.8	6.6
South Asia	8.2	8.1	4.0	4.1
Sub-Saharan Africa	7.3	7.6	8.6	9.1

Sources: ibid.

63. In the case of unemployment, both men and women have experienced slight declines or no changes in their rates across the world, except for East Asia and the Pacific and sub-Saharan Africa, but women's unemployment rates have remained higher than men's almost everywhere, the gender unemployment gap being largest in the Middle East and North Africa, and Latin America (table 2.3). North America is the only region where men's unemployment exceeds women's.

More women in paid jobs, but many still work without pay

64. Women's share of total wage employment in the non-agricultural sector is the indicator chosen for measuring progress in the achievement of the Millennium Development Goal (MDG) concerning gender equality and women's empowerment. In addition, data have been gathered for women's share in total wage employment, because in some countries export-

Table 2.4. Female shares in non-agricultural paid employment (MDG 3) and in total paid employment, 1995–2004 (percentages)

	Number of countries or areas	Female shares in non-agricultural paid employment		Female shares in total paid employment	
		1995	2004	1995	2004
World	**79**	**41.3**	**43.5**	**40.3**	**42.1**
East Asia and the Pacific	11	43.1	46.5	41.8	44.9
Europe (non-EU) and Central Asia	12	43.9	45.7	43.4	44.7
European Union	22	45.8	47.4	45.4	47.1
Latin America and the Caribbean	22	40.4	42.2	38.6	40.3
Middle East and North Africa	4	24.5	28.2	22.2	24.9
North America	2	48.1	49.0	46.5	47.4
South Asia	2	14.3	16.5	17.8	17.6
Sub-Saharan Africa	4	36.0	39.5	35.8	36.0

All values shown are medians.

Sources: Female shares in non-agricultural paid employment: United Nations Statistics Division: United Nations Common Database; female shares in paid employment: *KILM, Fourth edition*, table 3. When data were not available in KILM, the table was completed with data from the ILO database on labour statistics (LABORSTA), table 2D (mainly for data on 2004).

oriented agriculture has become an important source of paid work for women in the past decade (table 2.4).

65. Table 2.4 shows that the share of women in both non-agricultural wage employment and total paid employment has increased in all regions by roughly 2 percentage points. Moreover, the proportion of women in non-agricultural wage employment is higher than in total wage employment, with the exception of South Asia. This trend confirms that paid work in agriculture is a relatively important generator of income for women in that region compared to others.

66. While the Middle East and North Africa still have the lowest share of women in non-agricultural paid employment, the increase in this variable has been strongest in that region, followed by sub-Saharan Africa, and East Asia and the Pacific.

67. Although these two indicators have shown positive development across the world, in many regions the proportion of women working without pay remains significant (figure 2.1). This is an important indicator of women's status, as unpaid family labourers have no control over either the means of production or returns to work.

68. Sub-Saharan Africa is the only region where the proportion of women working without pay in total

female employment has increased (by 3.6 percentage points), while in all other regions this percentage has declined, although with significant variations. There are, however, important differences across regions in the proportions of women working without remuneration. South Asia, with two-thirds of all employed women working without pay, is the region with the highest share of unpaid female labour, but also registered the most important drop in that share in the period under review.

69. A significant proportion of employed women continue to be self-employed in many regions. Self-employment can be used as a proxy for informal work, which is characterized by low pay, poor working conditions and lack of protection. A recent ILO study confirms that women are disproportionately represented in informal employment and that, while roughly equal proportions of men and women are self-employed, women are concentrated among lower-quality jobs within self-employment.[1]

70. Another "face" of female informal work is domestic work. Despite the absence of global data, evidence shows that this form of employment absorbs important and growing shares of females, partly as a result of the growth of female migration for labour (see section on migrant workers below).

1. R. Galli; D. Kucera: "Gender, informality and employment flexibility in Latin America" (forthcoming).

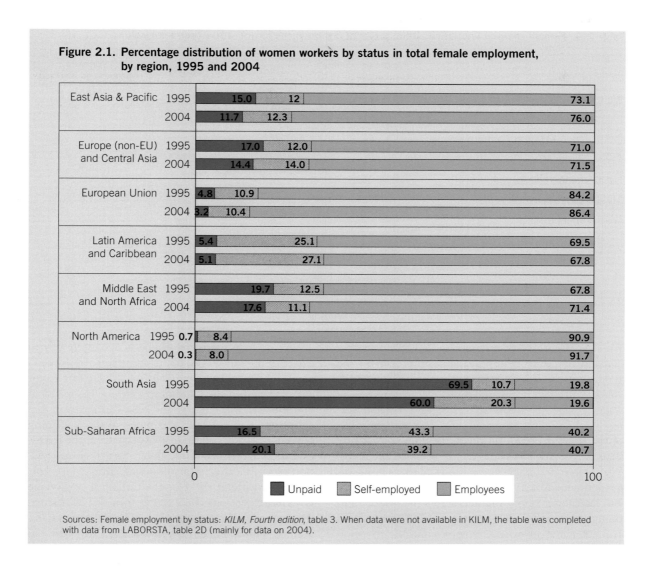

Figure 2.1. Percentage distribution of women workers by status in total female employment, by region, 1995 and 2004

Region	Year	Unpaid	Self-employed	Employees
East Asia & Pacific	1995	15.0	12	73.1
	2004	11.7	12.3	76.0
Europe (non-EU) and Central Asia	1995	17.0	12.0	71.0
	2004	14.4	14.0	71.5
European Union	1995	4.8	10.9	84.2
	2004	3.2	10.4	86.4
Latin America and Caribbean	1995	5.4	25.1	69.5
	2004	5.1	27.1	67.8
Middle East and North Africa	1995	19.7	12.5	67.8
	2004	17.6	11.1	71.4
North America	1995	0.7	8.4	90.9
	2004	0.3	8.0	91.7
South Asia	1995	69.5	10.7	19.8
	2004	60.0	20.3	19.6
Sub-Saharan Africa	1995	16.5	43.3	40.2
	2004	20.1	39.2	40.7

Sources: Female employment by status: *KILM, Fourth edition*, table 3. When data were not available in KILM, the table was completed with data from LABORSTA, table 2D (mainly for data on 2004).

71. As for the "employees" or wage earners' groups, the female share has registered a slight increase in all regions, except for Latin America and the Caribbean and South Asia, where it remained unchanged.

More women in high-status jobs, but the pay gap persists

72. If a country has a large proportion of women employed in legislative, senior official or managerial (LSOM) jobs, this is taken as an indication that good-quality jobs are available to women. Although women still represent a distinct minority in such positions throughout the world (28 per cent), the progress they have made in the past few years has been encouraging. Women's share in these high-status positions has increased in all regions (table 2.5). Although this indicator has seen the most growth in South Asia (where it has nearly doubled in nine years), this region is still the area where women hold the lowest share of LSOM jobs.

73. A country's stage of economic development does not seem to play a key role in determining the percentage of women in such jobs. Many other factors, such as anti-discrimination laws and policies, national job classifications and codification systems, the share of women in non-agricultural paid work and cultural norms, help explain variations in the female share of the LSOM group.[2]

2. R. Anker: "Women's access to occupations with authority, influence and decision-making power", Policy Integration Department Working Paper No. 44 (Geneva, ILO, 2005), at www.ilo.org/public/english/bureau/integration/download/publicat/4_3_414_wp-44.pdf.

Table 2.5. Female share in legislative and managerial positions, 1995 and 2004 (percentages)

	Number of countries or areas	1995	2004	Absolute percentage increase
World	**73**	**25.5**	**28.3**	**2.7**
East Asia and the Pacific	12	20.9	24.8	3.9
Europe (non-EU) and Central Asia	10	27.5	29.2	1.7
European Union	22	27.5	30.6	3.1
Latin America and the Caribbean	16	32.7	35.0	2.3
Middle East and North Africa	6	9.2	11.0	1.8
North America	2	38.6	41.2	2.6
South Asia	2	4.6	8.6	4.0
Sub-Saharan Africa	3	22.1	24.8	2.7

When data for 1995 and 2004 were not available, information on the closest year was used. All values shown are medians.

Source: ILO: LABORSTA, table 2C (Employment by occupation).

74. As stated earlier, accurate and reliable data on a global scale are not readily available for measuring the gender pay gap. Moreover, the relevant statistics available use different standards: some refer to gross hourly wages – whether across sectors or in particular sectors – while others are based on earnings. Regardless of the standard used, however, the data consistently show important disparities in pay between the sexes.

75. *Time for equality at work* showed that significant gender inequalities in pay were among the most resilient features of labour markets across the world. Even though the gender pay gap narrowed in some places and stagnated in others, women continue to work, on average, for lower earnings than men. This trend continues despite the striking advances of women in educational attainments relative to men (figure 2.2). In 2003, with the notable exceptions of South Asia and sub-Saharan Africa, female gross enrolment rates in tertiary education were considerably higher than men's, thus weakening the relevance of "productivity" differentials between men and women as an important explanatory cause of the persisting gender gaps.

76. Comparable data on wages by sex are more widely available for the manufacturing sector. Figure 2.3 shows the evolution of the gender pay gap in this sector between 1995 and 2004 for 37 countries and areas. While most countries saw a decline in the gap, especially Costa Rica and the United Kingdom, others experienced rocketing gender pay gaps (for example Egypt, Sri Lanka and El Salvador). But where the gender pay gap narrowed, this was due essentially to a decline in male wages, not to an increase in women's pay. The gender pay gap in the manufacturing sector also widened in the Commonwealth of Independent States (CIS) and Central and East European (CEE) countries. This has been attributed to the worsening of labour market conditions resulting from the transition to a market economy, along with the disproportionate impact this has had on women.[3]

77. Throughout the EU, the difference in average gross hourly earnings between women and men across the economy throughout all establishments has remained high at 15 per cent (figure 2.4). According to the European Commission, the difference in earnings levels between men and women results from "non-respect of equal pay legislation and from a number of structural inequalities such as labour market segregation, differences in work patterns, access to education and training, biased evaluation and pay systems and stereotypes".[4] The absence of gender-friendly work and family reconciliation measures in some of the EU countries also accounts for the persistence of the gender gap.

78. In Latin America, there has been a remarkable increase in women's earnings and wages as a percentage of men's in all countries, except for Argentina (the only country showing an increase in both gender gaps of about 10 percentage points). There are, however, significant differences in the size of the gender gap depending on whether earnings or wages

3. M. Corley; Y. Perardel; K. Popova: *Wage inequality by gender and occupation: A cross-country analysis*, Employment Strategy Papers, 2005/20, p. 19.

4. European Commission: *Report on equality between women and men, 2006* (Luxembourg, Office for Official Publications of the European Communities, 2006), p. 10.

Table 2.6. Female to male income differentials in Latin America, 1994 and 2004, percentages

	Earned income differential [1]		Wage differential [2]	
	1994	2004	1994	2004
Argentina	71	61	76	68
Bolivia	54	61	61	77
Brazil	56	66	61	87
Chile	67	64	70	83
Colombia	68	77	83	99
Costa Rica	69	75	75	85
Dominican Republic	75	68	90	89
Ecuador	67	67	76	87
El Salvador	63	73	79	100
Guatemala	55	58	70	80
Honduras	63	76	73	95
Mexico	57	63	68	78
Nicaragua	77	69	77	82
Panama	71	76	75	85
Paraguay	60	70	64	95
Peru	60	61	73	78
Uruguay	61	72	63	71
Bolivarian Republic of Venezuela	70	76	83	99

Differential calculated as the quotient of average female income and average male income, multiplied by 100. Where data for 1994 and 2004 were not available, information on the closest year was used. [1] Earned income corresponds to earnings of all employed people (self-employed, employees, employers). [2] Wages correspond to employees' earnings.

Source: Economic Commission for Latin America and the Caribbean (ECLAC): *Social Panorama of Latin America 2005* (Santiago, United Nations, 2006), Statistical appendix, table 26.

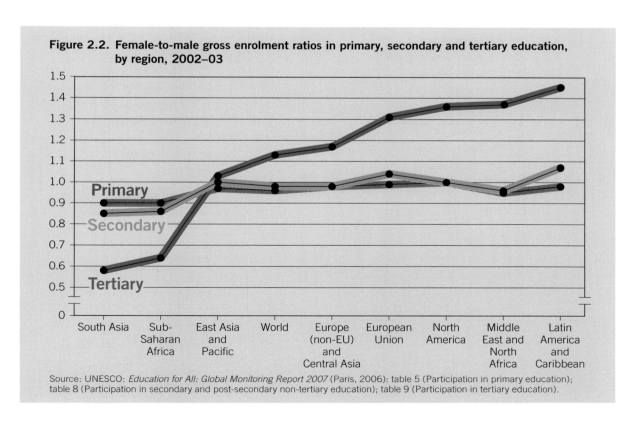

Figure 2.2. Female-to-male gross enrolment ratios in primary, secondary and tertiary education, by region, 2002–03

Source: UNESCO: *Education for All: Global Monitoring Report 2007* (Paris, 2006): table 5 (Participation in primary education); table 8 (Participation in secondary and post-secondary non-tertiary education); table 9 (Participation in tertiary education).

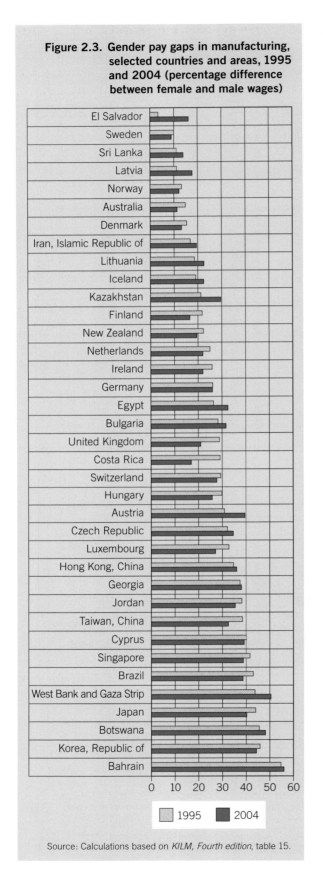

Figure 2.3. Gender pay gaps in manufacturing, selected countries and areas, 1995 and 2004 (percentage difference between female and male wages)

1995   2004

Source: Calculations based on *KILM, Fourth edition*, table 15.

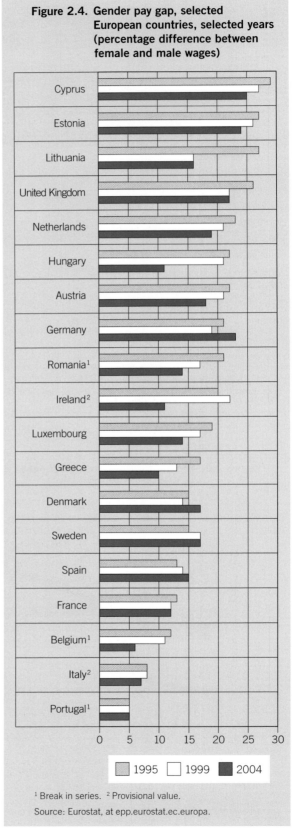

Figure 2.4. Gender pay gap, selected European countries, selected years (percentage difference between female and male wages)

1995   1999   2004

[1] Break in series.   [2] Provisional value.

Source: Eurostat, at epp.eurostat.ec.europa.

are being considered (table 2.6). The gender earnings gap remains roughly 10–20 percentage points higher than the gender wage gap, except in El Salvador, Paraguay and the Bolivarian Republic of Venezuela, where the difference is even stronger.

79.   Between 1994 and 2004 in all countries, except for the Dominican Republic, the decline in the gender wage gap has been much stronger than that of the gender labour earnings gap. The value of the latter increased in Argentina, the Dominican Republic and Nicaragua.

80.   In the past years, a growing number of studies have been conducted in industrialized, developing and transition economies alike with the aim of determining which proportion of the gender pay gap is due to discrimination and which part is due to objective factors, such as education, years of work experience and hours spent on paid work.[5] Most studies concur that discrimination, which is equated with the unexplained part of the gender pay gap, accounts for a not insignificant portion of the gender pay gap, although it varies considerably depending on the country and the methodology used. The unexplained portion of the gender pay gap in industrialized countries ranges between 5 and 15 per cent.[6] In South Africa[7] and the Republic of Korea[8] it represents 20 per cent of the overall pay gap, while in China[9] and Australia[10] the unexplained portion of the pay differential is 80 per cent. In France, the residual part of the gender pay gap increases with age: for women aged under 35 years 6 per cent of the pay differential between men and women is due to discrimination in remuneration, while for women over 35 this value doubles.[11]

81.   Discrimination in remuneration may be direct – when it relates to equal or similar jobs – or indirect when it concerns different jobs of equal value. Evidence shows that both remain an issue everywhere. In industrialized countries, problems of direct discrimination in remuneration have been noted in respect of professional and executive-level jobs and in the skilled trades.[12]

82.   Women have been making noticeable headway in the labour market across the world since 1995. While their employment rates, along with their participation rates, have been rising, and at a faster pace then men's, especially in countries where their participation has been traditionally low, progress in narrowing the gender gaps in high-status jobs and in pay has been considerably slower, despite remarkable advances in women's educational achievements. This suggests the need for continued efforts aimed at promoting equal opportunities for women in employment, tackling direct and indirect sex discrimination in remuneration and enabling them to juggle paid work and family responsibilities.

The persistence of racial and ethnic discrimination

83.   Racial discrimination[13] continues to be an obstinate problem: it shows a slow decline in countries such as Brazil and South Africa that have started addressing it more recently, considerable vitality in countries that still deny the problem, and resilience even in countries that have long recognized it.

84.   Past conflicts or civil wars along racial/ethnic lines have exacerbated racism in parts of Africa (Great

5.   A.Y.C. Liu: "Gender wage gap in Viet Nam: 1993 to 1998", in *Journal of Comparative Economics*, Vol. 32, No. 3 (Sep. 2004), pp. 586–596; C.J. Gerry; B-Y. Kim; C.A. Li: "The gender wage gap and wage arrears in Russia: Evidence from the RLMS", in *Journal of Population Economics*, Vol. 17, No. 2 (June 2004), pp. 267–288; T. Gálvez: "Discriminación de género en el mercado laboral de América Latina: La brecha de ingresos 2001", Ch. III, in L. Abramo (ed.): *Trabajo decente y equidad de género en América Latina* (Santiago, ILO, 2006), pp. 95–128.

6.   M. Gunderson: "Viewpoint: Male-female wage differentials: How can that be?", in *Canadian Journal of Economics*, Vol. 39, No. 1 (2006), pp. 1–21.

7.   C. Grün: "Direct and indirect gender discrimination in the South African labour market", in *International Journal of Manpower*, Vol. 25, No. 3/4 (2004), pp. 321–342.

8.   E. Monk-Turner; C. Turner: "The gender wage gap in South Korea: How much has changed in 10 years?", in *Journal of Asian Economics*, Vol. 15, No. 2 (2004), pp. 415–424.

9.   S. Demurger; M. Fournier; Y. Chen: "The evolution of gender earnings gaps and discrimination in urban China: 1988–1995", Research Paper, Hong Kong Institute of Economics and Business Strategy, 2005.

10. A.C. Preston: "Female earnings in Australia: An analysis of 1991 Census data", in *Australian Bulletin of Labour*, Vol. 26, No. 1 (2000), pp. 38–58.

11. Ministère de l'emploi, de la cohésion sociale et du logement: "Les écarts de salaires horaires entre hommes et femmes en 2002: Une évaluation possible de la discrimination salariale", in *Premières synthèses* No. 22/1 (June 2006), p. 6.

12. Pay Equity Task Force: *Pay equity: A new approach to a fundamental right*, Final Report 2004 (Ottawa, 2004), p. 171, at www.payequityreview.gc.ca.

13. The term "race" or "racism" is often used loosely in regard to linguistic communities or minorities whose identity is based on religious or cultural characteristics, or even on national extraction. Difference of colour is only one of the ethnic characteristics, but it is the most apparent, and is therefore often linked to the ground of race in constitutional or legislative provisions adopted by certain countries to prohibit discrimination. Generally speaking, any discrimination against an ethnic group is considered to be racial discrimination. See ILO: *Equality in employment and occupation*, Special Survey on Equality in Employment and Occupation in respect of Convention No. 111, Report III (Part 4B), International Labour Conference, 83rd Session, Geneva, 1996, paras. 30–31.

Lakes region) and in Eastern Europe (Caucasus and the Balkans). All over the world, the intensification of labour migration, and the feelings of anxiety that it has brought about in host societies, have fuelled an increase in expressions of hostility against migrant workers, as well as those of foreign origin, whether or not they have become nationals of the countries in which they work.

Racism and poverty: An inseparable duo?

85. Racial discrimination affects millions of different workers around the world, ranging from black people and ethnic minorities to indigenous peoples, nationals of foreign origin and migrant workers. Very often those who suffer racial or ethnic discrimination are very poor. Centuries of unequal treatment in all spheres of life, combined with persistent and deep ethnic socio-economic inequalities, explain their low educational and occupational attainments. Lower achievements, in turn, make them vulnerable to ethnic stereotyping, while social and geographic segregation perpetuates ethnic inequalities, reinforcing perceptions of "inferiority" or "distastefulness" by majority groups. The dynamics and manifestations of racial discrimination differ, however, depending on the groups concerned, and will therefore be examined separately below.

People of African descent

86. A small black middle class of people of African descent – commonly referred to as black people – has emerged in the past decades in several countries, but the majority continue to be overrepresented among the jobless and at the bottom of the job and pay ladder. This happens everywhere, regardless of the socio-economic circumstances of the countries in which they live.

87. In the United States, for instance, wage gaps by race remain significant: some policy analysts contend that no skill parity between blacks and whites is possible before at least 2050,[14] which implies that wage disparities will also persist.

88. Racial stereotyping does not seem to fade away: many employers continue to perceive black workers, especially young black men (see section on age discrimination in Part II, Chapter 2), as lazy, dishonest or violent.[15] Rising incarceration rates among young black males, together with their scant to non-existent track records in the workplace, make them especially vulnerable to stereotyping.[16] Although black women generally have higher educational levels than black men, and a higher likelihood of holding managerial and professional positions, black men earn more than comparable black women, pointing to sex discrimination in remuneration. As a result, a lower proportion of black men are in poverty than black women (22.8 compared to 26.7 per cent).[17]

89. In Britain, black people of African or Caribbean origin continue to experience higher unemployment rates and concentration in low-skilled, low-paid jobs and unfair treatment. According to the 2005 Citizenship Survey,[18] black people have the highest rate of being refused a job, and are more likely than others to have been denied a job in the past five years. As a result, the employment rate of black people remains low, while their unemployment rate is the highest, at 13 per cent for black Africans and 12 per cent for black Caribbean, more than double the unemployment rate of whites (5 per cent). All white respondents concur that racial prejudice has increased in Britain in the past five years.[19] If the employment rate for black workers remains as modest as it is at present, it is estimated that it could take 46 years before the employment gap between blacks and whites is closed.[20]

90. The introduction of democratic rule in South Africa in the mid-1990s was accompanied by an improvement in the relative earnings of the black Africans relative to all other racial groups, but these gains were almost totally eroded by 2001 as a consequence of economic openness and the unprecedented influx of new entrants in the formal labour market after the end of apartheid. The earnings gap remains signifi-

14. D. Neal: *Why has black-white skill convergence stopped?*, Working Paper 11090 (Cambridge, MA, National Bureau of Economic Research), Jan. 2005, at papers.nber.org/papers/w11090.pdf?new_window=1.

15. See J. Faundez: "Racism and employment", in *Dimensions of racism* (New York and Geneva, United Nations, 2005), p. 57.

16. E. McCrate: *Why racial stereotyping doesn't just go away: The question of honesty and work ethic*, Working Paper Series No. 115 (Apr. 2006), Political Economy Research Institute, University of Massachusetts, Amherst.

17. J.D. McKinnon; C.E. Bennett: *We the people: Blacks in the United States*, Census 2000 Special Reports (US Census Bureau, Aug. 2005).

18. S. Kitchen; J. Michaelson; N. Wood: *2005 Citizenship Survey – Race and faith topic report* (London, Department for Communities and Local Government, June 2006), at www.communities.gov.uk/pub/34/CitizenshipSurveyTopicreportraceandfaith_id1501034.pdf.

19. Commission for Racial Equality (United Kingdom): *Factfile 1: Employment and ethnicity* (Apr. 2006), at www.cre.gov.uk/research/factfiles.html.

20. Trades Union Congress (TUC): "Fifty years to plug ethnic minority employment gap, says TUC", 5 July 2005, at www.tuc.org.uk/equality/tuc-10161-f0.cfm.

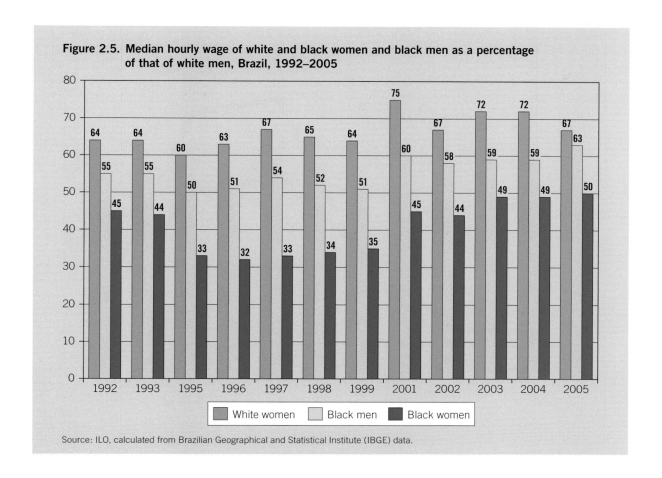

Figure 2.5. Median hourly wage of white and black women and black men as a percentage of that of white men, Brazil, 1992–2005

Source: ILO, calculated from Brazilian Geographical and Statistical Institute (IBGE) data.

cant today. Unemployment rates are highest among black Africans,[21] especially those with low skills or from rural areas.[22] Despite the important efforts by the Government and the social partners to tackle racial and other discrimination and some progress made, a recent survey by the National Labour and Economic Development Institute (NALEDI) shows that black people, and especially black women, still face discrimination in the workplace.[23] The main challenge lies in promoting economic equality for the vast majority of black Africans, through public policies that include but transcend anti-discrimination measures, such as inclusive education or land redistribution policies.

91. The mobilization of civil society, particularly the black movement, and government action have been key to starting change in Brazil. Data show that since 2001 there has been a significant improvement in the hourly wages of a majority of black women and men relative to those of white men (figure 2.5). Control over inflation and net gains in the real minimum wage have contributed to these results.[24]

The Roma people

92. The poor treatment and extreme poverty of Roma people, also commonly known as gypsies and the largest ethnic minority group in Europe at about 10 million people,[25] is one of the most pressing political, social and human rights issues facing an expanding Europe. This has led to the adoption of the Decade of Roma Inclusion (2005–15), the first

21. Statistics South Africa: *March 2006 Labour force survey*, at www.statssa.gov.za/publications/P0210/P0210March2006.pdf.
22. P.G. Leite; T. McKinley; R.G. Osorio: *The post-apartheid evolution of earnings inequality in South Africa 1995–2004* (Brasilia, International Poverty Centre, UNDP, 2006), Working Paper No. 32, Oct. 2006.
23. NALEDI: *The workers' survey for COSATU*, Aug. 2006, at www.naledi.org.za.
24. ILO: *Trabalho decente e desigualdade racial no Brasil* (forthcoming).
25. Directorate-General for Employment and Social Affairs of the European Commission: *The situation of Roma in an enlarged European Union* (Luxembourg, Office for Official Publications of the European Communities, 2004), p. 6, para. 7.

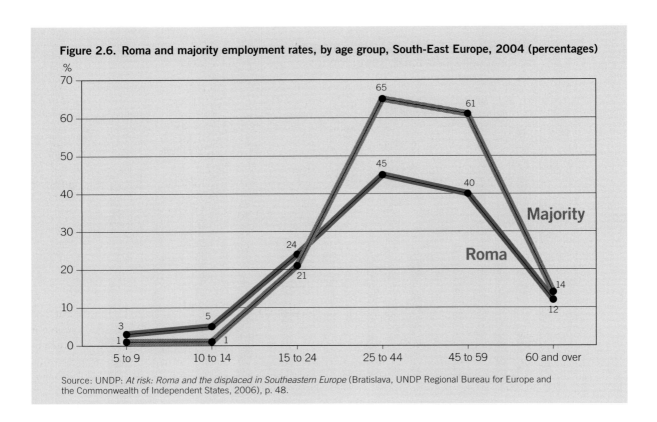

Figure 2.6. Roma and majority employment rates, by age group, South-East Europe, 2004 (percentages)

Source: UNDP: *At risk: Roma and the displaced in Southeastern Europe* (Bratislava, UNDP Regional Bureau for Europe and the Commonwealth of Independent States, 2006), p. 48.

cooperative transnational effort to change the lives of these people in that region.[26]

93.   The data on their employment status are not clearly documented; however, according to recent estimates of the European Commission[27] and the United Nations Development Programme (UNDP),[28] unemployment is at crisis level. In countries such as Albania, Bosnia and Herzegovina, Bulgaria, Croatia, Kosovo, the former Yugoslav Republic of Macedonia, Montenegro, Romania and Serbia and unemployment among Roma people, and especially Roma women, ranges between 50 and 90 per cent. Overall employment is low among them, but the employment rate is greater for Roma aged up to 24 years than for majority populations, suggesting a higher incidence of child labour among the former (figure 2.6).[29]

94.   A major underlying factor is low educational attainment, due to low attendance rates stemming from lack of resources for clothes, writing materials and meals, and over-representation in schools for the physically and mentally handicapped.[30] But even Roma with tertiary education have double the un-employment rate of equally educated majority community workers, while wage gains for each additional year of education are much lower for them than the majority, leading to a considerable ethnic pay gap.[31] Discrimination also manifests itself in a higher pro-portion of Roma workers engaged in unskilled la-bour irrespective of their level of education. Evidence shows, however, that in mixed and integrated settle-ments Roma people had completed secondary educa-tion and had formal jobs, regardless of gender, thus

26. This is a joint effort by eight countries in Central and South-East Europe supported by the international community, see www. romadecade.org.

27. *The situation of Roma in an enlarged European Union*, op. cit. p. 23. See also A. Gil-Robles, Commissioner for Human Rights: *Final report on the human rights situation of the Roma, Sinti and Travellers in Europe*, 15 Feb. 2006, Office of the Commissioner for Human Rights, Council of Europe, CommDH(2006) 1.

28. UNDP: *At risk: Roma and the displaced in Southeastern Europe* (Bratislava, UNDP Regional Bureau for Europe and the Common-wealth of Independent States, 2006), p. 41.

29. ibid., p. 48.

30. D. Ringold; M. Orenstein; E. Wilkens: *Roma in an expanding Europe* (Washington, DC, World Bank, 2005), p. xv.

31. UNDP, op. cit., p. 51.

> **Box 2.1.**
> **Court condemns discrimination against a Roma worker**
>
> On 16 November 2005 a Roma man won a judgement by the Sofia District Court in Bulgaria, based on Bulgaria's Act on protection against discrimination. The claimant had sought to apply in 2003 for a job as a food production worker with a company. He had been told by telephone that the only requirement was that the applicant be a male aged under 30, but that no Roma need apply. In 2004 when the advertisement reappeared, he applied for the job, and when invited for an interview he did not mention that he was a Roma. At that interview management discouraged him from expecting to be hired. Several weeks later he was told he had not been hired. The company failed to establish that the refusal was based on lack of proper qualifications. Instead, the court found that there was enough circumstantial evidence of a causal link between Mr Assenov's ethnicity and the company's refusal to hire him. This is an example of a court ruling recognizing and addressing direct ethnic discrimination in recruitment and hiring.
>
> Source: European Roma Rights Centre (ERRC): *Bulgarian court fines employer for denying access to employment to Roma*, 16 Nov. 2005, at www.errc.org.

suggesting that lower spatial segregation results in better social outcomes.[32]

95. Negative attitudes are not the only problem; legislation may also create barriers. In Romania, for instance, the law requires applicants for any job to have at least eight years of elementary education, thus seriously penalizing people whose levels of education are below average.[33] In other instances, however, the law has permitted Roma individuals to lodge discrimination cases successfully (box 2.1).

Indigenous and tribal peoples

96. Another group disproportionately represented among the poor, and the chronic poor in particular, are indigenous and tribal peoples: they account for over 15 per cent of the world's poor, although they make up 5 per cent of the world's population. The reason for this lies in societal and institutional racism during colonial times and after independence, together with the denial of their rights as distinct peoples, including access to and control over their ancestral lands.

97. Encroachment on and dispossession de jure or de facto of their traditional lands have continued apace, are the key cause of the pauperization of these peoples and remain central to their plight. But because of land deprivation, wage labour has become a vital source of livelihood, and is destined to continue to grow in importance. Similarly, migration for work – whether international or national – appears to be on the rise (box 2.2).[34]

98. In Viet Nam, only half of the differential in per capita expenditure between the Kinh majority and the Hoa minority, on the one hand, and the other ethnic minorities, on the other, is due to differences in physical and human capital; the remainder is the result of less favourable treatment or differences in returns to comparable characteristics.[35]

99. In Latin America, indigenous people are more likely than non-indigenous people to hold both informal and unpaid jobs, and to work in agriculture. Their lower educational attainments, despite the increased number of years of schooling for the population as a whole, are one important cause. But even after controlling for education, a large proportion of the pay gap between indigenous and non-indigenous workers remains unexplained. While indigenous workers make on average about half of what non-indigenous workers earn, between 25 and 50 per cent of the earnings gap is due to discrimination and non-observable characteristics, such as quality of schooling (figure 2.7).[36]

32. D. Ringold; M. Orenstein; E. Wilkens: op. cit., p. 74.
33. F. Nasture: "Comparing Romanian policies on employment: Lessons for the Roma Decade", at Eumap.org., Aug. 2005, at www.eumap.org.
34. I. Kempf: *Pobreza y pueblos indígenas: más allá de las necesidades*, Observatorio de conflictos, Serie identidades y pueblos indígenas (Madrid, Centro de Investigación para la Paz (Peace Research Center), 2003); International Organization for Migration (IOM), Secretariat of the Permanent Forum on Indigenous Issues: *Report of an Expert Workshop on Indigenous Peoples and Migration: Challenges and Opportunities*, Geneva, 6–7 April 2006, E/C.19/2006/CRP.5; M.A, Barrón Pérez: "Jornada de trabajo, ahorro y remesas de los jornaleros agrícolas migrantes en las diversas regiones hortícolas de México, Canadá y España", in *Análisis Económico*, No. 46, Vol. XXI (first quarter 2006), at www.analisiseconomico.com.mx/pdf/4605.pdf.
35. D. van de Walle; D. Gunewardena: "Sources of ethnic inequality in Viet Nam", in *Journal of Development Economics*, Vol. 65 (2001), pp. 177–207.
36. G. Hall; H.A. Patrinos (eds.): *Indigenous peoples, poverty and human development in Latin America 1994–2004* (Palgrave Macmillan, 2006).

Box 2.2.
Indigenous and tribal peoples migrating abroad for work

In Nepal the indigenous peoples from the hill areas, the Hill Janajatis, have the largest share of migrants working abroad (29 per cent) in countries other than India, and have the highest average remittance income (almost 35 per cent of annual household income). In Pakistan, official statistics show a growth since 2004 in the numbers of workers migrating from the tribal areas in search of jobs, mainly in the construction sector in the Gulf countries. Because of their limited access to official channels of migration and official travel documents, indigenous and tribal people appear to be more likely than other groups to become undocumented migrant workers. And indigenous women are especially vulnerable to falling prey to trafficking.

Sources: Department for International Development (DFID) and World Bank: *Unequal citizens. Gender, caste and ethnic exclusion in Nepal* (Kathmandu, 2006); IOM, Secretariat of the Permanent Forum on Indigenous Issues: *Report of an Expert Workshop on Indigenous Peoples and Migration: Challenges and Opportunities*, Geneva, 6–7 Apr. 2006, E/C.19/2006/CRP.5, p. 11.

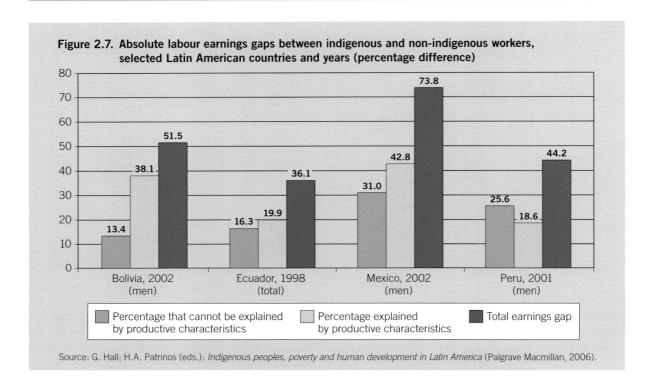

Figure 2.7. Absolute labour earnings gaps between indigenous and non-indigenous workers, selected Latin American countries and years (percentage difference)

Source: G. Hall; H.A. Patrinos (eds.): *Indigenous peoples, poverty and human development in Latin America* (Palgrave Macmillan, 2006).

100. The size of the gap increases with education, affecting mostly skilled indigenous workers and professionals. Returns to education are thus smaller for indigenous people than for non-indigenous people, which acts as a disincentive for indigenous households to invest in secondary and higher education. Gender is a further determinant of disadvantage: the wage penalty is higher for indigenous women than indigenous men (figure 2.8). During the 1990s the proportion of the earnings gap between indigenous and non-indigenous workers due to discrimination remained almost unchanged in Latin America.

101. Discrimination in remuneration against indigenous and tribal peoples consists of significantly lower wages for the same job, provision of remuneration partially or entirely in kind,[37] and delays in payment. A consequence of these practices is that a significant proportion of agricultural bonded labourers are indigenous in several regions,[38] including Africa (box 2.4). In Peru, abuse and deprivation of

---

37. J. Renshaw (ed.): *Indicadores de bienestar y de pobreza indígena* (Inter-American Development Bank (IDB), Oct. 2004) (unpublished document), p. 50.
38. ILO: *A global alliance against forced labour*, Global Report under the follow-up to the ILO Declaration on Fundamental Principles and Rights at Work, Report I(B), International Labour Conference, 93rd Session, Geneva, 2005.

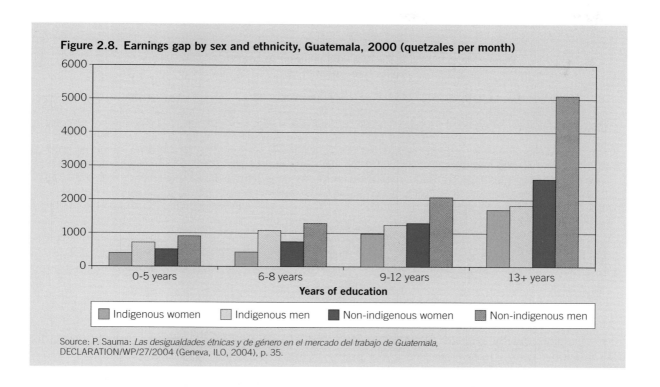

Figure 2.8. Earnings gap by sex and ethnicity, Guatemala, 2000 (quetzales per month)

Source: P. Sauma: *Las desigualdades étnicas y de género en el mercado del trabajo de Guatemala*, DECLARATION/WP/27/2004 (Geneva, ILO, 2004), p. 35.

Box 2.3.
Gathering data on indigenous and tribal peoples: Issues and challenges

Few countries collect and disaggregate data on the status and circumstances of their indigenous and tribal peoples. The main challenges include: the inadequacy of standard forms of question to capture their situation; the type and number of criteria to be used in order to determine the ethnic affiliation of respondents (place of residence, language(s) spoken, self-identification, etc.); the inaccurate reporting of indigenous identities because of misunderstanding of the questions asked; the fact that indigenous peoples often reside in war-stricken areas; and difficulties in capturing the situation of indigenous people migrating to other countries. Experts, including indigenous specialists, have stressed the importance of involving indigenous and tribal people in data collection, analysis and reporting. This would help define culturally appropriate indicators and overcome indigenous and tribal peoples' distrust towards data collection driven by the State. Collaborative efforts by government and indigenous peoples' organizations in Canada and New Zealand in this domain have been encouraging. Experts also recommend the use of multiple identification criteria and stress the need for gathering data that take account of issues of discrimination and exclusion in the economic, social and cultural arenas. This includes recognition of the value of indigenous work, e.g. "making a living" versus "having a job".

Sources: United Nations: *Report of the Workshop on Data Collection and Disaggregation for Indigenous Peoples*, Permanent Forum on Indigenous Issues, Third Session, New York, 10–21 May 2004, E/C.19/2004/2; United Nations: *Report of the Meeting on Indigenous Peoples and Indicators of Well-being*, Permanent Forum on Indigenous Issues, Fifth Session, New York, 15–26 May 2006, E/C.19/2006/CRP.3.

freedom are particularly severe in the most remote and semi-isolated indigenous communities, such as those of the Murunahuas, the Mashco-Piros and the Cashibo-Cacataibos, placed in "protected" natural areas.[39] Indigenous and tribal peoples are also vulnerable to child labour, which is significantly more prevalent and more persistent among indigenous children than among their non-indigenous peers.[40]

39. E. Bedoya Garland; A. Bedoya Silva-Santisteban: *El trabajo forzoso en la extracción de la madera en la amazonía peruana*, DECLARATION/WP/40/2004 (Geneva, ILO, 2005), pp. 12–13.
40. G. Hall; H.A. Patrinos: op. cit. ILO: *Guidelines for combating child labour among indigenous peoples* (Geneva, 2006).

**Box 2.4.
Bonded labour among the Mbororo pastoralists and the Baka, Bakola
and Bagyeli people (so-called "Pygmies") of Cameroon**

Participatory research undertaken by the ILO in 2004 and 2005 with indigenous representatives and communities revealed that in many areas, the so-called "Pygmy" communities, or individuals or specific families within these communities, are considered the property of their neighbours. "Pygmy" camps are not officially recognized in the administrative structures of Cameroon, and only exist in so far as they constitute attachments to neighbouring and officially recognized (non-indigenous) villages. This has a direct impact on their ability to own land and participate in decision-making processes. Most of the land and forest areas traditionally used by the "Pygmy" communities for subsistence purposes have been expropriated, sold, or converted into protected areas. As a result, these formerly nomadic, hunter-gatherer communities have been relying increasingly on wage labour and sedentary agriculture in neighbouring communities. Bonded labour and the underpayment of indigenous workers compared to workers of other ethnic groups were found to be widespread.

Sources: A.K. Barume: *Etude sur le cadre légal pour la protection des droits des peuples indigènes et tribaux au Cameroun*, PRO 169 (Geneva, ILO, 2005); B. Tchoumba: *Indigenous and tribal peoples and poverty reduction strategies in Cameroon*, PRO 169, ILO, and Centre for Environment and Development, Yaoundé (Geneva, ILO, 2005).

102. Despite growing evidence of labour market discrimination against indigenous and tribal peoples, policy initiatives aimed at improving their living conditions tend to disregard this matter. Policy prescriptions usually focus on their labour supply constraints, such as poor schooling and poor health conditions. While investments in more, better and culturally suitable schools and health services for indigenous and tribal peoples are badly needed and welcome, they will not succeed alone in eliminating discrimination at work. Measures explicitly geared towards removing biases on the labour demand side are required as well.

Others

103. In Japan, the United Nations Special Rapporteur on contemporary forms of racism, racial discrimination, xenophobia and related intolerance has recently expressed concern about discrimination against descendants of former Japanese colonies (e.g. the Koreans and Chinese), among other groups.[41] This is reflected in low wages, long and exhausting working hours, and violence. To protect them, Rengo,

the largest union in Japan, has created a union for Chinese workers.[42]

104. In the Russian Federation, racism and xenophobia have become more overt since the collapse of the USSR.[43] Rivalry, and sometimes conflicts, among the different nationalities of the Soviet Union also existed in the Soviet period but were kept under control. Anecdotal evidence shows an increase in racism against people from the former Soviet Republics, especially Caucasian and Central Asian countries.[44] With illegal labour migration estimated at between 5 and 14 million people,[45] a 2005 survey of the Moscow Bureau for Human Rights[46] reveals that about 40 per cent of Russians doubt that the economy will benefit from migrants and 70 per cent support immigration of Russians and Russian speakers, but feel that migration of other ethnic groups should be curbed.

Migrant workers

105. As noted in previous pages, migrant workers are often subject to discrimination because of their colour and race, or their actual or perceived religion, or a combination of these, and they may also be the target

41. United Nations Economic and Social Council: *Report of the Special Rapporteur on contemporary forms of racism, racial discrimination, xenophobia and related intolerance, Doudou Diène (Addendum: Mission to Japan)*, E/CN.4/2006/16/Add.2, 24 Jan. 2006.
42. S. Kakuchi: "Male migrant workers in Japan have it tough", in *Asia Times Online*, 9 June 2005, at www.atimes.com/atimes/Japan/GF09Dh02.html.
43. United Nations Committee on the Elimination of Racial Discrimination: *Concluding observations of the Committee on the Elimination of Racial Discrimination: Russian Federation*, document CERD/C/62/CO/7, 21 Mar. 2003.
44. C. Wyatt: "Racism on the rise in Russia", in BBC News, 16 July 2002, at news.bbc.co.uk/1/hi/world/europe/2131214.stm.
45. RIA Novosti: "Russia: Legal migrant workers up 63% on 2004", 26 Jan. 2006, at http://en.rian.ru/russia/20060126/43196003.html.
46. Moscow Bureau for Human Rights: "Racism, xenophobia, ethnic discrimination and anti-Semitism in Russia", June 2005, at www.antirasizm.ru/english_rep_017.doc.

Box 2.5.
Being migrant and a woman: A double burden

Jobs for female migrants are concentrated in less regulated sectors, making them more vulnerable to exploitation and unequal treatment than migrant men (e.g. agriculture, sex industry, domestic work). Domestic workers comprise mainly female migrants, not only in Western European countries, but also in the Gulf States and high- and middle-income Asian countries. In the Gulf Cooperation Council (GCC) countries women migrants represent about 20–40 per cent of the migrant workforce, and come mostly from South and South-East Asian countries. Many others work in Lebanon and Jordan (in 2000, 35,000 Sri Lankans and 7,000 Filipinas were employed as domestic workers in Jordan). Although their working conditions vary enormously, these workers are particularly vulnerable to discrimination, exploitation and abuse of all kinds, including harassment, violence by employers and coercion by employment agencies, forced labour, low wages and inadequate social coverage. Wage discrimination by nationality is also common in many countries in Asia and the Middle East (while workers from the Philippines earn relatively high wages, most Indonesian and Sri Lankan women are not paid the minimum wage).

Discrimination also affects skilled female migrants, especially when they belong to a racial, ethnic or religious minority. In Canada, for instance, a number of studies show that female migrants with university degrees belonging to visible minorities are offered jobs and pay that are inferior to those given to their male peers or non-minority women with an equivalent educational background. This is the result of both institutional obstacles to the recognition of foreign diplomas and university degrees, and biased recruitment practices at the workplace.

Sources: R. Jureidini: *Migrant workers and xenophobia in the Middle East* (Geneva, United Nations Research Institute for Social Development (UNRISD), Dec. 2003). at www.unrisd.org/; C. Kuptsch (ed.): *Merchants of labour* (Geneva, International Institute for Labour Studies, 2006); ILO: *A global alliance against forced labour*, Global Report under the follow-up to the ILO Declaration on Fundamental Principles and Rights at Work, Report I(B), International Labour Conference, 93rd Session, 2005; J. Salaff; A. Greve: "Gendered structural barriers to job attainment for skilled Chinese emigrants in Canada", in *International Journal of Population Geography*, Vol. 9 (2003), pp. 443–456, at www.chass.utoronto.ca/~agreve/IJPG_Salaff-Greve.pdf.

of unfavourable treatment simply because of their migrant status. Women migrant workers, who make up half the total, can be doubly penalized (box 2.5).

106. The plight of migrant workers is a growing concern, since foreign-born workers represent significant and rising proportions of the workforce in many countries. Estimated at 86 million over the world, and some 32 million in the developing regions, the movement of men and women seeking better job opportunities abroad is likely to increase in the coming years.[47] Ten per cent of the workforce in Western Europe is currently made up of migrants, while in a number of African, Asian or American countries percentages are higher, representing over 50 per cent of the workforce in some Gulf States.

107. One manifestation of discrimination against migrant workers is their concentration, often regardless of their skill levels, in "3D" jobs (dirty, dangerous and degrading) where protection is often inadequate or absent in law or in practice.[48]

108. Although most States tend to grant documented migrant workers de jure equality of treatment with nationals as regards remuneration, hours of work, holidays with pay, and minimum age, they face a variety of employment restrictions (box 2.6). The incidence and extent of differential treatment may vary depending on whether migrant workers are permanent or temporary, and according to whether they are high-skilled or low-skilled.

109. National migration policies are more inclined to provide for equal opportunities and treatment between nationals and migrant workers in high-skilled positions than those in unskilled and low-status jobs. High-skilled workers are usually offered more guarantees to shift towards permanent settlement than the low-skilled. Such preferences are doubly hard on low-skilled workers, who are already particularly vulnerable to exploitation and violations of their rights. If low skills are the result of denied equal opportunities in education or at work in their countries of origin because of their sex or religion or race, inferior treatment of low-skilled migrant workers in destination countries further aggravates discrimination.

47. See ILO: *Towards a fair deal for migrant workers in the global economy*, Report VI, International Labour Conference, 92nd Session, Geneva, 2004; OSCE; IOM; ILO: *Handbook on establishing effective labour migration policies in countries of origin and destination* (Vienna, 2006).
48. See ILO: *Towards a fair deal for migrant workers in the global economy*, op. cit., paras. 150–165 (agriculture), 173–178 (sweatshops), 181–194 (care economy, domestic work) and, to some extent, 166–172 (construction).

Box 2.6.
Migrant workers: Examples of employment restrictions

There are many ways in which migrant workers' free choice of employment and access to the labour market are restricted. The system of work permits allows governments to limit access of foreigners to certain categories of jobs (e.g. in Cyprus, Belgium, Czech Republic, Egypt, Jordan, Saudi Arabia and Syrian Arab Republic) and to restrict the job choices of migrant workers (e.g. Republic of Korea, where the Employment Permit System (EPS) prevents a migrant worker from switching jobs more than three times). Migrants may also be confined to a specific region of the country (Bulgaria and Switzerland). This system may be subject to quotas established by government (e.g. Kazakhstan) or associated with an employment authorization to be obtained by employers (e.g. Austria). Free access to the labour market may generally be obtained after a minimum period of employment in the country. Other restrictions include: limited access of migrant workers to certain administrative or political occupations which are reserved for nationals (political and administrative functions); non-recognition of diplomas and qualifications obtained in home countries; obligation to leave the country when the contract is terminated; and administrative and bureaucratic difficulties (e.g. unemployed workers in Spain, restrictive visa policies in the Gulf States). In some Arab States, foreign workers have limited rights to family reunification and reduced access to health insurance schemes. Saudi Arabia has adopted measures such as taxation on the recruitment of foreigners and taxation of foreigners to finance training programmes for nationals. Kuwait and the United Arab Emirates have also introduced indirect taxes, especially health and surgery fees, for migrants.

Sources: OSCE; IOM; ILO: *Handbook on establishing effective labour migration policies in countries of origin and destination* (Vienna, 2006), pp. 133–137, 102; United Nations Commission on Human Rights: *Specific groups and individuals: Migrant workers*, Report submitted by the Ms. Gabriela Rodríguez Pizarro, Special Rapporteur, in conformity with resolution 2003/46 of the Commission on Human Rights, doc. E/CN.4/2004/76/Add.2, 14 Jan. 2004.; N. Shah: *Restrictive labour immigration policies in the oil-rich Gulf: Effectiveness and implications for sending Asian countries*, United Nations Expert Group Meeting on International Migration and Development in the Arab Region, doc. UN/POP/EGM/2006/03, 5 May 2006, at www.un.org/esa/population/meetings/EGM_Ittmig_Arab/P03_Shah.pdf; P. Fargues: *International migration in the Arab region: Trends and policies*, United Nations Expert Group Meeting on International Migration and Development in the Arab Region, doc. UN/POP/EGM/2006/09, Rev. 5 Sep. 2006, at www.un.org/esa/population/meetings/EGM_Ittmig_Arab/P09_Fargues.pdf.

---

110. Resistance towards providing equal treatment with nationals is much stronger in respect of social security rights, employment mobility and access to employment and vocational training. The provision of alternative employment, relief work and retraining often depends on whether migrant workers are temporary or permanent settlers, which is contrary to the provisions of ILO standards, including the Migrant Workers (Supplementary Provisions) Convention, 1975 (No. 143). This is an important issue, especially in the light of the steady increase in temporary workers' programmes that often bind migrant workers to the same employer or may require them to leave the country immediately after termination of the contract, and to return only after a certain period of time. These temporary schemes discourage settlement of migrant workers in the country, which in practice often has the effect of excluding them from equal treatment rights.[49]

111. Regional integration schemes grant some nationalities privileges over others, with Member States extending equality of opportunity and treatment to migrant workers from countries within the regional bloc, but not to persons who are not citizens of a Member State (third-country nationals). However, there have been some encouraging developments in the form of the EU regulations granting equal treatment to third-country nationals legally residing in the country.[50] Moreover, despite the fact that the EU does not support permanent immigration, there seems to be a growing recognition that in some sectors it may be desirable.[51]

112. The circumstances of migrant workers in an irregular situation are of special concern. In the event of breach of national law by employers, they may find it difficult to claim the rights they do have or to seek redress in the courts, as some countries do not provide for such a possibility or for the right of these workers to have access to legal proceedings in a language they

---

49. See OSCE; IOM; ILO: op. cit., pp. 134–144.
50. Council Directive 2003/109/EC of 25 November 2003 concerning the status of third-country nationals who are long-term residents, *Official Journal* L 016, 23 Jan. 2004, pp. 0044–0053. Under the Directive, Member States will recognize long-term resident status after five years' continuous legal residence. They would be guaranteed equal treatment with EU nationals with respect to most socio-economic rights.
51. OSCE; IOM; ILO: op. cit., p. 125.

Box 2.7.
Easing tensions between religious requirements and established workplace practices

Workplaces, services and facilities frequently have rules about dress. These may take the form of a requirement to wear a particular uniform or protective gear or a prohibition on wearing a head covering. These rules may come into direct conflict with religious dress requirements. Certain creeds, for instance, do not permit men to cut their hair, while an employer, for health and safety reasons, may require men to have short hair. An example of a religious accommodation measure is to ask concerned employees to contain their hair with a net or other appropriate head covering. Some religions require that their members observe periods of prayer at particular times during the day. This practice may conflict with an employer's regular work hours or daily routines in the workplace. One way of overcoming possible tensions is by a modified break policy, flexible hours and/or providing a private area for devotions. An employee may request time off to observe a holy day because his/her religion may forbid him/her to work on those days. Flexible scheduling may be a solution, and may include alternative arrival and departure times on the days when the person cannot work for the entire period, or use of lunch times in exchange for early departure or staggered work hours. Where the person has already used up paid holidays to which he or she is entitled, the employer should also consider permitting the employee to make up time lost or use floating days off.

Source: Ontario Human Rights Commission: Policy on creed and the accommodation of religious observances, at www.ohrc.on.ca/english/publications/creed-religion-policy.shtml.

understand. Moreover, in many countries an undocumented migrant worker who is seized by the competent authorities does not have the opportunity or time to request payment of wages and benefits due or to lodge an appeal. The protection of fundamental rights of migrant workers in an irregular situation, including protection against racial, ethnic or sex discrimination, is illusory if they do not have access to legal procedures.

113.   On a positive note, trade unions around the world have increasingly taken steps to address the plight of migrant workers. For instance, there has been an increase in bilateral or multilateral agreements concluded by unions from origin and destination countries to assist migrant workers and combat their exploitation, one example being the agreement signed by Mauritanian and Spanish unions. Another interesting initiative is the "UNI Passport" launched by Union Network International (UNI), which, since 2001, allows a migrant worker who is already a member of a union in his/her country of origin to be "hosted" by a UNI member union in the host country. In Malaysia, the Malaysian Trade Union Congress (MTUC) Conference on Migrant Workers held in 2005 decided to initiate action and put in place mechanisms to ensure better protection of the 1.5 million documented migrant workers living in the country.[52]

Religious discrimination

114.   Discrimination based on religion has been on the increase in the past few years. Several factors have contributed to this: the deepening of economic inequalities along religious and racial or ethnic lines; the intensification of migration, and the cultural challenges it brings; and terrorist acts and the adoption of security policies in response to such acts.

115.   In the industrialized world, workplace discrimination against Muslims worsened after 11 September 2001. Situations range from harassment or offensive comments concerning religious beliefs or practices to the refusal by employers to accommodate the needs of a person arising from his or her religion that may conflict with a requirement, qualification or practice (see box 2.7).[53]

116.   Complaints of religious discrimination lodged before the Equal Employment Opportunity Commission (EEOC) in the United States rose by more than 20 per cent in 2002, most of the increase coming from Muslim employees, and stayed at the same level in 2003.[54] In 2005 the Council on American-Islamic Relations (CAIR) reported a 30 per cent increase over 2004 in complaints of anti-Muslim harassment, violence and discriminatory treatment.[55]

52. MTUC Conference on Migrant Workers (18–19 April 2005): Concluding resolution, available on the Global Union Research Network (GURN) web site, at www.gurn.info/topic/migrant/mtuc_conf_apr05.pdf.
53. P. Sappal: "Workplace intolerance rises for Muslims after Sept. 11", in *Career Journal*, 13 Jan. 2004.
54. ibid.
55. CAIR: *The status of Muslim civil rights in the United States 2006: The struggle for equality* (Washington, DC), at www.cair.com/cair-2006report/.

117. In the EU, the issue of the "Islamic veil" or *hijab* has thrown into relief the different perceptions prevailing among European countries regarding secularism and religious freedom and revealed some inconsistencies. For instance, in 2003, the Federal Constitutional Court of Germany ruled in favour of a teacher who wanted to wear an Islamic scarf to school; but at least four German states have banned teachers from wearing scarves, and in one state the ban applies to all civil servants.[56]

118. In many countries, religious discrimination continues to be strongly associated with race/ethnicity (for example, people of North African origin in France) or social origin (for instance, Dalits in India). Pasmanda and Dalits in India suffer even more extreme marginalization and socio-economic discrimination if they are either Muslim[57] or Christian.[58] In other countries (Afghanistan, Bangladesh and Pakistan) Hindus continue to be treated as unequal citizens and confined to low-skilled jobs.[59]

119. Religious discrimination is often worse in societies where no freedom of religion exists or where a state religion tends to disadvantage or exclude other religions. In Saudi Arabia, for instance, migrant workers who are not Muslim must refrain from public display of religious symbols such as Christian crosses or Hindu *tilaka*; other forms of discrimination consist of job advertisements excluding applicants belonging to certain religious groups (Hindus in particular), or of preventing migrant workers from practising their religion openly.[60] The situation of the Baha'i in the Islamic Republic of Iran has long been a subject of comment by both ILO and United Nations bodies.

120. In Senegal and Sudan, Christian job applicants are required to deny their faith or to convert to Islam if they want to be employed.[61] One of the most resilient forms of discrimination is that targeting Copts in Egypt, who are denied equal access to education and equal opportunities in recruitment and promotion. Very few are appointed to key positions in the Government or are candidates for parliament. Enrolment of Copts in police academies and military schools is restricted, and very few are teachers and professors.[62]

Discrimination based on social origin

121. Discrimination based on social origin arises when an individual is denied a job or certain economic activities or only assigned particular jobs because of the class or socio-occupational category or caste to which she or he belongs. Prejudices and institutional practices based on social origin thus limit the social mobility of certain people. A person's social origin continues to be a powerful obstacle towards equality of opportunities not only in highly stratified societies, but also in those where social segmentation has become less rigid. This is due to the fact that action to overcome this barrier covers a range of sectors and policy measures lying within the competence of different areas of government, which makes coordination and implementation difficult.

Rural migrant workers

122. In China, a person's place of residence is an important determinant of benefits and opportunities, including in employment and occupation. Rural dwellers have fewer entitlements than urban dwellers. The *hukou* system of resident registration, which tied people to a particular place of residence and has been in force since 1958, has been gradually dismantled since the 1980s to meet the increasing demand from industries in the major cities.[63] While movement has been made free irrespective of where migrants have their *hukou*, it is nonetheless hard for migrants from rural areas to obtain an urban *hukou*.

123. Of today's estimated 150 million rural migrant workers labouring in China's cities, however, only 40 per cent obtain either a permanent or a temporary permit; the others, called "floating population", do not have it. This is a matter of concern, considering

56. BBC: "The Islamic veil across Europe", 6 Oct. 2006, at news.bbc.co.uk/2/hi/europe/5414098.stm.
57. See Asian Human Rights Commission – Religious Groups for Human Rights: Ali Anwar: Letter to Justice Rajinder Sachar – Pasmanda and Dalit Muslims, 7 Nov. 2005, at www.rghr.net/mainfile.php/0743/1030.
58. See Dalitchristians.com: "Problems and struggles", at www.dalitchristians.com/Html/problems_struggles.htm.
59. Hindu American Foundation: "Hindus in South Asia and the diaspora: A survey of human rights 2005", at www.hinduamerican-foundation.org/reports.htm#hhr2005.
60. CEACR: Individual observation concerning Convention No. 111, Saudi Arabia, 2005.
61. ZENIT: *La persécution antichrétienne dans le monde* (interview with T. Grimaux), Mar. 2006, at www.ebior.org/Societe/Persecutions-I.htm.
62. See www.copts.com.
63. M. Tuñón: "Internal labour migration in China: Features and responses" (Beijing, ILO, Apr. 2006), at www.ilo.org/public/english/region/asro/beijing/download/training/lab_migra.pdf; and Bingqin Li: "Floating population or urban citizens? Status, social provision and circumstances of rural-urban migrants in China", in *Social policy and administration*, Vol. 40, No. 2 (Apr. 2006), pp. 174–195.

the phenomenal increase in rural to urban migration over the past two decades, from 2 million rural migrants in the mid-1980s to 150 million today.[64]

124.   Owing to their social status, rural migrants suffer from institutionalized discrimination.[65] In some cities, authorities deny them access to certain types of jobs (the better ones) that are kept for permanent residents. Rural migrant workers usually rely on informal networks (95 per cent found jobs through friends or by themselves) and end up working in informal, low-paid, menial jobs that urban workers refuse.[66]

125.   Most of them, especially those without a permit, have no labour contract. They may encounter difficulties in obtaining wages on time, they tend to work longer hours, are more vulnerable to workplace injuries and illnesses, do not have social security coverage and may be exposed to other risks, including trafficking. Many migrants from rural areas have a lower level of education and thus do not have access to skill training and promotion opportunities.

126.   In a period of rapid economic expansion and transition, rural migrant workers constitute an asset for China's economic development, as they account for 16 per cent of national gross domestic product (GDP) growth over the last 20 years, and represent 40 per cent of the urban workforce. Generally young (71 per cent are aged between 15 and 29), with little education (junior high-school diploma), they come from the less economically developed regions (western and central provinces).

127.   In the past few years, the Chinese Government has taken important steps to reform the *hukou* system and redress the disadvantaged situation of rural migrant workers. In 2002 and 2003, further to the recommendations of the State Council, a number of regulations were adopted providing for the suppression of unreasonable fees on migrants seeking permanent or temporary jobs in urban areas, the obligation on employers to sign labour contracts, and the prohibition of delayed payment of wages to migrant workers. In 2006, the State Council adopted further recommendations, including the guarantee of a minimum

wage to rural migrant workers, the enforcement of the labour contract system, access to employment services and job training, access to public services, and promotion of local economic development and village enterprises. Steps have also been taken to establish a social security system for migrant workers and to bring them within the scope of labour legislation.

128.   The amended Compulsory Education Law, which became effective in 2006, provides for nine years of compulsory schooling for children in both cities and rural areas, and grants the right to education of children of migrant workers no matter where they live. The 11th Five-Year Development Guidelines for 2006–10 include migration as an essential component of the national development strategy and, following the request of the Ministry of Labour and Social Security, the State Council approved the creation of the Joint Committee on Migrant Workers. The ratification of ILO Convention No. 111 in January 2006 is a further commitment to the elimination of employment discrimination based on social origin.

129.   Reforming the *hukou* system requires a number of institutional measures to be taken strategically, including reform of the labour protection system, reorganizing public resource distribution systems, building and expanding the capacity to offer public and social services (education, health care and housing) to rural migrants residing in urban areas. It also calls for a change in attitudes so that urban and rural workers are treated with equal dignity and respect.

Caste-based discrimination

130.   Violence, discrimination and segregation, because of their alleged "impurity" and inferiority, are a daily experience for millions of men and women in several regions of the world. Discrimination rooted in caste or similar systems of rigid social stratification has been observed in Africa, Asia and the Middle East, but the practice is most widespread in South Asia,[67] particularly in India and Nepal.[68] Although abolished by

---

64. M. Tuñón, op. cit.

65. Human Rights in China (HRIC): "Institutionalized exclusion: The tenuous legal status of internal migrants in China's major cities", 6 Nov. 2002, at hrichina.org/public/contents/article?revision%5fid=17138&item%5fid=3195; and "China's household registration *(Hukou)* system: Discrimination and reform", statement of Fei-Ling Wang to the Congressional-Executive Commission on China, 2 Sep. 2005, at www.cecc.gov/pages/roundtables/090205/Wang.php.

66. M. Tuñón: op. cit.

67. The study by the UN Sub-Commission on the Promotion and Protection of Human Rights presented in 2004 examines the situation in Bangladesh, Burkina Faso, India, Japan, Kenya, Mali, Federated States of Micronesia, Nepal, Pakistan, Senegal, Sri Lanka and Yemen (Commission on Human Rights: *Prevention of discrimination*, expanded working paper by Mr Asbjørn Eide and Mr Yozo Yokota on the topic of discrimination based on work and descent, doc. E/CN.4/Sub.2/2004/31, 5 July 2004).

68. In India, the Constitution abolished the caste system and provides for a reservations policy for "Scheduled Castes" to overcome de facto societal division. Civil rights and other protective legislation has been enacted. The Constitution and legislation of Nepal also prohibit any discrimination on the basis of caste.

Box 2.8.
Employment discrimination and poverty: The case of the Dalits in Nepal

The Dalits represent some 13 per cent or 2.9 million of Nepal's total population, which is comprised of different caste groups and indigenous people (Janajatis). Overall, the percentage of persons living below the poverty line dropped from 42 to 31 per cent between 1996 and 2004. All groups registered declines in poverty, but the Dalits and the Janajatis living in the hills benefited the least, and remain the groups most affected by poverty. In the case of the Dalits the incidence of poverty declined from 59 to 47 per cent, while among the Janajatis it dropped from 49 to 44 per cent. The highest caste group (Brahman/Chhetri) registered the deepest drop in poverty incidence (from 34 to 19 per cent), followed by Janajatis living in the plains (from 53 to 36 per cent).

A 2002 ILO survey of Dalits in Nepal[1] showed that 43 per cent of respondents were illiterate (male 34.6 per cent; female 62.2), 5 percentage points lower than the national average. Only 6.3 per cent of the survey population aged 15 years and above had undergone some sort of training – 80 per cent of them were male. Of the respondents, 71 per cent stated that if they obtained a job in the informal or private sector they were paid lower wages than persons belonging to other groups. Those working in occupations other than those typical of their caste were most likely to be agricultural wage labourers. Forty-eight per cent believed that open positions were not available for Dalits just because of their caste status and 21 per cent stated that they were refused jobs because of their caste status.

[1] A household survey conducted among 1,447 households from 60 Dalit settlement clusters in 18 of Nepal's districts.

Sources: DFID and World Bank: *Unequal citizens – Gender, caste and ethnic exclusion in Nepal* (Kathmandu, 2006); ILO: "Discrimination and forced labour of occupational castes in Nepal, 2003" (unpublished document).

law, which prohibits the practice of "untouchability", caste remains a dominant factor in defining the economic and social status of Dalit men and women throughout the subregion. The mobilization of Dalits in the countries concerned has helped raise the visibility of their plight nationally and internationally.[69]

131. Caste-based discrimination confines Dalits to occupations associated with their caste, often involving the most menial tasks such as "manual scavenging" or the removal of dead animals.[70] Dalits are generally not accepted for any work involving contact with water or food for non-Dalits or entering a non-Dalit residence. They are thus excluded from a wide range of work opportunities in the area of production, processing or sale of food items, domestic work and the provision of certain services in the private and public sectors (e.g. office helpers). Limited access to education, training and resources, such as land or

credit, further impair their equal opportunities for access to non-caste-based occupations and decent work. The deprivation stemming from discrimination in all areas of their life leads to higher levels of poverty among Dalits compared to non-Dalits (box 2.8).

132. A very encouraging and recent development, following efforts by the National Human Rights Commission, was the announcement by the Prime Minister of India of the abolition of the degrading practice of manual scavenging. Further to a number of meetings held by the Commission with representatives of the central and state governments and other stakeholders, the Planning Commission formulated a National Action Plan for Total Eradication of Manual Scavenging by the end of 2007.[71]

133. Where policies and laws are in place, enforcement and implementation are often lacking or unsatisfactory.[72] Affirmative action measures have assisted a

69. Dalits claim respect for their human rights and dignity through their own civil society organizations. The European Parliament and the UN Commission on Human Rights have adopted resolutions on discrimination based on work and descent. The US Congress held a hearing on the issue in October 2005. International non-governmental networking to raise awareness of the plight of the Dalits resulted in the adoption of the Kathmandu Dalit Declaration in 2004, available at www.nepaldalitinfo.20m.com/archives/KathDeclaration.pdf.

70. The practice of manual scavenging has been the subject of comments by the CEACR in respect of India. This practice involves the removal, under degrading and hazardous conditions, of human excrement from dry latrines that continue to be used throughout the country, despite the Government's efforts to abolish them. See CEACR: individual observation on India, Convention No. 111, published in 2006.

71. See *The Hindu*: "End manual scavenging, governments told", at www.thehindu.com/2003/12/30/stories/2003123001521200.htm.

72. In India, the National Commission for Scheduled Castes and Scheduled Tribes (now two separate commissions) has repeatedly called for measures to ensure the effective enforcement of the Protection of Civil Rights Act, 1995, the Scheduled Castes and the Scheduled Tribes (Prevention of Atrocities) Act, 1989, and the Employment of Manual Scavengers and Construction of Dry Latrines (Prohibition) Act, 1993.

small number of Dalits in obtaining formal jobs, but have failed to lead to more even progress in providing equal opportunities to all. Purely developmental approaches to improving the lot of the Dalits are insufficient, if the underlying structural causes and caste barriers are not simultaneously addressed.

134. Caste-based discrimination similar to the "untouchable" system in South Asia has also been identified in Africa and the Middle East. The Midgo community in the Somali region of Ethiopia is regarded as impure, unlucky, sinful, polluting and thus meriting avoidance and abuse by others. Midgos survive thanks to remittances from abroad. In Nigeria, the Osu are seen as untouchable and socially rejected. In Kenya, a subsection of the Samburu, known as the Ilkunono or blacksmiths, are despised and discriminated against. In Yemen, the Al Akhdam are a socially condemned group treated as non-citizens and engaged in the disposal of human waste.[73]

135. Social stratification in Niger remains a complex and highly sensitive issue. Historically, distinctions have existed within some social groups between "nobles" and "non-nobles", or between so-called "masters" and "slaves". Over time, such distinctions have become less pronounced, particularly among sedentary groups. There has been a certain degree of social and economic mobility, particularly as a result of outward seasonal or longer-term migration to work in neighbouring countries. For example, male Tuaregs of servile origin who migrate regularly from the region of Bankilaré develop strategies of avoidance of the social hierarchy on their return home, the first step in a gradual process of liberation.[74] Yet it would appear that persons of slave descent might still be subject to a range of exploitative and discriminatory practices, including some vestiges of forced labour.[75] Studies have drawn a distinction between "active" and "passive" forms of slavery.[76]

136. A recent positive step taken by the Government of Niger was the establishment in August 2006 of a national inter-ministerial commission to tackle remaining forced labour and discrimination problems, charged with promoting decent work and poverty reduction, as well as preventing such practices through the implementation of a national plan of action with ILO cooperation.

---

73. United Nations Human Rights Council, Sub-Commission on the Promotion and Protection of Human Rights: *Progress report of Mr Yozo Yokota and Ms Chin-Sung Chung, Special Rapporteurs on the topic of discrimination based on work and descent*, 58th Session, doc. A/HRC/Sub.1/58/CRP.2, 28 July 2006.

74. F. Boyer: "L'Esclavage chez les Touaregs de Bankilaré au miroir des migrations circulaires", in *Cahiers d'études africaines*, No. 179–180 (2005).

75. ILO: *A global alliance against forced labour*, op. cit., paras. 201–206.

76. M. Oumarou : *Défis et opportunités pour la Déclaration au Niger: Identification des obstacles à la mise en oeuvre des principes et droits fondamentaux au travail et propositions de solutions au Niger*, DECLARATION/WP4/2001 (Geneva, ILO), p. 24.

2. Newly recognized forms of discrimination

137. This chapter examines the latest developments concerning patterns of discrimination based on grounds not explicitly mentioned in Convention No. 111 but that have been recognized by law in many member States.

A workplace for all ages: A reachable goal?

138. Age is becoming an increasingly important determinant of people's occupational attainments and returns to work everywhere. Age discrimination affects both ends of the age spectrum, although its manifestations and the reasons leading to it differ depending on whether younger or older workers are concerned. Moreover, there is a deep-seated belief that a high rate of employment of older workers can only be achieved at the expense of new, younger labour market entrants or vice versa. This may lead to public policies favouring one group over the other, thus reinforcing discrimination against the latter.

139. The urgent need to create workplaces for all ages is apparent in the light of recent trends. In 2005, young people accounted for 44 per cent of the world's total unemployed, although their share of the total working-age population aged 15 and above was only 25 per cent – in other words they are three times more likely to be unemployed than adults. More than 300 million youth, or 25 per cent of the youth population, were living below the US$2 per day poverty line.[77]

140. On the other hand, by 2030, the EU will have 110 million people aged over 65, compared to 71 million in 2000, meaning a drop from 4.27 to 2.55 in the ratio of workers to persons over 65 years old.[78] In developing countries, the shares of people aged 60 and above in the total population are smaller, but growing at a much faster pace (figure 2.9).

Discrimination against younger workers

141. Less favourable treatment, often unjustified, on the basis of age seems to play an important role in explaining the lower occupational attainments of younger workers and, in particular, their over-representation in casual jobs with lower benefits, training opportunities and career prospects. Recent surveys show that, contrary to conventional wisdom, younger workers may be more vulnerable to age discrimination than their older peers. According to a report issued by the UK Employers Forum on Age, ageism at work is a bigger problem for people in their late teens than for those in their 50s.[79]

142. Biased treatment against younger workers can take many forms; one is the payment of lower entry wages to younger workers on the assumption that, as they are less experienced, they are entitled to lower pay. Lower wages are also intended to help reduce youth unemployment by creating incentives for employers to recruit them.[80] This practice may be justified for jobs demanding higher skills than those possessed by younger workers, the rationale being that employers would thus be encouraged to compensate their lower experience with investments in training. In other instances, however, it amounts to a breach of the principle of equal remuneration for work of equal value, embedded in the ILO Declaration. Moreover, lower wages for younger workers have proven not to be effective in curbing youth unemployment.[81]

143. Other manifestations of discrimination against younger workers include longer probation periods than for older workers, and much greater reliance on flexible forms of contract and special contracts to recruit younger workers.[82] The available evidence is inconclusive, but recent data from the European Commission show that over 30 per cent of young employees under temporary contracts found a more stable job after one year, but six years later 20 per cent had left employment, while about 16 per cent still held precarious jobs. An initial less favourable treatment may therefore have far-reaching consequences for the future working lives of young labour market entrants.

---

77. ILO: *Global employment trends for youth* (Geneva, 2006).
78. EQUAL: "A shrinking labour force? Not just a question of demographics", Policy brief, at europa.eu.int/comm/employment_social/equal/policy-briefs/etg3-working-life-cycle_en.cfm.
79. Employers Forum on Age (EFA): "Age stereotypes defunct", 17 Feb. 2005, at www.efa.org.uk/press/press-release005.asp.
80. G. Rosas; G. Rossignotti: "Starting the new millennium right: Decent employment for young people", in *International Labour Review*, Vol. 144, No. 2 (2005), pp. 139–160.
81. M. Godfrey: *Youth employment policy in developing and transition countries: Prevention as well as cure*, Social Protection Discussion Paper No. 0320 (Washington, DC, World Bank, 2003).
82. R. Diez de Medina: *Jóvenes y empleo en los noventa* (Montevideo, CINTERFOR, 2001).

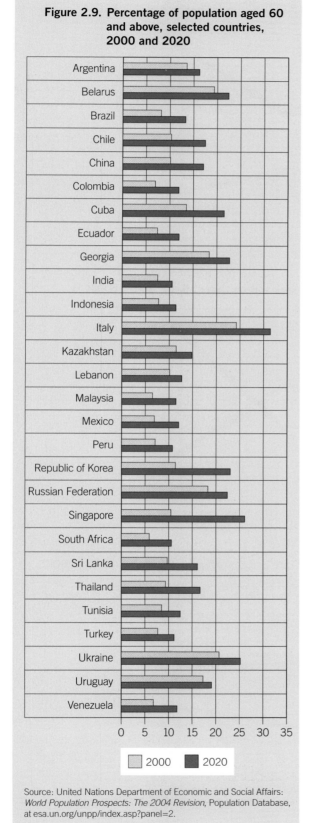

Figure 2.9. Percentage of population aged 60 and above, selected countries, 2000 and 2020

2000 ☐   2020 ■

Source: United Nations Department of Economic and Social Affairs: *World Population Prospects: The 2004 Revision*, Population Database, at esa.un.org/unpp/index.asp?panel=2.

144. Discrimination may also make it more difficult for some younger workers, because of their sex, nationality, race or ethnic origin, or a combination of these, to find a job or get training or obtain equal pay for equal work. Studies[83] reveal that discrimination in hiring and recruitment against second-generation younger immigrants in France is widespread, especially against those of both sexes of North African origin. Disparities in earnings between young French males and their immigrant peers are entirely due to occupational differences. But between young French females and immigrant females, unequal pay for equal work is an additional factor. All young women, however, irrespective of nationality and origin, suffer from additional discrimination in remuneration because of their sex.

145. In Brazil black and white male youth, in both the 15–19 and 20–24 age groups, experienced similar levels of employment and unemployment in 2004. Both white and black female youth registered higher unemployment and lower employment rates than their male peers, suggesting that gender barriers are stronger than racial ones, but black women were in the worst situation, with the highest unemployment and lowest employment rates (figures 2.10 and 2.11).

146. In the United States, black people aged 15–24 fared worse than their white peers in 2005. But black women outperformed black men: they registered higher employment and lower unemployment rates (figure 2.12). The better performance of young black women has been attributed to tight labour markets and an expanding demand in the service sector, the shift from welfare to workfare and the growth of income support, especially for working poor with children.[84]

Discrimination against older workers

147. Negative attitudes towards hiring and retaining older workers are rooted in perceptions that portray them as slow learners, less adaptable and in poor health. Age-unfriendly working conditions are a manifestation of discrimination against them, but innovative experiences show that age bias can be reduced by adjusting workplaces to older workers' needs through job redesign or work reorganization (box 2.9).

83. See P. Simon: "France and the unknown second generation: Preliminary results on social mobility", in *International Migration Review*, Vol. 37, No. 4 (2003), pp. 1091–1119; O. Joseph; S. Lemière: *La discrimination de genre et d'origine à l'encontre des jeunes sur le marché du travail: Mesures à partir de différents aspects des situations professionnelles*, Mar. 2005, at www.cereq.fr/pdf/Net-Doc-12.pdf.

84. P. Edelman; H.J. Holzer; P. Offner: *Reconnecting disadvantaged young men* (Washington, DC, The Urban Institute Press, 2006), pp. 18–19.

Figure 2.10. Employment and unemployment rates by race and sex, ages 20–24, Brazil, 2004

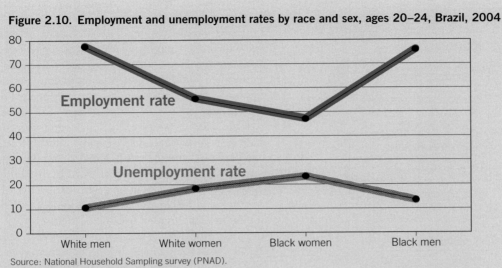

Source: National Household Sampling survey (PNAD).

Figure 2.11. Employment and unemployment rates by race and sex, ages 15–19, Brazil, 2004

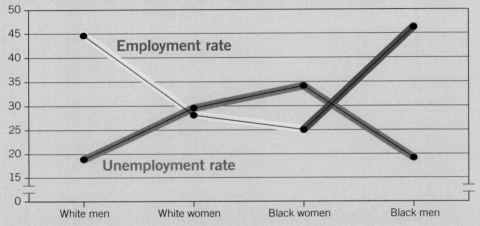

Source: ibid.

Figure 2.12. Employment and unemployment rates by race and sex, ages 16–24, United States, 2004

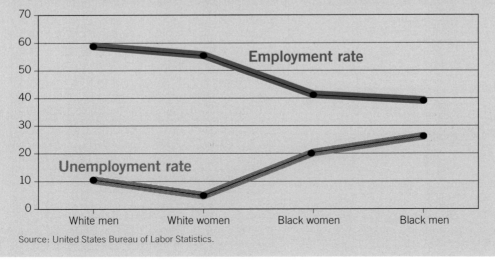

Source: United States Bureau of Labor Statistics.

Box 2.9.
Companies in action: Making workplaces "ageing-friendly"

Health and safety measures are very important, especially as older workers tend to suffer the most serious workplace accidents. Preventive measures, such as adapting the workplace to their needs or introducing more flexible working arrangements, can be very helpful. In the United States employers in the health sector have made nurses' work less strenuous by installing hydraulically functioning hospital beds. In Australia a distributor of medical products with a third of its workforce comprising women over 45 gave employees breaks during the day, part-time work and administrative assistance to workers who were not computer literate. As a result, the company did not have staff turnover in two years. In Austria, Polyfelt, a chemical production plant, has lowered the working week to 34 hours and introduced a new shift pattern, i.e. five shift groups instead of four, with three–four days off and six periods of night work per month (previously eight). In Germany, Volkswagen has devised a system of "time vouchers" that allows employees to save parts of their gross income, payments for extra shifts, additional payments, extra holidays and overtime work in a special fund. Workers may use it at their own discretion, and from the age of 55 can exchange their vouchers for periods of time off or receive higher pension benefits after retirement.

Sources: Chapter 4, "Age discrimination and human resource management in practice", in P. Thew; K. Eastman; J. Bourke (eds.): *Age discrimination: Mitigating risk in the workplace* (Sydney, CCH Australia Limited, 2005); and A. Jolivet; S. Lee: *Employment conditions in an ageing world: Meeting the working time challenge*, Conditions of Work and Employment Series, No. 9 (Geneva, ILO, 2004).

148. An additional obstacle to the recruitment of older workers may be the perceived higher cost of employing them and their declining productivity because of the deterioration of their physical and mental capacities. This belief is particularly common in countries where wage systems and benefits are strongly linked to age and length of service (Austria, Belgium, France, Japan and the United States).[85]

149. It is a misconception to think that older workers are less productive. Their productivity must be assessed on the basis of both their past work experience and the relevance of their skills and competences to the current job. Those who have worked under poor conditions for long periods and suffer from health problems are likely to experience a decline in productivity and are thus entitled to protection.

150. Interestingly, small and medium-sized enterprises (SMEs) appear more likely than large firms to recruit older workers, especially if they have had previous work experience in large companies.[86] This does not necessarily mean, however, that SMEs are less biased than larger firms; it may rather indicate that, as they do not invest as much in training, they are more eager to benefit from the training provided by larger enterprises.

151. Social perceptions are slow to change and laws banning age discrimination are one important means of accelerating the pace of change in behaviour. In countries such as New Zealand, Australia, Canada and the United States, the law has prohibited age discrimination for many years. More recently, under the impetus of the EU framework Directive on equality,[87] the majority of Member States have transposed into national law the provisions on age-based discrimination. For example, the UK Employment Equality (Age) Regulations, which came into force in October 2006, prohibit direct and indirect discrimination, harassment and victimization on grounds of age of people of any age, young or old.

152. In New Zealand, age equality legislation has contributed to eliminating the most blatant forms of ageism, such as discriminatory employment advertisements or Internet sites carrying discriminatory job vacancies, but has been less effective in tackling covert discrimination, especially at the recruitment stage and in the recruitment industry.[88] One of the reasons for its limited impact has been the fact that enforcement is based on individual complaints, with the burden of the proof on the plaintiff, which discourages victims from filing a complaint, especially when discrimination is indirect and thus more difficult to prove.

85. See OECD: *Ageing and employment policies* series, various countries (Paris, 2005).
86. See EIRO: "Industrial relations and the ageing workforce: A review of measures to combat age discrimination in employment: The case of France".
87. Council Directive 2000/78/EC of 27 Nov. 2000 establishing a general framework for equal treatment in employment and occupation.
88. J. McGregor: "Combating employment discrimination and older workers in New Zealand: The law, the rhetoric and reality", in P. Thew; K. Eastman; J. Bourke (eds.): *Age discrimination: Mitigating risk at the workplace* (Sydney, CCH Australia Limited, 2005), pp. 156-167.

Box 2.10.
Manifestations of discrimination based on sexual orientation at the workplace

Refusal of employment, dismissal, denial of promotion.

Harassment: unwanted jokes, innuendo and loaded comments, verbal abuse, malicious gossip, name calling, bullying and victimization, false accusations of child abuse, graffiti, abusive phone calls, anonymous mail, damage to property, blackmail, violence and even death threats.

Benefits denied to the same-sex partner (e.g. extra days off for a variety of reasons such as relocation, childbirth, parental leave, caring for a sick partner or bereavement; educational facilities for employees and their families; provision of the employer's goods or services free of charge or at a discount; survivor's benefit in occupational pension schemes or for the purposes of life insurance; health-care insurance for employees and their families).

Self-exclusion (e.g. when homosexual persons avoid certain jobs, careers or employers for fear of being discriminated against on the basis of their sexual orientation).

The fallacy of the substitution between older and younger workers

153. Empirical evidence shows that substitution between older and younger workers rarely occurs. Entries are much more concentrated in the service sector and smaller firms, while early retirement schemes have been popular in the industrial sector and in industrial occupations in big firms.[89] Even early retirement schemes with a replacement condition have had a minor impact, as new labour market entrants often lacked the experience and skills required by the jobs vacated by older workers. According to OECD research, in countries such as Belgium and France the use of these schemes led to a steep decline in employment rates for older people, but failed to increase youth employment or reduce youth unemployment.[90]

154. Shifting employment problems from one population group to another cannot be the solution: measures affecting older workers cannot be taken in isolation from those targeting younger workers, but must be framed in the context of an overall and well-balanced strategy for full employment which gives due attention to all population groups, in accordance with the ILO Older Workers Recommendation, 1980

(No. 162). A society for all ages requires rethinking the conventional course of working life and introducing more flexible and tailored working patterns.[91] This is imperative in order to shift from competition to solidarity among age groups.

Discrimination based on sexual orientation

155. A person whose sexual orientation does not conform to prevailing and established patterns can be the target of verbal, psychological and physical violence and acts of hate. Homosexuality is illegal in several States around the world, and in many of these it is subject to corporal punishment or imprisonment.[92]

156. In the workplace, employees may suffer from discrimination if they are known or believed to be lesbian, gay, bisexual or transgender[93] (increasingly referred to as LGBT) (box 2.10).

157. International and national human rights institutions and mechanisms are attaching increasing importance to fighting discrimination based on sexual orientation.[94] Certain countries have adopted legal provisions prohibiting discrimination at work based on sexual orientation (table 2.7). This has occurred

---

89. P. Auer; M. Fortuny: "Ageing of the labour force in OECD countries: Economic and social consequences", Employment Paper 2000/2 (Geneva, ILO).

90. OECD: *Live longer, work longer*, Ageing and Employment Policies synthesis report (Paris, 2006).

91. Commission of the European Communities: *Green Paper "Confronting demographic change: A new solidarity between the generations"* (Brussels, 16 Mar. 2005), COM (2005) 94 final.

92. See *Le Monde* and International Lesbian and Gay Association (ILGA): *State homophobia*, a "world legal map" of legislation affecting LGBT people (2004), at www.ilga.org/statehomophobia/StateHomophobia3.jpg.

93. "Transgender" is a very broad term, which may include persons who disagree with stereotypical gender norms and societal representations, or who feel discordant with their biological sex.

94. For instance, the issue of sexual orientation was placed on the agenda of the United Nations Human Rights Council in 2003 when Brazil submitted a draft resolution on human rights and sexual orientation. Sexual orientation has been addressed in the reports of the Special Rapporteur on extrajudicial, summary or arbitrary executions and the Special Rapporteur on violence against women, its causes and consequences (www.ohchr.org/english/bodies/chr/special/sexualorientation.htm). See also D. Sanders: "Human rights and sexual orientation in international law", 11 May 2005, at www.ilga.org/news_results.asp?FileCategory=44&ZoneID=7&FileID=577.

Table 2.7. Examples of legislation banning discrimination based on sexual orientation

Scope: General ban on discrimination based on sexual orientation	
Australia	Human Rights and Equal Opportunity Commission Act, 1986
Bulgaria	Act of 24 September 2003 on protection against discrimination
Canada	Canadian Human Rights Act, as amended on 20 June 1996
Ecuador	Political Constitution of the Republic of Ecuador of 5 June 1998 (article 23)
Fiji	Constitution Amendment Act (No. 13 of 1997)
Korea, Republic of	National Human Rights Commission Act (No. 6481 of May 2001)
New Zealand	Human Rights Act of 10 August 1993 (No. 82 of 1993)
Scope: Ban on discrimination based on sexual orientation with respect to employment	
Croatia	Labour Act of 1995, as amended in 2003
Denmark	Act No. 756 of 2004 respecting prohibition against discrimination in the labour market
Finland	Non-Discrimination Act (No. 21/2004)
Israel	Employment (Equal Opportunities) Law 5748-1988
Hungary	Act CXXV of 22 December 2003 on equal treatment and promotion of equal opportunities
Lithuania	Law No. IX-926 Labour Code of 4 June 2002
Malta	Equal Treatment in Employment Regulations, 2004
Norway	Working Environment Act (No. 62 of June 2005)
Slovakia	Anti-Discrimination Act No. 365/2004
Slovenia	Employment Relationships Act of 24 April 2002
South Africa	Employment Equity Act (No. 55 of 1998), as amended in 2006
Sweden	Act (No. 479 of 2005) to amend Act No. 133 of 1999 to prohibit discrimination in working life due to sexual orientation
Timor-Leste	Regulation No. 2002/5 on the establishment of a Labour Code for East Timor
United Kingdom	Employment Equality (Sexual Orientation) Regulations 2003 (No. 1661)

Source: ILO: NATLEX database, at www.ilo.org/dyn/natlex/natlex_browse.home?

in particular in the EU 25 in the past three years, following the adoption of the EU equality Directive prohibiting, among others, discrimination based on sexual orientation. Some shortcomings have nonetheless been observed with regard to the implementation of the Directive.[95] In some Member States, such as Estonia, the definition of harassment is more restrictive than in the Directive; in others, such as France, there is no specific provision making instruction to discriminate on this ground unlawful; in Latvia, discrimination based on sexual orientation in vocational guidance and training is not prohibited; and in many countries, national anti-discrimination bodies do not cover sexual orientation.

95. See J. Cormack; M. Bell: "Developing anti-discrimination law in Europe: The 25 EU Member States compared", report prepared for the European Network of Independent Experts in the non-discrimination field, Sep. 2005, at web20.s112.typo3server.com/fileadmin/pdfs/Reports/Law_Report_2005/05compan_en.pdf.

> **Box 2.11.**
> **Companies challenging the "cost" argument**
>
> Sixty-five per cent of Australian employers rated the financial cost of workplace accommodations as neutral and 20 per cent indicated an overall financial benefit. The average recruitment cost of an employee with a disability was 13 per cent of the average recruitment cost of an employee without a disability. DuPont has conducted surveys showing over 35 years that disabled employees perform equally or better compared to their non-disabled colleagues. Only 4 per cent of disabled people of working age require additional adjustments in the workplace. Costs are generally negligible. Marks and Spencer has shown that two-thirds of the adjustments for disabled people do not involve any costs.
>
> Source: See www.JobAccess.gov.au/ and www.csreurope.org.

Discrimination based on disability

158. Around 650 million people, or 10 per cent of the world's population, live with a disability – whether physical or mental. Statistics indicate that approximately one in five are born with a disability, while most acquire their disability after age 16, mainly during their working lives.[96] The vast majority, i.e. 80 per cent, live in developing countries.

159. Some 470 million people with disabilities are of working age.[97] There are considerable variations across countries in the relative size of the working-age disabled population, as well as in their unemployment and employment rates. These differences reflect in part the variety of definitions and methodologies used worldwide to capture disability (Part I, Chapters 1 and 2). Everywhere, however, their activity rates are considerably below average. This reflects, among other factors, their lower educational and skills development attainments, which, in turn, result from societal and institutional barriers to equal opportunities for people with disabilities in education and vocational training.

160. In Brazil, activity rates of women with a disability are lower than those of their male peers, and the activity gap between them is greater than that between disabled and non-disabled persons.[98] Once in employment, people with disabilities commonly earn less than their counterparts without disabilities and, while lower educational achievements explain a considerable portion of the earnings gap, discrimination also accounts for part of it. Equally important is the wage gap between men and women who are disabled. In Canada, for example, the difference is as high as 39 per cent and, while unionization helps bridge the gap between people with disabilities and those without, it is not as effective in helping women with disabilities obtain a higher level of wages compared to their male peers, which points to additional discrimination in remuneration based on sex.[99]

161. In the Middle East and North African countries, gender unemployment differentials are among the highest of the world (6 percentage points higher for women than for men in 2003), suggesting that disabled women face more obstacles than disabled men in finding a job.[100] Violence constitutes an additional manifestation of sex discrimination: women are at greater risk of violence, especially physical and sexual abuse. A study carried out in Zimbabwe in 2004 shows that 87.4 per cent of girls with disabilities had been sexually abused and, among them, 52.4 per cent tested HIV positive. The situation is similar in Namibia and Botswana.[101]

162. The likelihood for a person with a disability of finding a job seems to decrease as the level of disability increases.[102] In Europe, a person aged between 16 and 64 has a 66 per cent chance of finding a job;

96. See "Disabled employees: Labour standards, an Employers' Forum on Disability briefing for CSR practitioners", at www.csreurope. org/csrinfo/csrdisability/Disabledemployees.

97. Disability figures based on the World Health Organization's estimate that 10 per cent of the world's population have a disability, and United Nations Department of Economic and Social Affairs, Population Division: *World Population Prospects: The 2004 Revision*, Population Database, at esa.un.org/unpp.

98. A. Bercovich: "People with disability in Brazil: A look at 2000 Census results", Instituto Brasileiro de Geografia e Estatística, Population Census Committee, 2001, at iussp2005.princeton.edu/download.aspx?submissionId=52108.

99. See "There's room at the top for workers with disabilities: Canadian research shows union membership and gender are key factors", at www.disabilityworld.org/06-08_04/employment/canadianresearch.shtml.

100. World Bank: "A note on disability issues in the Middle East and North Africa", Human Development Department, June 2005.

101. G. Charowa: "Women with disabilities in Zimbabwe experience discrimination", 15 Nov. 2005, at www.disabilityworld.org/12-01_06/zimbabwewomen.shtml.

102. See ILO: "Trade unions and disabilities: Promoting decent work, combating discrimination", *Labour Education* 2004/4, No. 137.

Box 2.12.
Increasing number of complaints of disability discrimination in employment

In the United Kingdom, Employment Tribunals Service records show that the year 2004 was particularly costly for employers: disability discrimination attracted the highest amounts of awards, with the average total (£28,889) more than double the next highest – race discrimination (£13,720). Tribunals awarded over £100,000 in 9 per cent of disability cases (only 1 per cent of sex cases and 0 per cent of race cases). In Australia, the number of Disability Discrimination Act (DDA) complaints lodged before the Human Rights and Equal Opportunity Commission (HREOC) fell between 1994–95 and 1998–99 and has remained stable since then. In 2002–03, as in most years, over half of all DDA complaints (53 per cent) were related to the employment sector. In Hong Kong, China, the Equal Opportunities Commission recorded an increase in the number of discrimination-related complaints during the first five months of 2006. Out of 305 complaints (272 in the same period in 2005), 172 were lodged under the Disability Discrimination Ordinance (+6 per cent compared to the same period last year). Disability complaints thus represented over 56 per cent of the total number of complaints, ranking above complaints lodged under the Sex Discrimination Ordinance (40 per cent) and the Family Status Discrimination Ordinance (4 per cent). In the United States, from 1992 to 2005, over 70,000 charges were filed annually before the EEOC, of which around 19 per cent (220,000) were under the Americans with Disabilities Act (ADA). In 2005, 14,893 charges were filed under the ADA (19.7 per cent of the total number of charges) representing US$44.8 million in monetary benefits. In terms of lawsuits filed by the EEOC in court, those under the ADA accounted for 11 per cent (46) of the total number of suits in 2005 (417). This percentage has remained relatively stable since 2002.

Sources: Equal Opportunities Review, by LexisNexis Butterworths, Aug. 2005; Prime Minister's Strategy Unit (UK): *Improving the life chances of disabled people*, Final report, Jan. 2005; see also: www.hreoc.gov.au, www.eoc.org.hk and www.eeoc.gov/.

this rate falls to 47 per cent for a moderately disabled person and 25 per cent for a person with a severe disability.[103]

163. An important source of exclusion or disadvantage of people with disabilities is the fact that they are still often perceived as unproductive, unable to perform a job or too costly to employ. Some companies, however, have found that accommodation costs do not need to be high (box 2.11).

164. Discrimination is especially common at the hiring stage: a survey in France showed that under 2 per cent of people who mentioned their disability in their CV received an answer and were called for an interview.[104]

165. Several countries have seen an increase in both absolute and relative terms in the number of complaints filed concerning discrimination based on disability (box 2.12). This suggests a greater awareness of the injustice of this form of discrimination, but may also be due to the shift of the burden of the proof from the victim to the employer, or a combination of both.

Continued stigma and discrimination against people living with HIV/AIDS

166. Around 40 million people currently live with HIV/AIDS worldwide, compared to 37 million in 2003. The vast majority (95 per cent) are in developing countries, with sub-Saharan Africa being the hardest hit, with 10 per cent of the world population but over 60 per cent of all people living with HIV/AIDS. However, the epidemic is also spreading rapidly in Asia, Eastern Europe and Central Asia.[105] Prevalence is rising fastest among young adults (aged 15–29 years), especially girls and young women.

167. Thirty-six million people worldwide, or 90 per cent of those living with HIV/AIDS, are engaged in some sort of economic activity and most of them are in the 15–49 age group – the most productive segment of the labour force.[106] Three million working-age people die every year because of HIV/AIDS; around 28 million workers were lost by 2005 and, if current trends persist, 48 million and 74 million workers will be lost by 2010 and 2015, respectively.[107]

---

103. See www.csreurope.org/csrinfo/csrdisability/Disabilityandemployment.
104. Observatoire des Discriminations: "Discriminations à l'embauche: de l'envoi du CV à l'entretien", Apr. 2005, Paris, at cergors.univ-paris1.fr/docsatelecharger/Discriminationsenvoientretien.pdf.
105. Joint United Nations Programme on HIV/AIDS (UNAIDS): "UNAIDS/WHO AIDS epidemic update", Dec. 2005.
106. ILO: *Saving lives, protecting jobs*, International HIV/AIDS Workplace Education Programme, SHARE: Strategic HIV/AIDS Responses by Enterprises, Interim report (Geneva, 2006), p. viii.
107. ILO: *HIV/AIDS and work in a globalizing world* (Geneva, 2005), at www.ilo.org/public/english/protection/trav/aids/publ/globalizing.pdf.

Box 2.13.
"If I have AIDS, people will avoid me"

In South Africa, the Horizons programme, in cooperation with the South African power company ESKOM and Development Research Africa, launched a study on stigma and discrimination at the workplace. The greatest fear among respondents focused on relations with colleagues: three-quarters feared social isolation, 50 per cent mentioned rumours and gossip, 18 per cent verbal abuse. Around 90 per cent of workers surveyed agreed with the statement "if I have AIDS, people will avoid me". One-quarter of workers and 55 per cent of the workers' female partners or relatives said they were afraid of dismissal on account of AIDS. In France, two-thirds of HIV-positive persons (65 per cent) do not say anything about their HIV status at the workplace; the latter is often disclosed by another person.

Sources: J. Pulerwitz; J. Greene; E. Esu-Williams; R. Stewart: "Addressing stigma and discrimination in the workplace: The example of ESKOM, South Africa", *Exchange*, 2004-2, at www.kit.nl/exchange/html/2004-2_addressing_stigma.asp; and Sida Info Service: *Enquête sur les discriminations à l'encontre des personnes vivant avec le VIH, 2005*, at www.sida-info-service.org/.

---

168. Stigma (box 2.13) and discrimination on account of actual or perceived HIV/AIDS status are multiple and complex; they are hard to measure, and the data difficult to interpret.[108] All over the world, women's high vulnerability to HIV/AIDS is exacerbated by economic need, lack of employment, tradition, and poor access to education, training and information. Stigma generally affects more women than men, even when they are infected with the disease through their husbands. In an ILO study in India, a survey conducted among 292 persons (42 per cent of whom were women, with an average age of 30 years), showed that 90 per cent of women had been infected by their husbands. More women had suffered discrimination (74 per cent) than men (68 per cent).[109]

169. Because of their low social status, women are threatened by increased dependence and poverty. De-schooling of young girls has increased considerably because of HIV/AIDS, and lack of education fuels gender inequalities in the labour market.

170. Discrimination in employment remains prevalent worldwide, even in countries where AIDS policies and programmes have been in place for a long time, as shown by surveys conducted in France during the past five years by Sida Info Service.[110] A survey in Asia[111] shows that one in six respondents had been discriminated against in the workplace: a higher proportion of respondents experienced workplace discrimination in the Philippines (21 per cent) than in other countries (15 per cent in Indonesia, 12 per cent in India and 7 per cent in Thailand). In the Philippines, 33 per cent of discriminated workers lost their jobs, 44 per cent had their duties changed and 21 per cent were denied access to promotion. A large majority of respondents had no recourse for action.

171. Cases of discrimination in the hiring process are common, especially in the military[112] and the health sector.[113] Discrimination in the latter, however, goes far beyond the issue of testing. It can be practised by health-care workers towards other health-care workers, towards patients, or by employers towards health-care workers and takes various forms (for example, delayed or inappropriate treatment; breaches of confidentiality or unethical behaviour).[114] In Mexico in 2005, nine out of ten complaints received by the National Human Rights Commission from people living with HIV/AIDS involved the health sector. In France, a survey carried out in 2005 found that the highest rate of discrimination was experienced by respondents when seeking treatment in the health-care

---

108. See UNAIDS: *Protocol for the identification of discrimination against people living with HIV* (Geneva, 2000), which uses a list of 37 different situations in ten major areas of social life, including employment, social welfare and access to public accommodations or services. See also HIV/AIDS Survey Indicators Database, co-financed by USAID, UNAIDS and UNICEF, at www.measuredhs.com/hivdata/start.cfm.

109. ILO: *Socio-economic impact of HIV/AIDS on people living with HIV/AIDS and their families* (New Delhi, 2003), at www.ilo.org/public/english/region/asro/newdelhi/aids/download/socioec.pdf.

110. A national association for fighting AIDS created in 1990 by the French Agency against AIDS (AFLS); see www.sida-info-service.org.

111. Asia Pacific Network of People living with HIV/AIDS (APN+): "AIDS discrimination in Asia", 2004, at www.gnpplus.net/regions/files/AIDS-asia.pdf.

112. ILO: *HIV/AIDS and work in a globalizing world*, op. cit.

113. Sida Info Service: *Enquête sur les discriminations à l'encontre des personnes vivant avec le VIH, 2005*, at www.sida-info-service.org.

114. See ILO/WHO: *Joint WHO/ILO Guidelines on health services and HIV/AIDS* (Geneva, ILO, 2005).

Table 2.8. Types of legislation containing HIV/AIDS-related provisions, selected countries

Labour legislation	Provisions related to HIV discrimination and screening are integrated into the existing regulations. Prohibition of discrimination and mandatory HIV testing in employment.	Bahamas, Romania, Zimbabwe
Anti-discrimination and human rights legislation	Provisions on prevention and punishment of all forms of discrimination, including that against persons living with HIV/AIDS or "disfavoured groups".	Romania
Disability laws	Protection of people with disabilities; usually contain provisions on equal treatment and non-discrimination and require employers to make reasonable accommodations (working time, tasks and working environment). These laws may be extended to people living with HIV/AIDS, although their scope may vary depending on the definition of disability and its interpretation by courts.	United Kingdom, United States
Specific AIDS laws	Prohibition of discrimination in employment rights, training, promotion and career opportunities.	Cambodia, China, Costa Rica, Mozambique

sector (43.7 per cent of respondents), followed by discrimination at the workplace (33.7 per cent) and that encountered when requesting services in the bank and insurance sector (33.6 per cent).[115]

172. Up to 2006, 73 countries had included HIV/AIDS-related provisions in their labour legislation or anti-discrimination laws[116] (table 2.8 gives some examples of the types of legislation and HIV/AIDS-related provisions). However, even in countries where people living with HIV/AIDS benefit from legal protection, discrimination continues to occur.

173. Supplementing laws with non-legislative measures such as workplace initiatives is therefore essential to change employers' and co-workers' attitudes and behaviour towards those with actual or perceived HIV/AIDS status. Positive examples include the widespread adoption of the ILO code of practice on HIV/AIDS and the world of work and the signing of bipartite agreements in sectors, such as the transport industry, in which workers are more vulnerable to the disease (see Part IV, Chapter 1, section on promoting equal opportunities at the workplace).

115. Sida Info Service, op. cit.
116. ILO: *The workplace: Gateway to universal access* (Geneva, 2006), at www.ilo.org/public/english/protection/trav/aids/publ/access.pdf.

3. Emerging manifestations of discrimination

174. A number of practices have emerged in the past years, essentially in the industrialized world, which can result in the unfavourable treatment of certain people because of the perceived risks that their recruitment or continued employment may entail for the employer. These include individuals with a genetic predisposition to developing particular diseases, as well as people leading lifestyles that are deemed "unhealthy". These practices are relatively recent compared to those reviewed in the preceding pages, and the debate on their legitimacy and lawfulness is still open. They raise important questions about where to draw the line between employers' control over what employees do outside the workplace, and people's freedom to lead the life they choose. Moreover, given the rapid pace at which these practices are spreading, it is important to be aware of and monitor them. It should be borne in mind that efforts to change peoples' views on how they see other people's lifestyles need to start in the family, community and school.

Genetic discrimination

175. Rapid developments in genetics and related new technologies have made it easier to obtain information on genetic status. Genetic testing has been defined as "the use of a scientific test to obtain information on some aspects of the genetic status of a person, indicative of a present or future medical problem".[117] Genetic screening has important implications for the workplace, as employers may have an interest in excluding or dismissing employees whose genetic status shows a predisposition to developing a certain disease in the future. In some rare instances, employers may justify genetic screening of employees for safety and health reasons, especially when workers may be exposed to hazardous substances, such as radiation or chemicals, and are thus more likely to suffer subsequent health risk and damage.

176. Genetic testing may easily lead to unjustified dismissal or denial of employment. Making an employment decision on the basis of the probability of an individual's developing a certain disease, rather than on his/her actual capacity to perform the work, constitutes discrimination. Moreover, the test may indicate that an individual may be susceptible to developing a certain disease, but does not tell when it might occur or how severe it might be.[118]

177. Genetic discrimination at the workplace has been proven and contested in several courts around the world (box 2.14).

178. This has led many countries to adopt legal measures. Several EU Member States have introduced legislation prohibiting genetic discrimination (Denmark, Finland, France and Sweden). Others have prohibited or restricted the collection of genetic data from employees without their explicit consent (Austria, Greece, Italy, Luxembourg and Netherlands),[119] thus recognizing and guaranteeing people's right to privacy. In the United States, on 17 February 2005 the Senate unanimously passed bill S. 306, the Genetic Information Nondiscrimination Act of 2005, which prohibits the improper use of genetic information in health insurance and employment.[120]

179. Companies are also taking remedial action. IBM is the first major corporation that has revised its policy to prevent the use of genetic information in making personnel decisions[121] and for determining employees' eligibility for health-care or benefit plans.[122]

180. Trade unions are also active in this field. The Australian Council of Trade Unions (ACTU), in response to the inquiry of the Australian Law Reform Commission and Australian Health Ethics Commission on the protection of human genetic information, stated in 2002 that employers should not be allowed to gather genetic information about any employee.[123]

---

117. "Ethical aspects of genetic testing in the workplace", opinion of the European Group on Ethics in Science and New Technologies to the European Commission (28 July 2003), at http://ec.europa.eu/european_group_ethics/docs/avis18_en.pdf.

118. National Workrights Institute: "Genetic discrimination in the workplace fact sheet", at www.workrights.org/issue_genetic/gd_fact_sheet.html.

119. "Ethical aspects of genetic testing in the workplace", op. cit., para. 1.8, p. 11.

120. H.T. Greely, J.D.: "Banning genetic discrimination", in *New England Journal of Medicine*, No. 353:9, 1 Sep. 2005, at content.nejm.org/cgi/content/full/353/9/865.

121. A. Barrett: "IBM's smart stance on genetic testing", in *Business Week* online, 11 Oct. 2005, at www.businessweek.com/technology//content/oct2005/tc20051011_9733_tc024.htm.

122. *USA Today:* "IBM won't use genetic info for hiring, benefits", 10 Oct. 2005. at www.usatoday.com/money/industries/technology/2005-10-10-ibm-genetics_x.htm.

123. Australian Council of Trade Unions (ACTU): *ACTU response to the Australian Law Reform Commission and Australian Health Ethics Commission inquiry into protection of human genetic information*, Discussion Paper 66, Dec. 2002, at www.actu.asn.au/Images/Dynamic/oldsite/public/papers/genetic4/genetic4.doc.

Box 2.14.
Courts challenge genetic testing as a legitimate basis for personnel decisions

Germany: Darmstadt Administrative Court, Hessen, 2004

Teachers in Germany, like all civil servants, have to undergo a medical examination before obtaining a permanent job. A young female teacher was examined by the occupational health doctor and found to be in perfect health. But in response to questions about her family medical history, she indicated that her father had Huntington's disease. She refused genetic testing. The educational authorities denied her a permanent job in the German civil service on the grounds of this medical report. The teacher has since successfully contested the decision in the Administrative Court.[1]

United States: Equal Employment Opportunity Commission, 2001

The US Equal Employment Opportunity Commission (EEOC) alleged that the Burlington Northern Santa Fe Railway (BNSF) secretly subjected its employees to surreptitious testing for a genetic marker linked to carpal tunnel syndrome. The genetic testing programme was revealed when one of the workers diagnosed with carpal tunnel syndrome went to the company doctor with his wife for a mandatory exam. His wife, who is a nurse, became suspicious when the doctor drew seven vials of blood during the examination of the worker's wrist. Because the possibility of termination of employment was imminent, the EEOC acted swiftly and sought an emergency injunction in federal court, alleging that the tests were unlawful under the Americans with Disabilities Act (ADA) because they were neither job-related nor consistent with any business necessity. To condition any employment action on the results of such tests would be to engage in unlawful discrimination based on disability. Just two months after the suit was filed, the EEOC and BNSF reached a settlement in which the EEOC achieved everything it sought.[2]

Hong Kong, China: Hong Kong District Court, 2000

Three men were awarded damages by the Hong Kong District Court because the Government had denied them employment purely on the grounds that their parents were affected by schizophrenia. The three men had either been refused a job or dismissed from their post without a clear reason. An investigation by the Equal Opportunities Commission revealed the link to their family history and thus genetic discrimination.[3]

[1] D. Schmitz; U. Wiesing: "Just a family medical history?", in *BMJ*, Vol. 332, 4 Feb. 2006, at www.bmj.com. [2] See United States Equal Employment Opportunity Commission: "EEOC settles ADA suit against BNSF for genetic bias", Press Release, 18 Apr. 2001, at www.eeoc.gov/press/4-18-01.html. [3] R. McKie: "China is thwarted by jobs ruling: Hong Kong judge's decision on gene data hailed as civil rights landmark", in *The Observer*, 1 Oct. 2000, at Guardian Unlimited, www.guardian.co.uk.

While criticizing employers for inappropriate collection of employees' genetic data, the Commissions declared that they would consider permitting the use of genetic testing, where reasonable and relevant, and in a way that balanced the interests of employers, employees and the public at large.

181. While the debate is still open as to whether or not there are objective reasons or circumstances justifying the exclusion or less favourable treatment of an individual because of his/her genes, any such differential treatment must be objective, reasonable, appropriate and proportionate.

Discrimination based on lifestyle

182. Lifestyle and, more specifically, whether an individual leads a "healthy" life, is becoming a factor in obtaining or keeping a job. Being overweight or a smoker or suffering from hypertension can be an occupational disadvantage in several industrialized countries. Virtually every lifestyle choice, including driving fast cars, has some health-related consequence; the question therefore is where to draw the line between what an employer can regulate and the freedom of employees to lead the life of their choice.

183. Unfavourable employment practices against smokers are relatively easier to quantify because some companies have made it an official corporate policy to prohibit smoking. In the United States, for example, a number of enterprises do not recruit smokers or penalize former smokers by requiring them to pay

more for health insurance.[124] Companies' interest in employees' lifestyle is partly linked to their wish to avoid additional health insurance costs associated with unhealthy habits, especially in countries where employers are fully or partly responsible for their employees' health insurance. Eleven states in the United States allow insurance differentials between tobacco users and non-users when determining the price of coverage.[125] On the other hand, in response to anti-smoking corporate policies, around 30 states in the same country have adopted laws prohibiting discrimination against smokers or based on lifestyle, although they provide different levels of protection.[126] Company policies do not generally include provisions that expressly penalize people who are overweight or have high cholesterol, but the evidence suggests that adverse treatment against them is not infrequent.[127]

184. In recent years, unfavourable treatment against smokers has spread to other parts of the world. As of 1 December 2005, the World Health Organization (WHO) announced that it would no longer hire smokers or other tobacco users who did not agree to stop smoking.[128] The Human Rights Commission and the Department of Labour of New Zealand declared in August 2006 that refusal to hire smokers was not unlawful, as neither the national Human Rights Act nor the Employment Relations Act cover smoking as an illegal ground of discrimination.

185. These facts have given rise to a heated debate, including within the tobacco control community: some perceived it as too draconian a measure, which could be counterproductive to the anti-smoking agenda, while others considered it as a new step forward in the eradication of tobacco use.[129] Trade unions in Europe, such as the European Trade Union Confederation (ETUC) and the Italian General Confederation of Labour (CGIL), have expressed concern that tolerating discrimination against smokers would open the door to other kinds of discrimination.[130]

186. Curbing tobacco consumption or reducing cholesterol levels or obesity are all desirable and legitimate public health policies. Workplace initiatives, such as occupational health and safety (OSH) programmes[131] and smoking cessation programmes,[132] developed in consultation with the employees, and providing adequate assistance for smokers, while respecting non-smokers' rights, can effectively contribute to this goal.

187. One key aspect of the principle of non-discrimination and equality at work is that all employment decisions must be based on a person's capacity to perform a job. If obesity or smoking, including beyond working hours and outside the workplace, is proven to affect the accomplishment of work-related tasks, not recruiting an overweight person or a smoker is in order. Similarly, obesity or smoking could be a valid motive for dismissal if it is detrimental to co-workers or other people whom the overweight person or smoker may interact with in his/her daily work. Otherwise denying a job or dismissing qualified persons solely on the basis of their obesity or because they are off-duty smokers would amount to discrimination and constitute an undue intrusion in their private life.

124. U. Furi-Perry: "Butting in: Employers penalize smokers and overweight workers", 8 Nov. 2004, at www.lawcrossing.com/article/index.php?id=416.

125. Aon Consulting: "No-smoking policies must contend with state laws protecting smokers", in Forum, Oct. 2005, at www.aon.com/about/publications/pdf/issues/october_05_no_smoking_policies.pdf.

126. See R. Dotinga: "Can boss insist on healthy habits?", in Christian Science Monitor, 11 Jan. 2006, at www.csmonitor.com/2006/0111/p15s01-ussc.html.

127. See American Civil Liberties Union: "Lifestyle discrimination in the workplace: Your right to privacy under attack", 31 Dec. 1998, at www.aclu.org/workplacerights/gen/13384res19981231.html.

128. See WHO: "WHO policy on non-recruitment of smokers", at www.who.int/employment/recruitment/en/ and "Frequently asked questions", Nov. 2005, at www.who.int/employment/FAQs_smoking_English.pdf.

129. See K. Slama: "Schisms in the tobacco control movement", in International Journal of Tuberculosis and Lung Disease, Vol. 10, Nos. 4 and 5, Apr. and May 2006. See also Le Temps: "L'OMS est déterminée à ne plus recruter de fumeurs : Pour l'exemple", 1 Dec. 2005.

130. EUbusiness.com: "EU Commission's anti-smoking stand sparks cloud of complaints", 7 Aug. 2006, at www.eubusiness.com/Employment/060807154817.efj7kady; see also P. Pearson: "Smokers, the new deviants", 20 Aug. 2006, at www.smokersclubinc.com/modules.php?name=News&file=article&sid=3548.

131. See ILO Programme on Safety and Health at Work and the Environment (SafeWork), at www.ilo.org/public/english/protection/safework/tobacco/index.htm. On legislation, see C. Håkansta: Workplace smoking – Working paper: A review of national and local practical and regulatory measures, ILO/SafeWork (Geneva, ILO, 2004).

132. In the United States, a survey by Deloitte & Touche found that just over 50 per cent of employers offer smoking cessation programmes, while the National Business Group on Health reported that only 24 per cent of employers cover medical costs associated with tobacco use treatment. Out of 365 big companies surveyed in 2005, 56 per cent offer cessation programmes. See M. Hill: "Employer initiatives to stop smoking", in Journal of Employee Assistance, Vol. 36, No. 2, second quarter, 2006.

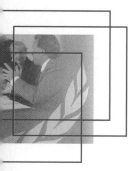

PART III

Institutions and policies: Trends, impact and challenges

188. The State has a major responsibility in ensuring equality at the workplace, but non-state actors and institutions, such as workers' and employers' organizations or collective bargaining, have an equally critical role to play. In the face of economic restructuring and global competition, problems of workplace inequity need to be addressed at the country level and beyond, as workplaces are increasingly affected by developments on global markets.[1] While the State and national policies and actors remain central to bringing about equality at the workplace, efforts at the international and global levels are also necessary.

189. This Part reviews the scope and impact of recent legal, institutional and policy trends at both the national and international levels with a view to identifying the best practices that have contributed to positive change.

190. Chapter 1 begins by focusing on state action at the national level, mainly in industrialized and middle-income countries: the number and scope of initiatives promoting equality are greater in these countries than in low-income countries, as is the availability of data. It also looks at international and regional initiatives.

191. The Chapter goes on to explore the potential and challenges for the achievement of equality at the workplace of recent developments in international lending and investment policies, as well as of trade policies and broader processes of economic integration.

192. Chapter 2 reviews the latest developments in relation to non-discrimination and equality within collective bargaining processes, as well as initiatives promoted by the social partners in this domain. It concludes by looking at how corporate social responsibility (CSR) can contribute to the attainment of equality objectives.

---

1. See ILO: *Changing patterns in the world of work*, Report of the Director-General, Report I(C), International Labour Conference, 95th Session, Geneva, 2006.

1. Trends in institutional and policy responses since 2003

Discrimination and law reforms: General trends

193. There is an increasing tendency worldwide to ensure that the four sets of fundamental principles and rights at work, including non-discrimination and equality, are embodied in labour law. Such a trend has clearly emerged in the last five years in many countries involved in a labour law reform process, including some newly independent countries such as Timor-Leste.

194. Another clear trend is global recognition of the need for specific legal provisions on non-discrimination and equality issues at the workplace. This general acceptance can be seen as a major achievement of the United Nations Fourth World Conference on Women held in Beijing in 1995.

195. Provisions on non-discrimination and equality, especially in the industrialized world, are increasingly being adopted or consolidated in the form of a text encompassing different grounds of discrimination (EU Directives, Australia and the United Kingdom). This approach, which is also gaining ground in the UN system, especially in the field of human rights, is based on the acknowledgement that certain individuals may face discrimination on more than one ground. It tries to ensure a more coherent support to victims of discrimination, regardless of the ground, and is consistent with the tendency to establish multi-ground or umbrella specialized bodies (see following section).

196. At the same time, however, adopting special legislation focusing on a specific issue may be preferable in certain circumstances, and easier than amending an existing law. A specific law may also reflect a strong political commitment to addressing issues of crucial importance: this is typically the case in many African countries that have adopted legislation concerning discrimination based on HIV/AIDS.[2] An increase in specific laws prohibiting discrimination based on disability can be expected in coming years, as a result of the adoption in December 2006 of the United Nations Convention on the rights of persons with disabilities. Employment and workplace rights feature prominently in this new instrument, which thus recognizes the importance of achieving decent work opportunities for people with disabilities, not as an element of social welfare policy, but as a matter of human rights and social inclusion.

197. Another interesting development has been the greater emphasis on sanctions. This is reflected in the punishment of discrimination as a penal offence, or as a civil and/or administrative offence, depending on the ground and country concerned. Dealing with discrimination from this varied perspective responds to a concern to ensure more effective and expeditious protection of victims of discrimination in their daily lives.

198. Protection against discrimination is also enhanced through the prohibition of indirect discrimination and the reversal of the burden of proof, by placing it on the person or enterprise accused of discrimination once a prima facie case of discrimination has been established. Under the impetus of the EU Directives mentioned above (Introduction and Part II, Chapter 2),[3] the national laws of Member States have enlarged the grounds on which the burden of the proof lies with the employer, and prohibit direct and indirect discrimination, as well as harassment or an instruction to discriminate, both deemed to amount to discrimination. The EU Directives also require protection to be provided against victimization as a key condition for enabling individuals to assert their rights. Positive action measures are also permitted in order to ensure full equality in practice for protected groups. Attitudes towards positive action differ considerably across the Member States, however: it is allowed in the Netherlands only where there is evidence of structural discrimination on grounds of sex, race and disability, and in Slovakia the Constitutional Court found positive action to be unconstitutional.[4]

199. Another discernable trend, mentioned in Part II of this Report, has been the inclusion in a range of legal texts of provisions banning discrimination in

---

2. See J. Hodges: *Guidelines on addressing HIV/AIDS in the workplace through employment and labour law*, InFocus Programme on Social Dialogue, Labour Law and Labour Administration (IFP/DIALOGUE) Paper No. 3 (Geneva, ILO, 2004).

3. Council Directive 2000/43/EC of 29 June 2000 implementing the principle of equal treatment between persons irrespective of racial or ethnic origin and Council Directive 2000/78/EC of 27 Nov. 2000 establishing a general framework for equal treatment in employment and occupation.

4. Commission of the European Communities: *Communication from the Commission to the Council and the European Parliament: The application of Directive 2000/43/EC of 29 June 2000 implementing the principle of equal treatment between persons irrespective of racial or ethnic origin* (Brussels, 30 Oct. 2006), COM(2006) 643 final, p. 8.

the workplace on grounds such as age, sexual orientation or genetics. This tendency is more common in the industrialized world, and the protection provided is uneven, as it does not necessarily cover all aspects of employment.

200. As for sex discrimination, there has been considerable progress across the regions in the scope of protection provided by law. Of particular interest are laws focusing on sectors that have traditionally discriminated against women. Austria, for instance, provides for equal treatment for women in forestry and agriculture. Cyprus has adopted laws encouraging the provision of long-term contracts to women or protecting the rights of persons in short-term employment, in which women tend to be concentrated. Peru has removed the prohibition of women's access to the military and police force, and the United Republic of Tanzania and Burkina Faso have developed provisions to prevent women's exclusion from government.

201. Another positive development has been the growing attention to and awareness of sexual harassment, which is a form of sex discrimination.[5] While certain countries have enacted laws that address this problem exclusively (Belize, Costa Rica, Israel, Philippines and Uganda), others provide for courses of action within other branches of law, such as criminal, tort or labour law. In Chile, for instance, recent amendments to the Labour Code define and punish sexual harassment as contrary to human dignity and require employers to include provisions on the subject in enterprise regulations, thereby ensuring its regular monitoring by management, staff delegates and bipartite committees.[6] In Japan, the revised Equal Employment Opportunity Law provides that, as of 1 April 2007, both women and men shall be protected from sexual harassment, and requires employers to take workplace measures to address it. Companies contravening these provisions will be publicly denounced, with detrimental effects on their image.

202. On the pay equity front, Finland, France and Spain adopted proactive laws in 2005 and 2006 requiring employers not just to abstain from discriminating in remuneration on the basis of sex, but to take measures to promote equal opportunities in pay, for example through equal pay reviews and job evaluation methods, and to correct any pay differentials due

to discrimination. Experience has shown that proactive laws are particularly effective in revealing and addressing problems of sex discrimination in remuneration, in particular because they help overcome employers' reticence to disclose information on wages.

203. Despite these encouraging developments, problems persist. Some countries, for instance, still do not prohibit sex discrimination in all aspects of employment (Republic of Korea, Sudan and Viet Nam); others maintain protective measures with potentially discriminatory effects (Indonesia, Mongolia and Yemen); while yet others apply provisions for equal remuneration only to the basic or ordinary wage or only to certain allowances (Kyrgyzstan, Pakistan, Slovakia and Thailand), or maintain sex-based differences in the payment of additional allowances, including family allowances (Senegal and Trinidad and Tobago).

204. Labour law reforms may have the effect of reducing the protection of groups that are already vulnerable to discrimination. One telling example is the experience of countries that adopted laws providing for lower dismissal costs for groups such as younger workers, as a means to curb their unemployment, without achieving the intended results (see section on age discrimination in Part II, Chapter 2). Conversely, a law on outsourcing, adopted in Chile in 2006, amended the Labour Code to grant outsourced workers equal treatment with regular workers, including in relation to maternity protection.[7]

The rise in specialized institutions dealing with discrimination and equality

205. The institutional landscape concerning discrimination and equality matters has been marked by the emergence or restructuring of national specialized bodies. These may be vested with a variety of powers, ranging from assisting individuals in taking legal action to recommending reforms of existing laws, advising the social partners on how to give practical effect to equality, or designing and overseeing the implementation of national action plans. These institutions may be separate from government or established within or among existing government bodies and operating at different levels of government. They reflect a shift from a narrow focus on discrimination

---

5. In its general observation concerning Convention No. 111 (2003), the Committee of Experts on the Application of Conventions and Recommendations (CEACR) defines sexual harassment as sex-based or sexual behaviour that is unwelcome and offensive to its recipient.

6. Act No. 20,005 of 8 March 2005 defining and punishing sexual harassment.

7. Act No. 20,123 of 16 Oct. 2006 governing work under outsourcing arrangements, the functioning of temporary service providers and temporary service contracts.

Table 3.1. Pros and cons of equality institutions dealing with more than one ground of discrimination

Advantages	Disadvantages/challenges
Tackling multiple discrimination, as some people may face more than one type of discrimination	Possible loss of focus on any particular ground, and difficulty of reconciling a general concern about non-discrimination and equality with the need to address the specificities of each ground of discrimination
Transfer of knowledge from areas where law and policy are more developed, i.e. sex and race, to "newer" grounds, such as sexual orientation	Possible different levels of protection depending on the grounds of discrimination concerned
More coherent support to victims of discrimination, regardless of the ground	Possible potential difficulties in working with a greater number of communities and discriminated groups
More coherent and effective guidance and support to employers, trade unions and policy-makers	Possible financial and staff constraints, especially in the event of merger of existing bodies
More cost-effective use of resources, e.g. support staff, office costs, etc.	

Sources: F. Palmer: "Specialized national institutions to combat discrimination in Europe", background paper prepared for this Global Report; J. Niessen; J. Cormack: "Organismi specializzati istituiti a livello nazionale in seguito all'adozione delle direttive antidiscriminatorie comunitarie", in S. Fabeni; M.G. Toniollo (eds.): *La discriminazione fondata sull'orientamento sessuale: L'attuazione della direttiva 2000/78/CE e la nuova disciplina per la protezione dei diritti delle persone omosessuali sul posto di lavoro* (Rome, Ediesse, 2005), p. 280.

to one based on equal treatment and opportunities at work, with an emphasis on outcomes and proactive action.

206. As of 2000, under the impetus of the EU Directive on racial equality, which requires Member States to designate a national body to address discrimination on the grounds of racial or ethnic origin,[8] 19 out of 25 countries in Europe have either extended the mandates of existing institutions so as to encompass race or ethnic origin (e.g. Austria, Lithuania and the Netherlands) or established new entities covering all the types of discrimination banned by national law and the EU Directives (e.g. France and Hungary) or focusing only on racial or ethnic discrimination (e.g. Italy and Spain).

207. In Europe, there are more institutions dealing with multiple forms of discrimination, beyond race/ethnicity or sex, than bodies focusing on a single ground. This reflects a commitment towards the elimination of discrimination beyond what is required by the EU law and the acknowledgement that all victims of discrimination have an equal right to protection.[9] But their establishment has been accompanied by a lively debate about the advantages and drawbacks of institutions dealing with a single ground of discrimination compared to those covering multiple grounds (table 3.1).

208. The 25 EU Member States have widely differing experiences in dealing with racial or ethnic discrimination and, as noted earlier, display different understandings of how to bring about racial or ethnic equality. The harmonization of notions and strategies to advance racial and ethnic equality is therefore important in an enlarged Europe. The European Commission against Racism and Intolerance (ECRI), an independent human rights monitoring body established by the first Summit of Heads of State and Government of the Member States of the Council of Europe, held in Vienna in 1993, seeks to contribute to this goal by providing a forum for exchanging good practices on key issues such as ethnic data collection, enforcement of national law against racial discrimination, and mediation and other forms of dispute resolution.[10]

209. In Latin America, after a long history of denial,[11] thanks to the mobilization of civil society and the backing of governments, racial and ethnic inequalities feature prominently on the public agendas of several countries, such as Brazil (box 3.1). In March 2003, for the first time in the history of the country,

8. Council Directive 2000/43/EC, op. cit., article 13.
9. J. Niessen; J. Cormack: "Organismi specializzati istituiti a livello nazionale in seguito all'adozione delle direttive antidiscriminatorie comunitarie", in S. Fabeni and M.G. Toniollo (eds.): *La discriminazione fondata sull'orientamento sessuale: L'attuazione della direttiva 2000/78/CE e la nuova disciplina per la protezione dei diritti delle persone omosessuali sul posto di lavoro* (Rome, Ediesse, 2005), p. 280.
10. European Commission against Racism and Intolerance (ECRI): *Examples of good practices: Specialised bodies to combat racism, xenophobia, antisemitism and intolerance at national level* (Strasbourg, Council of Europe, Jan. 2006).
11. A.E. Dulitzky: "A region in denial: Racial discrimination and racism in Latin America", in A. Dzidzienyo and S. Oboler (eds.): *Neither enemies nor friends: Latinos, Blacks, Afro-Latinos* (Houndmills, Palgrave Macmillan, 2005).

Box 3.1.
Follow-up in Latin America to the 2001 World Conference against Racism,
Racial Discrimination, Xenophobia and Related Intolerance (Durban)

A Regional Conference of the Americas organized by Brazil and Chile was held in Brasilia in July 2006 on progress made and challenges remaining regarding the effective implementation of the Durban Declaration and Programme of Action against Racism, Racial Discrimination, Xenophobia and Related Intolerance. The final document of the Conference contained the following provisions:

● recognition of the positive role played by national institutions in fighting racism;

● the need for national monitoring systems and the creation of indicators to measure the impact of national policies and programmes;

● the development of human rights training programmes, especially in the administration of justice;

● the need for positive action policies;

● a call to governments to establish reliable disaggregated data on race, sex, geographical distribution and socio-economic indicators.

Source: United Nations General Assembly: *Global efforts for the total elimination of racism, racial discrimination, xenophobia and related intolerance and the comprehensive implementation of and follow-up to the Durban Declaration and Programme of Action*, Report of the Secretary General, doc. A/61/337, 12 Sep. 2006, paras. 57 and 59.

---

the Government created the Special Secretariat for Policies to Promote Racial Equality (SEPPIR) with ministerial rank.

210.   In the developing world single-ground institutions appear to be more common than bodies tackling multiple grounds of discrimination. There are, however, a few interesting exceptions, such as the Equal Opportunities Commission of Hong Kong, China, and the National Council for the Prevention of Discrimination (CONAPRED) in Mexico (box 3.2).

211.   Established in 1996, the Equal Opportunities Commission of Hong Kong, China, works against discrimination on the grounds of sex, marital status, pregnancy, disability and family status. It has investigation and conciliation powers; issues codes of practice and guidelines on equal opportunities; produces research on discrimination; and builds partnerships with enterprises and governmental and non-governmental organizations alike. A major achievement of the Commission has been the reform of the Secondary School Places Allocation (SSPA) system that for a quarter of a century had led to the systematic lowering of the best girls' scores and scaling up of the best boys' scores, and gender quotas that restricted girls' access to the best schools arbitrarily.[12]

The challenge of making laws work

Labour courts

212.   Even when specialized institutions in the areas of human rights and equality exist, the courts and the labour administration frequently share responsibility for the supervision and enforcement of anti-discrimination law. The courts hear and decide individual cases, establish whether or not discrimination has occurred, and determine legal consequences, through a decision that is binding on the parties in dispute. Court proceedings enable justice to be restored for victims through the remedies available under the law, such as cessation of discrimination and payment of compensation or damages for the injury suffered. Courts also clear the defendant of unfounded allegations. The equality jurisprudence of higher courts has led to efforts to strengthen and develop legislation.[13]

213.   In many countries victims of employment discrimination still do not benefit fully from the possibility of seeking relief in court, as shown by the very small number of cases brought to ordinary courts or labour tribunals. Victims of discrimination, who often belong to socially and economically disadvantaged

---

12. Equal Opportunities Commission: *Annual Report 02/03* (Hong Kong, China), p. 4.

13. For instance, EU rules provide for shifting the burden of proof to the respondent, after the European Court of Justice held that the rules on the burden of proof must be adapted when there is a prima facie case of discrimination: Council Directive 97/80/EC of 15 December 1997 on the burden of proof in cases of discrimination based on sex, *Official Journal of the European Communities*, L 014, 20 Jan. 1998, pp. 6–8.

Box 3.2.
Mexico: National Council for the Prevention of Discrimination (CONAPRED)

CONAPRED was established in 2003 by the Federal Act for the prevention and elimination of discrimination, which prohibits discrimination based on sex, ethnic origin, health condition, age, disability, social or economic status, pregnancy, language, opinion, marital status, sexual orientation, nationality or religion. CONAPRED relies on a variety of strategies aimed at putting an end to discrimination in Mexico. It develops projects and programmes to fight discrimination in employment as well as other spheres; proposes relevant legal reforms; launches awareness-raising campaigns; carries out studies to document the incidence and manifestations of different forms of discrimination; investigates any alleged discriminatory practice by an individual or federal authorities; applies administrative measures prescribed by the Federal Act and verifies the adoption of preventive and corrective measures by public and private organizations. CONAPRED has launched separate programmes for people with disabilities and for those with a sexual orientation other than heterosexuality. CONAPRED is currently developing a set of indicators to measure the extent of discrimination and influence public policies with a view to mainstreaming discrimination and equality concerns. In May 2006, the first national public policy ever to combat discrimination was launched under the auspices of CONAPRED.

Sources: A. Becerra Gelover: *Fighting discrimination in Mexico: The case of the National Council for the Prevention of Discrimination*, paper prepared for this Global Report, May 2006; CONAPRED web site at www.conapred.org.mx.

groups, may not perceive legal action as a means to overcome injustice, or may not take legal action out of fear of reprisals or because they see little chance of winning their case. In some instances, the incompatibility between positive and customary justice systems, especially where the former lack legitimacy and political outreach, while customary systems are the prevalent form of regulation and dispute resolution, may reinforce discrimination against marginal groups. At the same time, customary law may legitimize and reinforce certain inequalities, especially those stemming from gender discrimination, denial of women's rights to land or other assets, or those underpinning ethnic-based structures of power. A step in the right direction is being taken by countries such as South Africa, in their efforts to integrate customary law into constitutional reforms while addressing possible inconsistencies between fundamental rights, as enshrined in positive law, and customary rights.[14]

214. Lack of accessible legal assistance and appropriate procedural rules plays a role in restricting access to justice by members of groups subject to discrimination. "My rights", a television show that uses mock trials to depict real-life disputes in courts in

Armenia, has increased Armenians' understanding of their rights and redress procedures, and reduced widespread distrust of the courts.[15] Other innovative experiences include the Roma Anti-Discrimination Customer Service Network in Hungary (box 3.3).

215. In a number of jurisdictions the courts are able to rely on international labour standards as a source of law.[16] ILO training activities for judges and lawyers on international labour standards have been well received and show positive results, with participants starting to use acquired knowledge in their work (Part IV, Chapter 1).[17]

Labour inspection: An underutilized potential

216. With the inclusion of non-discrimination provisions in labour legislation, the labour inspection system also has competence to deal with discrimination matters. Where comprehensive anti-discrimination laws exist, the labour inspection services are sometimes charged with supervising its provisions dealing with work and employment.[18] Unlike the courts, labour inspection services can monitor legal

14. World Bank: *World Development Report 2006: Equity and development* (Washington, DC, 2005), box 8.3, p. 160.

15. ibid., box 8.1, p. 157.

16. See C. Thomas; M. Oelz; X. Beaudonnet: "The use of international labour law in domestic courts: Theory, recent jurisprudence and practical implications", in J.-C. Javillier and B. Gernignon (eds.): *Les normes internationales du travail: un patrimoine pour l'avenir. Mélanges en l'honneur de Nicolas Valticos* (Geneva, ILO, 2004), pp. 249–285.

17. See A.A. Sanches: *Evaluation d'impact des cours sur les normes internationales du travail pour juges, juristes et professeurs de droit (1999–2003)* (Turin, International Training Centre of the ILO, 2005).

18. For instance, under the Finnish Non-Discrimination Act (No. 21/2004), as amended by Act No. 50/2006, compliance with the Act in employment relationships and service relationships governed by public law shall be supervised by the occupational safety and health authorities.

Box 3.3.
Hungary: The Roma Anti-Discrimination Customer Service Network

The Network is a joint initiative of the ministries responsible for Justice, Roma Affairs, and Equal Opportunities, the Office of National and Ethnic Minorities and the National Roma Self-Government. The purpose of the Network is to provide legal assistance to Roma free of charge. In 2005 the Network was comprised of 30 attorneys. Between 1 May 2003 and 31 May 2005, the Network handled 256 cases of employment discrimination. In these cases, the primary objective was to eliminate the discriminatory measure or situation and included reinstatement in the job. Lawsuits and administrative proceedings before the competent bodies were only instituted as last resort if the cases could not be resolved otherwise. The Network's lawyers prepare monthly reports on their activities, which are then analysed by its governing structure.

Source: 2005 report provided by the Government of Hungary under article 22 of the ILO Constitution in respect of Convention No. 111.

compliance without waiting for an alleged victim of discrimination to take the initiative. Labour inspectors have the power to inspect workplaces at will and to obtain and examine information to which victims have no access and which may reveal instances of discrimination. Moreover, even where inspections are carried out following reports from individuals or groups, the complainant does not become a party to the proceedings, thus considerably lessening the burden on the complainant.

217. In some jurisdictions labour inspectors are able to bring cases before the courts or intervene in court proceedings instituted by another party. The examples of Argentina, Dominican Republic, Guatemala and Mexico show that some governments in Latin America may be gradually assigning greater importance to the enforcement and advisory services provided by labour inspectors and are prepared to increase the financial resources for strengthening labour inspection.[19]

218. Labour inspectors can also play a role in preventing discrimination by providing information and technical advice. The impact of these activities is greater if they are part of a broader and integrated national policy for the promotion of non-discrimination and equal opportunities. The experience of the *núcleos*, or units for promoting equal opportunities and fighting discrimination in employment and occupation, in Brazil, is a case in point (box 3.4).

219. Addressing discrimination requires the capacity and a clear mandate to do so; experience in a number of countries shows that labour inspection can fulfil its potential in combating discrimination when certain enabling steps are taken (box 3.5). The labour

administration in Belgium has set up a unit to advise and train labour inspectors on discrimination issues. As a part of this effort, a handbook was made available to help inspectors deal with discrimination at the workplace. In Cyprus, the Equal Pay Act of 2002 assigns a specific supervisory and advisory role to the labour inspectorate regarding equal pay. The annual training course for labour inspectors in Uruguay regularly includes training in the area of equality. In Poland, the authorities have declared compliance with equality provisions a priority for labour inspections during a specified time frame, and the National Labour Inspectorate carried out gender equality inspections on the basis of a detailed questionnaire. In Pakistan, the Labour Protection Policy 2005, supported by the Labour Inspection Policy 2006, identifies the elimination of gender discrimination at work as a major objective.

220. In a number of countries the role of labour inspection in combating discrimination is restricted because discrimination falls within the remit of other administrative bodies or is considered to be a matter that should be dealt with by the courts. In Croatia, the Labour Act (consolidated text of 2004) does not provide for penalties for violation of the equal remuneration provisions and, as a result, the labour inspection service has no mandate to monitor these provisions.[20] In addition, the scarcity of resources and infrastructure allocated to labour inspection units may be a practical obstacle preventing labour inspectors from taking action in this area.

221. Where judicial procedures do not offer victims of discrimination real access to the remedies available under the law, the very purpose of legal protection is

19. M.J. Piore; A. Schrank: "Trading up: An embryonic model for easing the human costs of free markets", in *Boston Review,* at boston-review.net/BR31.5/pioreschrank.html.
20. CEACR: Direct request, 2006, Convention No. 100.

Box 3.4.
**Brazil: Lessons learnt from the *núcleos* for promoting equal opportunities
and fighting discrimination in employment and occupation**

In 1995, the Ministry of Labour and Employment, with ILO technical assistance, instituted the programme "Brazil, Gender and Race – United for Equal Opportunities" and established units for promoting equal opportunities and fighting discrimination in employment and occupation, known as *núcleos*, within the Regional Departments of the Ministry at the state level. The units receive and examine complaints of discrimination, provide mediation services, and engage in awareness-raising activities. An assessment of five selected *núcleos* was carried out in 2005 with ILO support. The study revealed some positive results but also shed light on a few shortcomings. It found that little attention had been paid to racial discrimination, compared to discrimination based on disability (partly because of the quotas imposed on employers by law). Attention had focused primarily on discrimination in formal wage employment, while a significant proportion of black people worked informally or were self-employed. The *núcleos* did not share a common method of work, and did not operate according to common targets and impact indicators. There were thus also differences in the relative weight given to labour inspection compared to sensitization/education activities, and cooperation/constructive dialogue with enterprises, although in all cases labour inspection was prevalent. However, in some cases contacts had been developed with universities and NGOs and, in the *núcleo "Pro-Dignidade"* (Natal), NGO representatives had been involved in a mediation procedure regarding an HIV-based discrimination complaint. The assessment study stressed the need to standardize the *núcleos'* focus and modes of operation, and to develop a common set of criteria for assessing performance. It urged the *núcleos* to establish synergies with other programmes of the Ministry of Labour (such as those related to the solidarity-based economy or *"Economía solidaria"*), and other public partners (e.g. the Secretariat for Policies for Women, the Labour Prosecutor and the Special Secretariat for Policies to Promote Racial Equality (SEPPIR) and human rights institutions). The monitoring and evaluation activities had to be improved and better coordinated at national level. On this basis, the ILO, in cooperation with the Ministry of Labour, carried out capacity building for the staff of the units to address some of these constraints. The ILO was also involved in discussions about the reorganization of the Ministry that culminated with the creation, in 2006, of a Special Advisory Unit on discrimination and equality that reports directly to the Executive Secretary of the Ministry of Labour, thus raising the profile of these questions in the Ministry's organizational structure.

Source: P. Cappellin; J.C. Alexim; C. Letierre: *A experiência dos núcleos de promoção da igualdade de oportunidades e combate à discriminação no emprego e na ocupação* (Brasilia, ILO, 2005), at www.oitbrasil.org.br.

Box 3.5.
Equality inspections in the Czech Republic

The Ministry of Labour of the Czech Republic has issued a methodological instruction to labour inspectors regarding equal opportunities for men and women, which entered into force on 1 January 2003. The document describes the relevant legal provisions and provides concrete guidance on how to conduct gender equality inspections. The list of questions to be asked during equality inspections covers issues that arise in relation to recruitment, training and promotion, working conditions, sexual harassment, breastfeeding, maternity and parental leave. An additional document provides guidance on how to evaluate jobs with a view to establishing whether equal remuneration is being paid for work of equal value. The new Labour Inspection Act of 2005 provides that violations of the principles of equal treatment and equal remuneration for work of equal value are offences subject to fines. During the second half of 2004 and the first half of 2005 labour inspectors identified a total of 757 breaches of the provision on equal remuneration.

Source: 2003 and 2006 reports provided by the Government of the Czech Republic under article 22 of the ILO Constitution in respect of Convention No. 100.

undermined. Nonetheless, an emphasis on enforcement, penalties and sanctions does not mean that other ways to deal with discrimination, such as prevention and mediation, are less important. Alternative dispute resolution works best when enforcement exists as an option of last resort. The possibility of facing legal action or penalties serves as an effective incentive for employers to avoid and prevent discrimination in their enterprises.

222. To strengthen legal protection against discrimination, training and capacity building should target workers and employers and their organizations, legal

educators and lawyers, as well as judges and labour inspectors. Given that little experience in handling discrimination cases is available in most jurisdictions, lawyers and judges would particularly benefit from practical training that integrates comparative jurisprudence and relevant international law (Part IV, Chapter 1). In addition to training on issues of law and litigation to these audiences, victims should be able to rely on structures or mechanisms that provide support, counselling and advice, including legal assistance.

223.   In addition, information on the number, nature and outcomes of cases involving discrimination should be collected and assessed regularly, as an indicator to measure the practical impact of anti-discrimination legislation.

Changing labour demand

224.   By adopting affirmative action or positive action measures as part of their human resource development and management policies, employers can play an important role in creating more equal and inclusive workplaces. By doing so, they can achieve a more positive demonstration effect in promoting non-discriminatory human resource practices.

Affirmative or positive action: What has it achieved?

225.   As mentioned earlier, affirmative or positive action is based on the recognition that the prohibition of discrimination alone may be insufficient to level the playing field, once inequalities have become entrenched. In such cases, different treatment of members of disadvantaged groups may be necessary until the causes justifying the adoption of these measures cease to exist. Positive action does not imply that beneficiaries have something wrong with them or need to change; rather, it highlights and seeks to address the failure of labour market institutions to provide equal opportunities to all. Such measures may target one or more groups and may apply to public and/or private enterprises (table 3.2).

226.   Eligible employers are generally asked to prepare reports at regular intervals, providing information on the demographic composition of their workforce and changes over time, on the causes of under-representation of particular groups, and on

measures taken to correct them. The focus is not on statistics alone, but also on the review of companies' human resource management policies and practices.

227.   What has been the impact of these measures? Have they undermined overall efficiency by lowering standards and deterring members of both beneficiary and non-beneficiary groups from performing at their best? Or have they been able to redress a situation of disadvantage due to past and present discrimination, without undermining overall productivity?

228.   These are important questions that need to be answered, especially in the light of the ongoing debate on these matters, which is often tarnished by ideological bias. Despite data constraints, as not all designated employers may comply with their reporting requirements, and the difficulty of determining to what extent affirmative action measures or other policies may be responsible for improvements in the status of under-represented groups, we can draw some conclusions on their impact.

229.   In South Africa, affirmative action appears to have had an impact on the workforce profile of employers covered by the Employment Equity Act, although progress has been uneven among beneficiary groups, black men having benefited the most. In 2003, they accounted for 18.5 per cent of people in top management positions and 20 per cent of those in senior management positions, compared to 5.3 and 7.4 per cent, respectively, of black women and 8.8 and 15 per cent of white women. Black women and men together accounted for almost 37 per cent and over 37 per cent of all promotions to top management and senior management positions, respectively, in the years 2002–03. Recruitment played an equally important role in raising their representation at the top. The position of black women, especially African women, appears to be worsening, while the number of people with disabilities has remained low, and variations in their representation in top management positions insignificant.[21]

230.   In Namibia, the representation of previously racially disadvantaged men increased at the special/skilled/supervisory level, where they formed the dominant group, and the share of their female peers also improved. However, men, especially white men, dominated both top and senior management positions, while women, both white and black, were still under-represented.[22] As in South Africa, persons with disabilities were hardly represented at any level of employment. The public service is at the forefront in

---

21. Commission for Employment Equity: *Annual Report 2003–04* (Pretoria, Department of Labour), at www.labour.gov.za.
22. V. Usiku: "Affirmative action in employment: The Namibian experience", paper presented at the International Dialogue on Advancing Equity and Racial Inclusion, Brasilia, 11–14 April 2005.

Table 3.2. Characteristics of affirmative action programmes in seven countries

	United States	Canada	India	Malaysia	Namibia	South Africa	United Kingdom (Northern Ireland)
Law	Executive Order 11246, 1965 – Equal Employment Opportunity	Employment Equity Act, 1995	Constitution	New Economic Policy 1970	Affirmative Action (Employment) Act, 1998	Employment Equity Act, 1998	Fair Employment and Treatment (Northern Ireland) Order, 1998
Target groups	Racial minorities, women	Women, visible minorities,[1] aboriginal peoples, persons with disabilities	Scheduled castes, scheduled tribes, other "backward classes"[2]	Bumiputeras, (ethnic Malays), persons with disabilities	Racially disadvantaged persons, women, persons with disabilities	Black people (Africans, coloureds and Indians[3]) women, persons with disabilities	Catholic minority
Scope	Public and private sector contractors	Public and private sector	Public and private sector (voluntary)	Public and private sector	Public and private sector	Public and private sector	Public and private sector
Rationale	Compensation for past discrimination	Compensation for past discrimination and building a more racially egalitarian society	Elimination of societal and employment discrimination	Compensation for lack of development	Compensation for past discrimination and building a more racially egalitarian society	Elimination of employment discrimination and building a more racially egalitarian society	Elimination of employment discrimination
Quotas or goals and timetables	Goals and timetables	Goals and timetables	Quotas or "reservations"	Quotas	Goals and timetables	Goals and timetables	Goals and timetables

[1] The term "visible minorities" means persons, other than aboriginal peoples, who are non-Caucasian in race or non-white in colour. [2] "Backward classes" in India do not constitute a clearly defined category, and the identification of groups entitled to these special rights has been the subject of regular disputes and reviews. [3] This racial classification, in use under apartheid, has been maintained after 1994. The term "African" denotes the indigenous people of South Africa, as opposed to people whose origin can be traced to other continents; "coloured" refers to mixed-race South Africans; and "Indian" refers to those of Indian descent.

terms of appointing members of all designated groups in senior and middle management positions; private companies claim they cannot compete with parastatal or state companies in attracting qualified members of designated groups since they cannot afford to pay the same remuneration.[23]

231. In Northern Ireland, the 1990s have seen an increase in employment of the under-represented religious community and greater religious balance in the workforce composition of the firms that reached agreements concerning both Protestant and Catholic under-representation.[24]

232. In Canada, annual reports on performance in the federal public service highlight sustained progress and positive results overall, although significant challenges remain, especially for "visible minorities". The public service is considerably behind with regard to its representation goal of just over 10 per cent of its

23. D. Motinga; T. Mbuende: *Progress on affirmative action and employment equity: Still a man's world!*, IPFR Briefing Paper No. 26, Nov. 2003.
24. C. McCrudden; R. Ford; A. Heath: "Legal regulation of affirmative action in Northern Ireland: An empirical assessment", in *Oxford Journal of Legal Studies*, Vol. 24, No. 3 (2004), pp. 363–415.

workforce for visible minorities. This is a moving target because of the steady flow of immigrants from Asia, Africa, the Caribbean and Latin America. Under-achievement by the public service is compensated by better results in the federally-regulated private sector – also covered by the Employment Equity Act – in which employers regard employment equity as a key tool for attaining greater corporate success.[25]

233. This brief review shows that in several countries where thorough analyses have been conducted, affirmative action has been shown to improve the representation of protected groups at the workplace, although its impact has varied depending on the group.

234. Key to the success of these measures is employers' commitment and the effectiveness of the enforcement mechanisms. The employers in South Africa that have made the most progress in attracting, advancing and retaining suitably qualified persons from designated groups engaged in affirmative action measures long before the Employment Equity Act had become law. These employers viewed these measures as one key strategy to pursue corporate goals of productivity, excellence and global competitiveness. The high prominence of skill development schemes in the list of affirmative action measures adopted by these employers is consistent with this approach.[26]

235. Equality commissions can also play a crucial role in improving enforcement. In Northern Ireland, for instance, the former Fair Employment Commission (FEC), which in 2000 became the Equality Commission for Northern Ireland (ECNI), concluded agreements with eligible employers containing similar enforcement provisions. Regardless of whether the agreements were binding or voluntary, they included a "review of progress" clause, providing for FEC staff to liaise with the employers to ascertain that agreed action was being undertaken, and to review regular reports on employment trends. Over time the FEC's focus shifted from large to smaller enterprises, resulting in greater reliance on voluntary agreements, and priority moved from signing new agreements to ensuring the effective implementation of those already reached.[27]

236. Capacity-building and training sessions for management are also essential. The preliminary

evaluation of the Embracing Change Initiative (ECI) and Action Plan, adopted by the Government of Canada in 2000 to address the under-representation of visible minorities in the public service, recommends greater investment in the education of managers on ECI. It also advocates human resource planning oriented towards visible minorities, as well as the inclusion of ECI-specific goals in the performance of managers responsible for selection and recruitment. These initiatives are intended to accelerate the representation of visible minorities which, despite steady increases each year since 2000, has reached only half of the one-in-five external recruitment benchmark set for 2003.[28] In 2005, the Government further committed itself towards the elimination of racism in the workplace under federal jurisdiction through "A Canada for all" – Canada's action plan against racism.

237. Laws may also increase or reduce the likelihood of human resources management practices to bring about more inclusive workplaces. In countries that rely largely on voluntary action (e.g. the United Kingdom) or on rigid and strict requirements, such as quotas (e.g. India and Malaysia, with regard to the public sector), enterprises may have limited incentives to establish formal human resource management practices. The reduced risk of litigation on the basis of unfair employment leads employers to use greater discretion in the type of measures they may decide to implement. On the other hand, a strict requirement to meet certain quotas may discourage the development of formal testing procedures for job applicants.

238. In countries such as Canada, South Africa and the United States, where laws impose costs on employers in the event of non-compliance, but do not enforce rigid measures such as quotas, employers have greater incentives to develop more sophisticated human resource systems. Formal job evaluation, testing for job applicants, training needs assessment, training evaluation, formal career paths and performance-related pay may be more likely to develop in such contexts.[29]

239. Affirmative action needs to be backed up by effective enforcement, combined with building capacity for implementation, strengthening accountability,

25. W. Boxhill: "Employment equity in Canada", paper presented at the International Dialogue on Advancing Equity and Racial Inclusion, Brasilia, 11–14 April 2005.
26. Commission for Employment Equity, *Annual Report 2001–2002*, at www.labour.gov.za.
27. McCrudden; R. Ford; Heath, op. cit.
28. Consulting and Audit Canada: "Preliminary evaluation of the Embracing Change Initiative", paper prepared for the Employment Equity Branch, Public Services Human Resources Management Agency of Canada, June 2004, p. v.
29. S. Taggar: "A comparative look at the impact on human resources management of employment equity legislation", in H. Jain; P. Sloane; F. Horwitz (eds.): *Employment equity and affirmative action: An international comparison* (Armonk, NY, M.E. Sharpe Inc., 2003), p. 71.

and developing tools to support practitioners and those responsible for implementation.

240. Although essential, affirmative action measures alone are not enough to create more inclusive workplaces. They need to be supported by action in the community and at school. Racial segregation of housing, for instance, may maintain labour market segregation by preserving recruitment practices through local networks that keep members of racial minorities away from decent jobs, regardless of their qualifications. Similarly, significant and consistent investment in quality education of the younger members of disadvantaged groups to reduce their drop-out rates and increase their university enrolment are essential to close the socio-economic divide between mainstream and subordinate groups.

Procurement policy:
Does it work against discrimination?

241. *Time for equality at work* stressed that public procurement policies were increasingly being used to complement national law in furthering social goals, including equality in employment. Procurement policies can attain these objectives by requesting contractors to modify the racial or gender or ability/disability make-up of their workforce, or by encouraging contractors who are female or belong to racial or ethnic minorities to participate in public tenders. Considering the scale and economic importance of public tenders, the potential impact of equality clauses on removing discriminatory practices and diversifying the profile of companies' workforces and ownership is significant. Moreover, ILO Recommendation No. 111,[30] accompanying Convention No. 111, explicitly refers to the use of contracts for this purpose, and the CEACR has stressed the desirability of the use of public contracts for securing both equal opportunities in employment and equal pay for work of equal value.[31]

242. But are these policies effective or mere window dressing? Under what circumstances do they result in workplaces that are more inclusive as regards race, gender and/or disability? Do procurement policies aimed at promoting equality increase costs? Do they exclude small and medium-sized enterprises (SMEs) or make it more difficult for them to tender successfully?

243. The United States is among the countries with the longest experience in this area. Since the mid-1960s all government contractors and subcontractors with federal contracts totalling US$10,000 or more are required to analyse their workforce, ascertain the impact of their personnel practices on their performance from an equal employment opportunity (EEO) perspective, identify related barriers, and take corrective action. This may consist of back pay and reinstating a person found to have been discriminated against, or setting targets or benchmarks to ensure greater representation of under-represented groups. The Office of Federal Contract Compliance Programs (OFCCP) is responsible for both developing and enforcing the rules and regulations implementing Executive Order 11246 (Equal Employment Opportunity), the cornerstone of US efforts to link federal contracting and EEO.[32]

244. Over the decades different methods have been applied in the United States to assess the outcomes of public procurement for equality goals. Originally, the main indicator used was the scope and content of the written affirmative action programmes prepared by contractors. In the early 1980s, attempts were made to measure the impact of the law by looking at changes in the numbers of under-represented groups at all levels of the enterprise workforce. Eventually, the number of evaluations carried out by the OFCCP, the number of compensated victims and the amount of financial remedies obtained became the yardstick.

245. Compliance appears to be strongly correlated with the level of management commitment: the greater the endorsement of EEO goals by company boards and chief executive officers (CEOs), the higher the impact of public procurement policies. The size of the enterprise also plays a role: smaller companies, even when willing to abide by the law, have fewer means and other competing demands that prevent them from assigning dedicated staff to EEO matters.

246. In cases of non-compliance, written conciliation agreements are drawn up between the employers concerned and the OFCCP. An important step was

30. Paragraph 3 of the Recommendation provides that each Member should promote the observance of the principles of non-discrimination "where practicable and necessary" by such methods as making eligibility for contracts involving the expenditure of public funds dependent on observance of the principles, and making eligibility for grants to training establishments and for a licence to operate a private employment agency or a private vocational guidance office dependent on observance of the principles.

31. ILO: *Equal remuneration*, General Survey by the Committee of Experts on the Application of Conventions and Recommendations, Report III(4B), International Labour Conference, 72nd Session, Geneva, 1986, para. 158. Idem: *Equality in employment and occupation*, General Survey by the Committee of Experts on the Application of Conventions and Recommendations, Report III(4B), International Labour Conference, 75th Session, Geneva, 1988, para. 177.

32. This and the following paragraphs are based on J. DuBray: "Use of public procurement policies in the United States to combat discrimination and to promote equal employment opportunities", background paper prepared for this Global Report.

Box 3.6.
Business Unity South Africa (BUSA) and black economic empowerment (BEE)

As part of its contribution to the achievement of black economic empowerment (BEE) goals, BUSA has developed a step-by-step guide for its members on how to formulate sector transformation charters (voluntary agreements to ensure the implementation of BEE objectives in a given sector). It spells out the process underpinning such charters; the criteria to be included in the scorecard to determine the status of enterprises with regard to BEE; the steps required to identify the substantive transformation matters to be addressed; and guidelines on how to monitor and evaluate the effective implementation of the charters.

Source: Business Unity South Africa (BUSA): *A guide on BEE sector transformation charter facilitation and formulation*, at www.busa.org.za.

the development in the early 1980s of industrial liaison groups that brought together, on a regular basis, groups of contractors from a variety of industries with representatives from the OFCCP to share information on EEO matters in a non-adversarial context. This helped create trust between the parties, and led to the creation of the Exemplary Voluntary Efforts (EVE) award programme, under which the Secretary of Labor recognizes every year three to as many as 12 contractors that have taken affirmative action measures above and beyond what is required by law.

247. In South Africa the use of public procurement to transform the country's social landscape is a much more recent development and features prominently on the national public agenda. "Preferential procurement" is part of the strategy adopted under the Broad-based Black Economic Empowerment Act, 2003.[33] This strategy is founded on a host of laws and policies introduced since the mid-1990s with the aim of "deracializing" business ownership and control. Preferential procurement, in particular, is geared towards changing the racial make-up of the suppliers of both government and large private companies, thus contributing to black entrepreneurship development.

248. Preferential procurement is a key element of many of the Black Economic Empowerment (BEE) sector transformation charters mandated by the Broad-based Black Economic Empowerment Act. These charters are negotiated voluntary agreements among all the key stakeholders of a particular sector

establishing indicators, targets and timeframes within which to measure progress in meeting BEE obligations (box 3.6). Many charters tend to go above and beyond what is required by law. Preferential procurement provides for example for a 10–20 per cent price preference system for black- and women-owned enterprises during the adjudication of tenders.[34]

249. It is too early to assess the impact of preferential procurement in South Africa, but its potential is apparent: in 2004 alone the State and state-owned enterprises spent over US$123 billion in purchasing good and services.[35] The success of preferential procurement, however, depends on several conditions: the availability of competent, reliable and racially and gender-diverse providers of services and goods, and strict monitoring of quality standards and corruption. The supply of a diverse pool of providers requires considerable investment in education and skills enhancement, as well as the adoption of supportive policy measures to boost black entrepreneurship and facilitate their transition from micro to small and medium-sized businesses. On the other hand, an independent and strict monitoring system of suppliers, as envisaged by many charters, is important to prevent white-controlled, established companies from using blacks or women as fronts to gain access to tenders.

250. In Europe, the use of procurement policies for promoting equality at the workplace is a more recent development, and does not have the visibility it has achieved in the countries mentioned above. The

33. The aims of broad-based black economic empowerment, as stated in the Act, include increasing black ownership and management of business; achieving substantial change in the racial composition of skilled occupations of new and existing enterprises; facilitating community and worker ownership of enterprises and productive assets; increasing the extent to which black women own and manage existing and new enterprises; and encouraging investment in businesses owned by black people (defined as Africans, Coloureds and Indians). Economic empowerment complements efforts aimed at fostering employment equity within enterprises, as required by the Employment Equity Act of 1998. The purpose of the latter is to ensure equitable representation of and promote equal opportunities for disadvantaged groups.

34. Some of these charters require companies to allocate up to 50per cent of their total discretionary spending to black- and women-owned enterprises by 2010: L. Mbabane: "Preferential procurement in South Africa's Black Economic Empowerment Policy and its prospects for combating discrimination and reducing economic inequalities", background paper prepared for this Global Report.

35. Bureau for Economic Research, Stellenbosch University, 2005, cited ibid.

Table 3.3. Evolving models of European practice in linking procurement policies to equality objectives

Models and goals	Examples	Advantages	Challenges
Tenderer qualification model: Focuses on the pre-qualification stage and prohibits the award of government contracts to firms that fail or have failed to meet equality requirements	West Midlands (UK): Six local authorities developed a "common standard" to assess whether a firm's policy on race relations met the national legal requirements on racial equality	Minimizes the risk of contracting unsuitably qualified or dubious firms All potential contractors, not just those awarded the contract, are encouraged to adopt anti-discrimination measures	Used for narrower anti-discrimination goals, not for broader equality purposes Limits competition by excluding potential competitors that might be financially sound and technically competent, but not suitable from an anti-discrimination angle More as a means to discipline a company, rather than an incentive to improve their human resources practices
Contract conditions model: Focuses on the post-contract award stage; requires compliance with certain conditions in implementing the contract	Since 2001 a Danish municipality requires contractors to design an equal treatment policy for people with different ethnic backgrounds, setting measurable goals for the period of the contract Non-compliance with these conditions is deemed equivalent to non-fulfilment of the contract	Does not reduce competition, as it does not exclude potential contractors on the basis of their previous activities	Relatively inflexible, as the same conditions are applied to all; no incentives to do more than what is required Conditions apply only to the contract Enforcement relies completely on post-award monitoring. For the monitoring to be effective, equality issues must receive the same attention as those pertaining to the primary purpose of the contract Need to develop a control instrument to assess compliance and determine appropriate remedy in the event of breach of contract (financial penalties or denial of future contracts)
Award criteria model: Tendering firms that meet equality requirements, in addition to being financially sound and technically competent, are at an advantage in the award of contract	A Northern Ireland pilot scheme required tenderers to use unemployed people in public contracts. Among equally qualified tenderers, a firm is selected on the basis of the way in which it addresses equality issues	Promotes competition between tenderers on equality issues	Greater emphasis on equality may lead to increased overall cost of the bid, to the financial detriment of the public body awarding the contract
Technical specifications model: Successful contractors meet technical specifications laid down by the public body and also offer equality-friendly options	Office of Government Commerce (UK): Bids that do not include fair trade options are not rejected or considered non-compliant A bid including fair trade options would be chosen if not substantially above the bids that do not include these options	Likely to reduce the costs associated with the "award criteria" model	Procedures of compliance are complicated, tender documents must invite tenderers to offer equality-friendly options and specify the minimum equality specifications to be met and the way in which these options have to be presented

Source: C. McCrudden: *Public procurement: How effective is it in combating discrimination?*, May 2006, background paper prepared for this Global Report.

reasons for this are varied. An important factor is the stricter limits placed by EU law on affirmative action measures, compared to South Africa or the United States. Another reason is the complexity of the legal requirements under both EU law and the Agreement on Government Procurement of the World Trade Organization (WTO), and the uncertainty as to whether they permit the use of procurement policies for social goals.[36]

251. To address this situation, the European Commission issued a communication in 2001 clarifying its position on the use of public procurement for social policy purposes. Ever since, through the supply of information, it has tried to harmonize standards in the public procurement context with a view to avoiding the erection of new barriers to trade in the EU internal market.[37] One example of this effort is the *Build-for-All Reference Manual*, issued in 2006, which provides guidance on the use of accessibility criteria in public procurement in order to remove architectonic barriers to access by people with disabilities.[38]

252. Five questions dominate the present European debate on the use of public procurement policies for equality goals: (a) what groups should be targeted (e.g. racial or ethnic minorities, people with disabilities) – this would have different implications in terms of approaches and instruments; (b) what areas of equality they should focus on – only employment or also areas such as housing and provision of essential services; (c) where procurement policies should seek to produce effects – inside the jurisdiction of the competent public authorities or abroad; (d) to what extent companies can be required to go beyond the existing legal obligations; and (e) which level of government should be involved in the use of public procurement for equality goals.[39]

253. The four different models of public tendering for equality that have emerged up to now in Europe (table 3.3) reflect these concerns.

254. The cases examined show that contract compliance for equality goals has considerable potential for promoting equality at the workplace, including along supply chains, provided that certain conditions are met. The political importance attached to the elimination of discrimination and the promotion of

equality by society at large is the number one factor in fostering the acceptance and impact of contract compliance for building a more equal society.

255. Another crucial condition is clarity and transparency about the rules and implications of public procurement for equality goals. A useful approach is the supply and dissemination of user-friendly information about how to accomplish the link between procurement and equality, what kind of clauses would serve this purpose, what kind of consideration on racial or gender or other forms of equality should be addressed, and what have been the experience and outcomes of companies nationally and abroad. Knowledge-sharing forums of the sort developed in South Africa and the United States provide suitable conduits for disseminating the necessary know-how, while building the required legitimacy.

256. An area that requires closer scrutiny is the implications of social procurement for SMEs' involvement in tendering processes. It is also important to show businesses how they can benefit from addressing equality issues, thus dispelling the perceived tension between promoting equality and achieving "value for money".[40]

Addressing labour supply constraints through inclusive active labour market policies

257. Active labour market policies comprise a host of measures: job search, recruitment and placement activities, training, hiring subsidies, job-creation programmes and various support services. Many countries around the world have such policies, although they differ in scale, types of measures and effectiveness.[41] Given the disproportionate representation of groups vulnerable to discrimination among the unemployed, the underemployed and the inactive, these policies have a strong potential for increasing or stabilizing their job opportunities and earning prospects, thus narrowing inter-group inequalities.

258. Evidence shows, however, that while members of discriminated groups may join job placement and training schemes, they often fail to achieve similar levels of success to those of their peers belonging

36. C. McCrudden: "Public procurement: How effective is it in combating discrimination?", May 2006, background paper prepared for this Global Report.
37. Interpretative communication of the Commission on the Community law applicable to public procurement and the possibilities for integrating social considerations into public procurement, COM/2001/0566 final, *Official Journal* 333, 28 Nov. 2001, at eur-lex. europa.eu.
38. The *Build-for-All Reference Manual* (Luxembourg, Info-Handicap and the "Build-for-All" Project, 2006), at www.build-for-all.net.
39. C. McCrudden: "Public procurement", op. cit.
40. See IRIS Consulting: *Department for Work and Pensions: Review of race equality and public sector procurement*, Sep. 2005.
41. P. Auer; U. Efendioglu; J. Leschke: *Active labour market policies around the world: Coping with the consequences of globalization* (Geneva, ILO, 2005).

Box 3.7.
Gender mainstreaming and the European Employment Strategy (EES):
An assessment of the first phase

The EES has been a major catalyst for the integration of equal opportunity issues into the employment framework. With the conclusion of the first phase of the EES, progress has been most notable in narrowing the gender employment gaps and the expansion of leave entitlements and childcare facilities, even in countries that already had relatively good coverage, such as France. The initiatives aimed at narrowing the gender pay gap have been inadequate, however, while available evidence is still insufficient to assess the impact of measures addressing gender occupational segregation. Outcomes vary significantly from one Member State to another, as their starting points also differed considerably, but progress was more apparent in countries with no tradition of taking a gender perspective into account. Political change at the national level, for example in Italy and Portugal, also contributed to slowing down gender mainstreaming efforts.

The guidelines on gender mainstreaming relating to the pillar on equal opportunities between men and women in the first phase of the EES called upon governments to develop and reinforce consultative systems with gender equality bodies, develop indicators to measure progress in gender equality, and apply procedures for gender impact assessment of policies. Efforts to promote gender mainstreaming by training equality actors were deployed, including in Greece, where concerned officials were made more gender-conscious in the use of the European Social Fund (ESF). There has been continued improvement in the quality and range of indicators to measure gender equality, although the poor quality and lack of data disaggregated by sex in some cases mean that gender equality indicators are not available for all countries. Most countries failed to mainstream gender issues into the other three pillars of the EES, but a few managed to do so in relation to active labour market policies. These include Austria, which required all public employment services (PES) to spend up to 50 per cent of their budgetary resources on women, and Denmark, which introduced a gender mainstreaming strategy in the PES, as well as pilot projects to break down gender segregation and raise women's presence in key sectors to overcome labour supply and skill bottlenecks. In Austria, Belgium, France and Germany, access to labour market policies has been opened up to jobseekers, regardless of whether or not they are eligible for unemployment benefits. Entrepreneurship development has been the area where most countries either set gender targets within existing programmes or developed targeted schemes. Conversely, lifelong learning policies and measures aimed at addressing skill shortages have paid little, if any, attention to gender issues.

Sources: J. Rubery: "Gender mainstreaming and gender equality in the EU: The impact of the EU employment strategy", in *Industrial Relations Journal*, 33:5, pp. 500-522; J. Rubery; D. Grimshaw; C. Fagan; H. Figueiredo; M. Smith: "Gender equality still on the European agenda – but for how long?", in *Industrial Relations Journal*, 34:5, pp. 484-486.

---

to non-discriminated groups. It is important to acknowledge and redress existing structural inequality in the labour market.

259. Active labour market policies and programmes can address discrimination in three ways:

- by developing comprehensive policies to address workplace discrimination;
- by improving the job placement function in the public and private sector; and
- by building the employability of those vulnerable to discrimination.

Developing comprehensive policies
to address workplace discrimination

260. The experience of mainstreaming gender and promoting gender equality in the European Employment Strategy (EES) is unique in the world and sheds light on the advantages and challenges of gender mainstreaming (box 3.7). Launched in 1997, the EES requires Member States to develop annual National Action Plans on employment based on common agreed targets. Gender equality was incorporated in this process through the requirement that gender issues and impacts be addressed by the action plans, the adoption of a specific female employment rate target of 60 per cent by 2010 (2000 Lisbon Summit), and the introduction in the period 1997–2002 of a specific pillar – one of four – on promoting equal opportunities between men and women. In the subsequent phase of the EES gender equality became one of the ten priorities for action, but the requirement to mainstream gender in the remaining priority areas was kept. Some countries set national targets and timeframes for substantially reducing the gender employment, unemployment and pay gaps, but did not always specify the policies needed to this end. The involvement of the social partners in tackling these gaps has been an important feature in many countries.

Box 3.8.
ACCEDER: Increasing job opportunities for unemployed Roma in Spain

ACCEDER is a Spanish programme widely recognized as a good practice. It began in Madrid in 1998 and has been subsequently expanded to 13 regions in Spain. It aims to increase opportunities for the Roma community to integrate into the labour market. For the period 2000–06, the target was to secure 2,500 labour contracts for unemployed persons, approximately 70 per cent of whom would be Roma. The programme was designed to meet individual needs of jobseekers: it provided guidance on selecting jobs compatible with the applicants' skills, facilitated research of and contact with enterprises, and offered training to improve employability. In 1999 there were 304 active jobseekers enrolled in ACCEDER, and 63 per cent found employment. However, the job retention rate is unknown. The programme's strengths are its individualized approach in assessing and matching skills and jobs, and the use of mediators who can bridge the gap between Roma and non-Roma. Its weaknesses include the difficulty of providing adequate and appropriate training for individuals with low education levels and persistent discrimination on the labour market. The programme had not addressed the problem that participants might be unwilling to accept low-paying jobs and, consequently, lose access to social assistance benefits.

Sources: D. Ringold; M. Orenstein; E. Wilkens: *Roma in an expanding Europe: Breaking the poverty cycle* (Washington, DC, The World Bank, 2005), box 6.3, p. 166; Fundación Secretariado Gitano (FSG): "The Multiregional Operational Program Fight against Discrimination ACCEDER: Actions aimed at the Romani community in Spain", in *Roma Rights Quarterly*, No. 1, 2006, at www.errc.org.

Improving the job placement function in the public and private sectors

261.   The effectiveness of job placement services carried out by private employment agencies and public employment services is assessed by measures such as rates of placement and costs per placement. The pressure in both sectors to meet standards of accountability pushes placement organizations to recruit the most qualified and job-ready individuals. This puts less skilled individuals with more real or perceived barriers to employment at a disadvantage.

262.   In the public sector, economic efficiency goals are often balanced with social equity goals, as in the EES mentioned above.

263.   A variety of activities are used to promote equity in job search assistance and placement of the persons who need them most (box 3.8). Job coaching designed to help integrate people with disabilities directly into the workplace (Australia, Norway, United Kingdom and United States) has proven effective.

264.   Another example is the Ethnic Minority Outreach (EMO) initiative, launched in 2002 by the UK government as part of its New Deal Next Phase, which seeks to facilitate the transition of jobless people from ethnic minorities into employment. Its main features are: a territorial focus (it operates in five regions where 75 per cent of working-age ethnic minority adults live) and partnerships established between local private institutions and Jobcentre Plus (the public employment service) and/or other local service providers. The host of outreach techniques (ranging from SMS text messages, television and radio advertising to offering home visits and going to local markets) used by EMO operators, alongside their language skills, made it possible to reach those who had never approached Jobcentre Plus, especially Indian and Pakistani women.[42]

265.   As part of their recruitment and placement activities, job placement services have an important role to play in tackling employers' discriminatory hiring practices. Employers may provide either implicit or explicit instructions on the qualifications of the job applicants to be recruited; sometimes the qualifications demanded are not related to the actual work to be carried out. The example of the Red CIL PRO-Empleo programme in Peru provides evidence of discriminatory practices in public employment services (box 3.9).

266.   To address these discriminatory practices, Job-Centre Plus in the United Kingdom has introduced a procedure for recording and addressing direct and indirect discrimination by employers (the *Dealing with Discrimination* guide provides guidance on the procedure). If an employer is found to be attempting discrimination, or if jobseekers submit written complaints alleging discrimination by employers, staff are required to talk with the employers about their behaviour and

---

42. H. Barnes et al.: "Ethnic Minority Outreach: An evaluation", Department for Work and Pensions, Research Report No. 229 (2005), at www.dwp.gov.uk.

Box 3.9.
Red CIL PROEmpleo (*Red*) in Peru

Red was created with the aim of boosting employment opportunities, especially for disadvantaged social groups. It works through a network of public and private agencies in the main cities countrywide, but the bulk of operations are concentrated in Lima. Performance is assessed against the numbers of: (a) registered jobseekers; (b) enterprises using *Red*; and (c) job vacancies that are filled. In 2004, 80,064 individuals, representing 5.4 per cent of total unemployment, approached *Red* and, of these, 24 per cent found work, thus filling 80 per cent of job vacancies. Over 60 per cent of jobseekers were men, like non-*Red* jobseekers, but younger, more educated and with less work experience. Eighty-two per cent of job vacancies require no education or primary school, as enterprises look for skilled workers through other channels, i.e. private employment agencies or personal contacts. The proportion of manufacturing enterprises is higher among *Red* enterprises than non-*Red* enterprises (43 per cent compared to 28 per cent), as is the share of those with more than 100 employees (27 per cent compared to 15 per cent of non-*Red* enterprises). Wages offered to *Red* jobseekers are much lower than average market wages. *Red* operators use two types of forms: one containing jobseekers' personal data (age, sex, civil status and whether or not head of household) and qualifications (education, training, work experience), and their present/recent and expected earnings, and another form with only the characteristics and requirements (education, computer literacy, linguistic skills, work experience) of advertised jobs. This information is to be introduced in the *Red* database to facilitate and speed up "job matching" and monitor the programme's performance, but *Red* operators prefer to use the forms manually because this way they can add information that is relevant to employers, i.e. sex, age and height, among others. A recent study showed that for all levels of education, "sex" and "age" are among the most prevalent requirements of employers, who clearly prefer young men. A particular "appearance" (being "thin", "light-skinned", "good-looking") is mostly required for occupations entailing contact with the public, and for which only women, and young women, are in demand. A particular "height" is required mainly for occupations for which only men are requested, some of which involve the use of high equipment or machinery.

Source: P. Vera Rojas: *La discriminación en los procesos de selección de personal*, DECLARATION Working Paper No. 46 (Geneva, ILO, 2006).

legal standards. Little use has been made of this procedure, however. One reason is the limited number of written complaints by jobseekers owing either to lack of knowledge of the procedure or to scepticism about staff's willingness to use it. Other factors include the often covert and subtle nature of employers' discrimination, which is difficult to prove, lack of clarity on the part of staff about the specifics of the reporting complaint procedure and, last but not least, the fact that staff may avoid sending jobseekers to workplaces where they anticipate that discrimination may occur.[43] Discriminatory selection can take the form of interviews or tests requiring a high level of analytical ability or communicative competence that are not demanded by the job.[44] This can be avoided through employment agencies providing guidance to employers.

267. Another means to lower barriers for members of disadvantaged groups in the selection process consists of providing employers with an anonymous curriculum vitae (that does not include the name, age or photo of the jobseeker). Since 2003, the National Employment Agency (ANPE) of France has used this measure to combat racial discrimination. The identity of the candidates is revealed to the employer only once he/she contacts them.[45] The rationale is to overcome the obstacles that members of ethnic minorities face from the very early stages of the selection process, as shown by recent surveys.[46]

268. Private employment agencies have taken steps to combat discriminatory treatment as well. In France, for instance, Manpower and the private association Agefiph signed a two-year agreement in

43. M. Hudson; H. Barnes; K. Ray; J. Phillips: "Ethnic minority perceptions and experiences of JobCentre Plus", Research Report No. 349, Department for Work and Pensions, 2006, pp. 108–118, at www.dwp.gov.uk.
44. C. Roberts; S. Campbell: "Talk on trial: Job interviews, language and ethnicity", Research Summary No. 344, Department for Work and Pensions, at www.dwp.gov.uk.
45. R. Fauroux: *La lutte contre les discriminations ethniques dans le domaine de l'emploi* (Paris, Ministry of Employment, Social Cohesion and Housing, 2005).
46. J.F-Amadieu: "Enquête 'Testing' sur CV", Adia/Paris I Observatoire des Discriminations, at cergors.univ-paris1.fr/docsatelecharger/pr%E9sentation%20du%20testing%20mai%202004.pdf.

Box 3.10.
France: Private employment agencies and discrimination

After two discrimination cases, Adecco, the leading private employment agency for temporary jobs, introduced, as of 2001, a number of corrective measures, such as a free telephone call line for temporary workers alleging discriminatory treatment, diversity training for 2,000 of its 4,700 employees, and the obligation on staff not to accept discriminatory job requirements by employers, under the threat of sanctions including dismissal. More recently, however, one of Adecco's affiliates has been sued for recruiting, upon the client's request, only young, white French women.

See Y. Philippin: "L'entreprise prend des couleurs", in *Le Journal du Dimanche*, 14 May 2006, p. 15.

2005 focusing on six priorities: raising the number of temporarily employed disabled workers; supplying training programmes for disabled workers; more partnerships with regional and local structures; awareness raising activities among enterprises; training of Manpower staff; and assistance to temporary workers who are victims of industrial accidents. Especially for large private employment agencies, the need to avoid damage to their reputations stemming from a discrimination case may prevail over fears of losing existing or potential clients, although actual enforcement of an anti-discrimination policy may not always be easy (box 3.10).

Building the employability of those vulnerable to discrimination

269. Fighting discrimination in the workplace does not begin at the point of job search assistance and placement.

270. Employment and training programmes to develop the employability of those who face discrimination may be funded by government and administered by public employment services, local governments, community organizations, the private sector or employers' organizations or trade unions. The benefits arising from participating in such schemes depend on the extent to which schemes and those delivering them acknowledge and address the specific needs of members of discriminated groups. This is why consultations with, and involvement of, members of the groups concerned in the design and implementation of policies are crucial to their relevance and legitimacy.[47]

271. Career guidance, whether provided by secondary or tertiary education, the public employment service, community organizations or employers,[48] can be an important tool for empowering workers and addressing discrimination. Special training schemes are often required to address the needs of members of disadvantaged groups, as conventional training programmes are not designed for people with limited literacy or numeracy and often overlook the fact that they are employed in informal jobs.[49]

272. The programme "Trabalho doméstico cidadão" in Brazil, which is part of the country's national vocational training policy (PNQS), is of special interest because of its pioneering approach. This is the first time in the history of Brazil that a national public policy targets domestic workers, who numbered over 6 million in 2004, representing 20 per cent of total female employment,[50] comprising mainly black women with little education. The programme acknowledges and addresses the triple disadvantages that domestic workers face because of their sex, race and class. The novelty of this programme lies in its integrated approach, which combines vocational training, formalizing domestic work, which is largely unregistered, promoting unionization among domestic workers and providing a housing programme for them. Practical action covers different fronts: media awareness-raising campaigns on the situation and plight of these workers; tax incentives

---

47. E. Ogbonna; M. Noon: "A new deal or new disadvantage? British ethnic minorities and Government training", in *International Journal of Manpower* (Bradford), Vol. 20, No. 3/4 (1999).

48. For a comparison of different systems, see A.G. Watts; R.G. Sultana: "Career guidance policies in 37 countries: Contrasts and common themes", in *International Journal for Educational and Vocational Guidance*, Vol. 4, No. 2–3 (2004), pp. 105–122.

49. See I. Zoon; J. Kiers: "Report on the Council of Europe Project 'Roma Access to Employment in SEE'" (Stability Pact for South Eastern Europe, Apr. 2005), at www.coe.int/T/DG3/RomaTravellers/stabilitypact/activities/FYROM/accessemplymentregional_en.asp.

50. L. Abramo; M.E. Valenzuela: "Inserción laboral y brechas de equidad de género en América Latina", in L. Abramo (ed.): *Trabajo decente y equidad de género en América Latina* (Santiago, ILO, 2006), p. 50.

to employers who give them regular labour contracts; training courses for domestic workers on labour rights and basic education; and vocational training to broaden their occupational prospects.[51] Providing subsidies to cover transportation costs or childcare services have proven important enabling conditions for their attendance. The programme is implemented by the Ministry of Labour and Employment in cooperation with domestic workers through their unions.

273. In Cambodia, mobile courses were offered in rural areas during the 1990s and early 2000s, thus allowing many rural women to receive training. Previously, their access to training opportunities had been restricted by the lack of adequate means of transportation, and cultural constraints that limited their physical mobility (social norms do not allow women to leave their households or family obligations for protracted periods of time, nor is it considered appropriate for them to ask for a ride from neighbours to attend a course outside their communities).[52]

274. Labour market programmes, such as public works or community works, are designed to generate temporary wage opportunities for low-income and unskilled workers; they constitute a key component of employment policies in most developing countries and economies in transition. They represent an important policy instrument to reduce underemployment and raise wages for casual labour, especially in contexts where the prospects of increases in formal wage employment are bleak or where such new jobs are more likely go to better qualified people – whether unemployed or not yet in the labour force.

275. The National Rural Employment Guarantee Act 2005 (NREGA) in India has institutionalized a minimum wage for rural unskilled labour and aims at ensuring at least 100 days' employment. It also provides for unemployment allowances if a job is not offered to a rural household. It is premature to draw any conclusions about the impact of the scheme on poverty and gender equality, but concerns have been voiced about possible tensions within families over the selection of the member to be given the job and about women being left out. Experiences elsewhere show, however, that the level and mode of payment, system of recruitment and mobilization, conditions of work at the worksite, and type of job-generation schemes are key determinants of women's inclusion or exclusion from these programmes, and the benefits they may obtain.[53]

276. Surveys are being conducted at the initiative of the ILO in selected districts in India to examine the decent work and gender equality aspects of the National Rural Employment Guarantee Programme (NREGP) and the effects on distress migration. In particular, the gender dynamics at the household, community and worksite levels are analysed to see how they shape the extent and forms of women's participation in the Programme. The ultimate goal is to devise the necessary safeguards to be put in the place in the NREGP so that men and women can benefit from it equally.[54]

277. The case of "A Trabajar Urbano", a programme which generates temporary employment through the construction of social and economic infrastructure in Peru, is illustrative. This programme targets heads of households – whether males or females – with at least one child under the age of 18 years, belonging to the first two lowest quintiles, and living in carefully selected urban areas. While women represent the majority of the beneficiaries overall, their participation varies over time and by region. Women's participation is higher in Lima than elsewhere because the wages paid are very low – less than the average earnings of potential male beneficiaries. But in the other cities, the same wage is higher than the local average earnings of potential beneficiaries and hence attractive to men, who account for the majority of participants. A change in the type of projects financed by the programme also led to a sudden change in the gender composition of participants. The shift from an almost exclusive focus on projects aimed at beautifying Lima and its parks through the construction of social or economic infrastructure, and the programme's call for the selection of "suitable" candidates, led to the massive incorporation of men into these public works. Eventually, the programme rectified this requirement on the ground that it had led to misinterpretations and the unintended exclusion of women.[55]

51. S. Sanches: "Mainstreaming gender and race in active labour market policies: Some reflections and experiences in Brazil", May 2006, background paper prepared for this Global Report.

52. ILO, EIC and UNIFEM: *Decent work for women and men in the informal economy: Profile and good practices in Cambodia* (Bangkok and Phnom Penh, ILO, 2006), p. 67.

53. A. King Dejardin: "Public works programmes, a strategy for poverty alleviation: The gender dimension", Issues in Development Discussion Paper No. 10 (Geneva, ILO, 1996), pp. 18–20.

54. Institute of Social Studies Trust (ISST): "Women and the NREGA", report of the first phase, June 2006; and Decent Work Country Programme for India 2006–09.

55. M. Tostes: "Igualdad de oportunidades y promoción del empleo en el Perú: Una radiografía" (unpublished paper, 2006), p. 49.

Table 3.4. Causes and dimensions of the gender pay gap

Causes	Dimensions
Differences in productivity characteristics of men and women	• Years of education • Field of specialization • Years of work experience • Seniority in the job
Differences in the characteristics of enterprises and sectors employing men and women	• Size of the enterprise • Type of industry • Unionization of enterprises and sectors
Differences in the jobs held by women and men	• Women under-represented in higher-paid jobs • Women over-represented in a smaller and lower-paying range of occupations than men • Women and men concentrated in different segments of the same broad occupations • Women over-represented in part-time work
Differences in the number of hours devoted to paid work	• Men work longer hours (in paid work) than women
Discrimination in remuneration	
Direct discrimination	• Different pay for men (higher) and women doing the same or similar jobs • Different job titles (and pay) for the same or similar occupations
Indirect discrimination	• Undervaluation of the skills, competencies and responsibilities associated with "female" jobs • Gender biases in job evaluation methods • Gender biases in job classification and job grading systems • Gender biases in job remuneration systems

Policies for closing the gender gap in employment and pay

278. The facts tell us that in most regions of the world opportunities for women to participate in paid employment have continued to rise, although with considerable variations by region, and that growing numbers of women have entered careers once regarded as exclusively masculine (Part II, Chapter 1). But despite phenomenal advances in their educational achievements, women continue to earn, on average, less than men in all countries, and for many women (and some men too), especially those at the bottom of the occupational ladder, reconciling parenthood with paid work continues to be a daily challenge.

279. Family responsibilities may constitute a disadvantage in the labour market when they conflict with work demands, because of the way society is organized and care work is shared.[56] As women still shoulder the bulk of family responsibilities in most societies, these responsibilities are a source of gender inequality. Work–family tensions reduce women's options as to whether to work, where and in what types of jobs. This, in turn, affects their seniority and work experience, as well as their training and career prospects, thus contributing to keeping their earnings down. However, even when women with family responsibilities manage to remain and advance in the labour market and occupy high-status jobs, they continue to earn less than their male counterparts. This suggests the existence of discrimination in remuneration.

280. Accordingly, the promotion of gender equality at the workplace requires a set of short-term and long-term policies that address all these issues together.

56. C. Hein: *Reconciling work and family responsibilities: Practical ideas from global experience* (Geneva, ILO, 2005), pp. 10–11.

Promoting pay equity

281.   The gender pay gap has many causes, including sex discrimination in remuneration. Table 3.4 highlights the reasons underlying the gender pay gap, with a breakdown of the different factors leading to discrimination.

282.   The persistence of sex discrimination in remuneration shows that specific policy measures are needed to tackle this problem. To this end, ensuring equal remuneration for work of equal value, a fundamental right enshrined in ILO Convention No. 100, is essential. Pay equity is not about men and women earning the same; nor is it about changing the work that women do. Pay equity is about redressing the undervaluation of jobs typically performed by women and remunerating them according to their value. This is not necessarily a reflection of market factors or skill requirements, but may mirror differences in collective bargaining power, preconceived ideas about scarce skills/market rates or the historical undervaluing of "female" jobs.[57]

Job evaluation methods free from gender bias: An effective tool to achieve pay equity

283.   Achieving pay equity requires comparing and establishing the relative value of two jobs that differ in content, by breaking jobs down into components or "factors" and "sub-factors" and assigning points to them. According to analytical job evaluation methods, such factors generally include skills/ qualifications, responsibility, effort and working conditions.[58] Two jobs that are found to have the same numerical value are entitled to equal remuneration. Job evaluation is concerned with the content of the job and not with the characteristics or the performance of the persons doing the job.

284.   To assess "male" and "female" jobs fairly, job evaluation must be free from gender bias, otherwise key requirements of women's jobs are either disre-

garded or scored lower than those of male jobs, thus reinforcing the undervaluation of women's jobs.[59] The process whereby job evaluation methods are developed and applied is at least as important as these methods and their technical content (box 3.11). Possible and unintentional gender biases and prejudices may arise at any stage in its design and application.

285.   A number of job evaluation methods (JEMs) free from gender bias, such as "Steps to Pay Equity" in Sweden,[60] the ABAKABA and EVALFRI methods in Switzerland and the ISOS method in Spain, have been developed in various industrialized countries.

286.   Experience shows that it is important that job evaluation be carried out jointly by management and employees, men and women. In Quebec, Canada, for instance, all companies with 100 employees or more are required to establish a pay equity committee consisting of two-thirds employee representatives, who may or not be trade union members, and 50 per cent of these must be women. Transparency about pay or aspects of flexible remuneration is equally important to ensure that the employees perceive the outcomes to be fair and in conformity with the law.

287.   Pay equity commissions or commissions with broader anti-discrimination jurisdictions can play a very helpful role in the achievement of pay equity, particularly for SMEs. In Sweden, for instance, since 2001 the Equal Opportunities Ombudsman has undertaken information and education measures to assist the social partners in meeting their obligations under the Equal Opportunities Act, with special emphasis on wage mapping. Similarly, in the United Kingdom the Equal Opportunities Commission has developed a set of useful materials to promote effective equal pay practices in the workplace including in small businesses. The establishment of tripartite committees to develop job evaluation tools for use in a particular sector is especially relevant for SMEs. Such committees help reduce the administrative costs of job evaluation processes (see section on the ILO's action plan on the elimination of discrimination in Part IV, Chapter 1 – EQUAL project in Portugal).

---

57. See Women and Work Commission (United Kingdom): *Shaping a fairer future* (Feb. 2006), at www.womenandequalityunit.gov. uk/research/index.htm.

58. There are two major types of job evaluation method: global/ranking evaluation method, and analytical job evaluation methods. Global/ranking methods examine the whole job rather than its score components, thus leading to the identification of the characteristics of the jobholder with the job characteristics. Hence the evaluators' judgement tends to be influenced by the traditional value of the job. These methods are difficult to use when there are more than ten job classes. The comparison and ranking process must be repeated each time a new job class is introduced. See Pay Equity Task Force: *Pay equity: A new approach to a fundamental right*, Final Report 2004 (Ottawa, 2004), at www.payequityreview.gc.ca and www.canada.justice.gc.ca.

59. Conventional analytical job evaluation methods (JEMs) place a heavy emphasis on skills, mental effort and responsibility, favouring high-ranking positions in which men predominate, and disregarding aspects, such as caring and being responsible for other people, which characterize women's jobs. See C. Katz; C. Baitsch: *L'égalité des salaires en pratique – Deux outils d'évaluation du travail non discriminatoire à l'égard des sexes: ABAKABA et VIWIV* (Geneva, vdf and Georg Éditeur, 1996), p. 27.

60. A. Harriman; C. Holm: *Steps to pay equity: An easy and quick method for the evaluation of work demands* (Equal Opportunities Ombudsman, 2001).

Box 3.11.
Main phases of an analytical job evaluation free from gender bias

Establishment and training of the job evaluation committee

Usually a job evaluation committee is established at the workplace to carry out a job evaluation. It should comprise an equal number of men and women; the women should not all be from low-graded jobs and the men should not all hold management positions; and there should be an equal number of employees and managers. The committee must be trained in the technical aspects of the job evaluation method (JEM) that will be used and in sex discrimination in remuneration.

Selecting the jobs to be evaluated

This requires identifying female- and male-dominated jobs. One key criterion is the proportion of women or men performing a particular job: a job where 60 per cent or more of the workforce is of either sex is considered female- or male-dominated. For the purposes of selecting the jobs to be compared, all jobs – whether part-time or full-time, short-term or without limit of time – must be taken into account.

Selection of the method

Analytical JEMs are most appropriate to identify and redress sex discrimination in remuneration. Once the method has been chosen, the factors and sub-factors or job requirements should be identified. All the relevant aspects of "male" and "female" jobs must be described, because what is not recognized is neither measured nor counted. Moreover, each sub-factor has to be given an evaluation scale with a certain number of levels of intensity or frequency that help differentiate job classes. In setting the levels it is important not to introduce gender bias and automatically attribute a longer scale to sub-factors that are commonly associated with male jobs.

Gathering job-related information

The content of the jobs selected for comparison must be known. Information can be obtained through formal job descriptions and/or questionnaires, whether open-ended or closed-ended, for jobholders to fill in, or face-to-face interviews, or a combination of both. It is important that the language used in the questionnaire or interviews not contribute to the perpetuation of gender biases, for example using the term "coordinating" rather than "managing" to describe tasks associated with female jobs or using the passive rather than the active tense. Jobholders as well as supervisors must be involved in data gathering and both parties must endorse the information. Possible disagreements must be discussed and resolved.

Examining the results of the job evaluation

On the basis of both the information gathered and the agreed set of factors, sub-factors and corresponding evaluation scales, the committee draws up the job descriptions of the evaluated jobs.

Determining the value of the evaluated jobs

This requires assigning weights to the various factors and sub-factors, as not all factors are equally important to the work of an enterprise. The factors' weighting must reflect these differences and must be transparent and free from gender bias. On this basis, points are then assigned to the jobs reviewed. These are grouped in point intervals.

Analysing and adjusting score outcomes

Once the evaluation work and the point calculation have been concluded, the score outcomes must be examined. This entails verifying if there are systematic differences in the way "male" and "female" jobs scored, and in the wage rates for those jobs.

Measuring and correcting the wage gaps

After identifying the portion of the pay gap that is due to discrimination, the pay of the undervalued job is raised accordingly.

Source: ILO: "Promoting pay equity through job evaluation free from gender bias: A step-by-step guide" (forthcoming).

Table 3.5. Different methods of promoting pay equity

Model 1	Model 2	Model 3
Comprehensive approach aimed at the elimination of discriminatory remuneration practices and the pay gap due to discrimination	Partial approach aimed at the elimination of discriminatory remuneration practices	Mixed approach aimed at eliminating certain discriminatory practices and the overall gender pay gap
Sweden and Quebec, Canada	UK, Netherlands	France, Switzerland
Compulsory	Voluntary	Compulsory
• Requires the development of a JEM free from gender bias • Focuses on and compares female- and male-dominated jobs • Measures wage gap between jobs of equal value • Adjusts the wages of female-dominated jobs to eliminate the gap within a set time frame	• Requires the development of a JEM free from gender bias • No precise guidelines on measuring wage gaps • No precise guidelines on eliminating wage gaps	• Requires regression analysis of wages according to sex, if residual gap higher than 5 per cent, further analysis leading to corrective measures (Switzerland) • Assessment of wage distribution by sex, average monthly salary by sex and proportion of women in ten highest-paid occupations (France) • No requirement to develop a JEM free from gender bias • No precise guidelines on measuring wage gaps • No precise guidelines on eliminating wage gaps

Source: M.-T. Chicha: *A comparative analysis of promoting pay equity: Models and impacts*, DECLARATION Working Paper No. 49 (Geneva, ILO, 2006).

288. There is a clear tendency, especially in industrialized countries, to incorporate pay equity concerns in collective agreements. While this constitutes a positive development, if left entirely to collective bargaining, pay equity runs the risk of being subordinated to other concerns (see section on collective bargaining in Part III, Chapter 2).

289. Job evaluation methods and processes contribute to pay equity to the extent that they lead to the measurement and correction of pay gaps stemming from discrimination in remuneration. In practice, however, this does not always happen, as countries have different understandings of what pay equity entails, ranging from the removal of discriminatory remuneration practices to the partial elimination of such practices, coupled with measures aimed at addressing other causes of the overall pay gap (table 3.5).

290. For many developing countries, analytical job evaluation remains a challenge, and many countries do not have methods for carrying out an objective appraisal of jobs. A number of national laws and regulations, including recent ones, merely refer to "iden-

tical" or "similar" work and do not include the broader notion of "work of equal value".[61] Furthermore, provisions on equal remuneration often apply only to the basic or ordinary wage, remuneration in cash, or certain allowances, thus allowing sex discrimination in respect of the flexible part of remuneration.[62]

291. This also mirrors perceptions that equal pay for work of equal value is a "luxury" that only more industrialized countries can afford, especially in contexts with a high incidence of informal work, labour surplus and poverty. Some countries, however, such as Lebanon, Mauritius and Nigeria, have requested specific assistance from the ILO in this field.

292. Since 2001 Public Services International (PSI) has tried to show, with some encouraging results, that pay equity programmes contribute to broader goals such as poverty reduction, social inclusion and increased quality of public services.[63] This has helped increase social and political acceptance of pay equity objectives. Other benefits stemming from pay equity include better knowledge of job requirements, better targeted firm-level training, and greater efficiency in

---

61. For example, Burkina Faso, Central African Republic, Congo, Cuba, Democratic Republic of the Congo, Egypt, Estonia, Fiji, Honduras, India, Jamaica, Kyrgyzstan, Mexico, Nepal, New Zealand, Nicaragua, Panama, Peru, Romania, Rwanda, Slovakia and Thailand; K. Landuyt: "Equal remuneration for men and women for work of equal value: Convention No. 100", International Labour Standards Department (Geneva, ILO, Feb. 2006), p. 1.

62. For example, Norfolk Island (Australia), Democratic Republic of the Congo, Kyrgyzstan, Pakistan, Rwanda, Slovakia and Thailand; ibid., p. 2.

63. A. Hegewisch; S. Hammond; K. Valladares: "Report of the evaluation of the PSI Pay Equity Campaign", 31 Oct. 2006, at www.world-psi.org.

remuneration, as well as in recruitment and selection practices (see box 4.1 in Part IV).

293.   More and more countries recognize that measures and policies to promote equality of opportunities and treatment between men and women in employment and occupation in general also help to reduce pay inequalities. Steps to promote gender equality at work, such as reconciling work and family, can help to close the wage gap by improving women's seniority and work experience, as well as training and career prospects.

Workplace policies to expand opportunities for workers with family responsibilities

294.   Family-friendly arrangements are not just for women, but for men as well, and the notion of "family" goes beyond childcare responsibilities to include any other family member dependent on a working family member – whether male or female (for example, an elder dependant or a disabled partner).

295.   It is estimated that around the world 340 million children under six and 930 million children under 15 live in households in which all of the adults work for pay. This situation is the result of the global movement of women into the labour force, which has not been matched by an equal decline in men's labour, and family-unfriendly public and workplace policies.[64]

296.   Current trends in working time in industrialized, developing and transition economies alike make it increasingly difficult for workers with family responsibilities to juggle work and family care. The industrialized world has seen an intensification and "densification" of working time, i.e. the elimination of unproductive time during the working day, especially of managers and the self-employed.[65] Long working hours seem to be a distinct feature of the ten new EU Member States, and overtime, especially for some low-wage and low-skilled workers, is the norm in Thailand,[66] as well as in countries such as Argentina, Brazil, Colombia, Chile and Mexico.[67]

297.   Long working hours have a disproportionate impact on women, as they are still the main care providers, thus reducing their options as to whether to work, where and in what types of jobs. In industrialized countries, excessively long working hours represent a barrier to the hiring and retention of women in management positions, thus reinforcing sex-based job segregation and, consequently, the gender pay gap. In Canada, for instance, women, particularly those with family responsibilities, are more likely than men to take on regular weekend jobs that are part-time, temporary and seasonal, as they appear to be trying to accommodate the work schedules of their spouses, who work during the week (Monday to Friday).[68]

298.   In the informal economy, time demands are especially pressing on particular categories of workers, such as market traders, often women, who bring their children to work, and have to contend with seasonal demands as well as changing weather and trading patterns that may entail early starts or late evenings.

299.   These working patterns reinforce the unequal division of paid and unpaid work between women and men, undermining women's job prospects, careers and pay, while increasing their overall workload (figure 3.1).

300.   Public family-friendly measures can help effectively address these challenges, provided that they are also sensitive to gender equality issues (box 3.12). Such policies can also assist in countering the alarming decline in fertility rates facing a number of industrialized countries, such as Japan or Italy. OECD studies show that in some countries the correlation between female labour force participation and total fertility rate turned from negative to positive after the introduction of a set of initiatives aimed at reducing work–family tension such as wide childcare availability, lower direct costs of children, more opportunities to work part time and longer leaves.[69]

Part-time work

301.   The growth of part-time work in the OECD and EU 15 countries has been significant and steady in the past ten years, and its availability has resulted in greater female labour participation rates. Nonetheless, despite its growing incidence, there are significant

64. J. Heymann: *Forgotten families: Ending the growing crisis confronting children and working parents in the global economy* (New York, Oxford University Press, 2006), pp. xi and 7.

65. J.-Y. Boulin; M. Lallement; F. Michon: "Decent working time in industrialized countries: Issues, scopes and paradoxes", in J.-Y. Boulin; M. Lallement; J.C. Messenger; F. Michon (eds.): *Decent working time: New trends, new issues* (Geneva, ILO, 2006), p. 32.

66. K. Kusakabe: *Reconciling work and family: Issues and policies in Thailand*, Conditions of Work and Employment Series No. 14 (Geneva, ILO, 2006).

67. M. L. Vega Ruíz (ed.): *La Reforma laboral en América Latina: 15 años después – Un análisis comparado* (Lima, ILO, 2005), pp. 41–43.

68. I.U. Zeytinoglu; G.B. Cooke: "Who is working at weekends? Determinants of regular weekend work in Canada", in J.-Y. Boulin et al. (eds.): *Decent working time*, op. cit., pp. 411–412.

69. A.C. D'Addio; M. Mira d'Ercole: *Trends and determinants of fertility rates in OECD countries: The role of policies*, OECD Social, Employment and Migration Working Papers No. 27 (Paris, OECD, 2005).

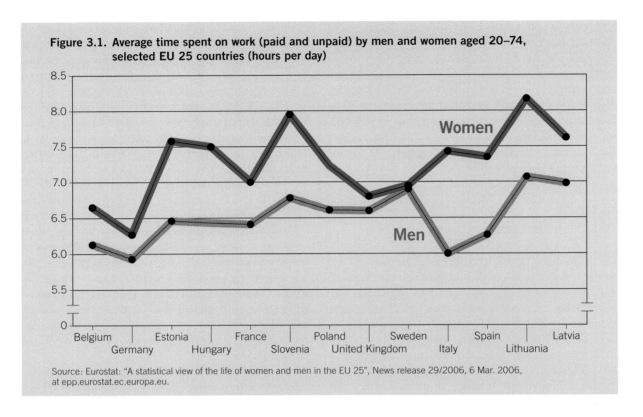

Figure 3.1. Average time spent on work (paid and unpaid) by men and women aged 20–74, selected EU 25 countries (hours per day)

Source: Eurostat: "A statistical view of the life of women and men in the EU 25", News release 29/2006, 6 Mar. 2006, at epp.eurostat.ec.europa.eu.

variations in the relative sizes of part-time employment shares and distribution across sectors and occupations within OECD countries (figure 3.2). Differences in national policies and institutions explain these variations, but in most countries part-time work remains women's work and is synonymous with low status, low training and limited career opportunities, despite its being often presented as available to both working mothers and fathers. Moreover, part-time may often be involuntary, in the sense that it is a second-best option to a full-time job.

302. Part-time work, however, can help reconcile work and parenthood, without reinforcing gender inequalities in employment and pay, and in the family. A study comparing part-time work in Germany, Netherlands and the United Kingdom finds that the Netherlands has managed to eliminate some of the disadvantages for women's labour market status generally associated with this form of employment. First, it has "normalized" part-time work by levelling the differences between part-timers and full-timers in terms of rights, benefits and incomes, while in Germany and the United Kingdom these jobs have very short weekly working hours (less than 16 hours in the United Kingdom), with lower levels of wage costs, and are low paid and excluded from social protection

---

Box 3.12.
Key requirements for family-friendly measures to be gender equality-friendly

Recognizing men's caring role: Offering paternity leave and making parental leave, after the initial maternity leave, available to both men and women and non-transferable.

Making "normal" work more family-compatible: Flexible arrangements with regard to working schedules, rest periods and holidays; provision of annual leave, short leave for emergencies; (good) part time, flexitime, time banking, teleworking, reduction of daily hours of work and of overtime.

Making family responsibilities more compatible with work: Availability of affordable and good-quality childcare for preschoolers and young children.

Promoting a more equal sharing of family responsibilities between men and women.

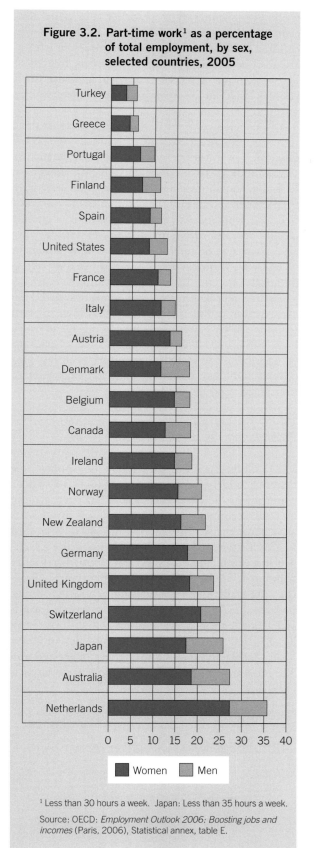

Figure 3.2. Part-time work[1] as a percentage of total employment, by sex, selected countries, 2005

Legend: ■ Women ■ Men

[1] Less than 30 hours a week. Japan: Less than 35 hours a week.

Source: OECD: *Employment Outlook 2006: Boosting jobs and incomes* (Paris, 2006), Statistical annex, table E.

benefits. Second, the Netherlands has managed to introduce part-time work throughout all sectors and occupations, and, unlike the other two countries, part-time is evenly distributed among all groups of women. As a result, involuntary part-time is very low, and more widespread among men than in other countries.[70]

303. These results can be attributed to greater labour market regulation, mobilization of women's activist groups and supportive social partners. Nevertheless, part-time workers still have fewer training and career opportunities, and limited childcare facilities continue to be a problem.

304. Moreover, although in the three countries mentioned above recent legislative reforms entitle employees, under certain circumstances, to request changes to their working hours, take-up rates have been very low. This may suggest that employees fear that requests for shorter working hours may compromise their career prospects.

Childcare arrangements

305. The availability of affordable and reliable childcare facilities is key to enhancing female labour participation, retaining mothers in the labour market, and enabling lone and married fathers to reconcile paid work with family duties. Childcare facilities and arrangements must address the needs of different groups of children, ranging from toddlers to pre-schoolchildren and schoolchildren who need supervision after school.

306. There have been encouraging developments across the world in respect of the coverage of pre-primary education, i.e. from age 3 up to the age of entry into primary school.[71] But the expansion of early childhood services, i.e. for children under 3 years old, has been limited in industrialized countries and has not been a priority in many developing countries and the transition States.[72] After the collapse of the Soviet bloc, long paid and unpaid parental leave for mothers was maintained in countries such as the Czech Republic, Hungary,[73] Poland, Belarus

70. M. Yerkes; J. Visser: "Women's preferences or delineated policies? The development of part-time work in the Netherlands, Germany and the United Kingdom", in J.-Y. Boulin et al., op. cit., p. 257.

71. UNESCO: *Education for All: Global Monitoring Report 2006: Literacy for life* (Paris, 2005), p. 40.

72. Soo-Hyang Choi: *Pre-primary education: The valid investment option for EFA*, UNESCO Policy Brief On Early Childhood, No. 31, Mar.–Apr. 2006.

73. See E. Fultz; M. Ruck; S. Steinhilber (eds.): *The gender dimensions of social security reform in Central and Eastern Europe: Case studies of the Czech Republic, Hungary and Poland* (Budapest, ILO, 2003).

and Ukraine.[74] Extended leave has been used to reduce the demand for and investments in childcare
services.[75] The decline in the CEE countries in the
supply of affordable and reliable childcare provision,
especially outside big cities, appears to have led to
greater workplace discrimination against women.[76]

307. Private-public arrangements can prove ex-
tremely important in reducing childcare subsidies. In
China there has been a tendency towards privatiza-
tion and cooperation with the private sector in the
delivery of pre-school services. Enterprise-run kin-
dergartens have been dissolved or transferred to local
educational departments, non-state institutions are
to become the main providers of nurseries and kin-
dergarten for 3–5 year-olds, with funds to be raised
from various sources, including companies, citizens
and communities, and steps have been taken to provide better guidance to early childhood care providers
in rural areas.[77]

308. In Kenya parents and communities are the
most important partners in the management of pre-
school education centres, which, in 2000, covered
34 per cent of 3–5 year-olds. While 80 per cent
of these centres are public, and public authorities
shoulder the running cost of pre-schools in town,
parents and communities provide land and funds for
the construction of physical facilities, and supply the
furniture and materials, as well as the salaries of the
teachers. Decentralization and respect of the country's rich and varied cultures are other key features of
the programme.[78]

309. Trade unions and companies can also effectively join forces to help overcome work–family tensions. One example is a childcare centre in Bangkok,
Thailand set up in response to the need to assist the
employees of the company TOT PLC in looking after
their children. The company provided premises and
the union pays the teachers' salaries, while the parents
bring children's blankets, diapers and bottles of water
and milk. The centre receives children aged between
1½ and 5 years.[79]

310. The specific circumstances and needs of
workers with family responsibilities in the informal
economy warrant special attention. The costs associated with inaction on this front are well-known:
children brought to hazardous workplaces, or left un-
attended at home with the risk of being injured or
ill, or taken out of school in order to look after their
younger sisters and brothers, or left in inadequate care
settings.[80]

311. Experience shows that something can be done
to reverse this situation, and that a focus on specific
categories of informal workers and on particular
sectors appears to produce encouraging outcomes.
In India, mobile crèches on construction sites have
been created to cater for the children of migrant construction workers. At present the system of mobile
crèches operates through a network of 450 day care
centres, located on building sites and slum clusters in
New Delhi, Mumbai and Pune and reaching out to
600,000 children.[81] In South Africa, StreetNet, an organization representing street vendors, has placed the
construction of water and childcare facilities in plans
for new market places on its bargaining agenda with
local authorities. This is part of a broader package
of demands that includes simplified licensing procedures and a halt to harassment and confiscation of
unlicensed vendors' goods.

Paternity and parental leave

312. Childcare leave entitlement is a policy area
that has undergone significant changes in various
countries in the past years. There has been a move
towards encouraging fathers to take up care-related
leave through the introduction of paternity leave or
modifying parental leave. Recently introduced paternity leave entitlements, a short leave immediately after
childbirth, can be optional or obligatory: in Italy fathers are entitled, but not obliged, to take two weeks'
post-natal leave, while in Portugal paternity leave is
of 20 days, of which five days are compulsory. It can
be of varied length (ranging from one day in Chile,
Saudi Arabia and Tunisia to 90 days in Iceland and
Slovenia) and paid or unpaid (although the latter is

74. See United Nations Economic Commission for Europe (UNECE): "Employability policies in transition countries: Issues, good
practices, and policy options", background paper submitted to the Regional Symposium on Mainstreaming Gender into Economic
Policies, 28–30 Jan. 2004, Geneva, p. 12.
75. L. Haddad: *An integrated approach to early childhood education and care*, UNESCO Early Childhood and Family Policy Series, No. 3,
Oct. 2002, p. 7.
76. S. Steinhilber: "Women's views on social security reform: Qualitative survey", in E. Fultz et al. (eds.), op. cit., pp. 319–320.
77. L. Haddad, op. cit., pp. 9–10.
78. ibid., pp. 15–16.
79. K. Kusakabe, op. cit., p. 58.
80. J. Heymann: *Social transformations and their implications for the global demand for ECCE*, UNESCO Policy Brief on Early Childhood, No. 8, Nov.–Dec. 2002.
81. See www.mobilecreches.org.

often the case), and financed by the employer, through social security or by a combination of both.[82]

313. In Iceland, since the 2001 law reform, no distinction is made between paternity and maternity leave, but a nine-month paid leave (at 80 per cent of salary) after childbirth is granted instead. This leave is split into three equal parts between the mother, the father (whose share is non-transferable) and the couple.

314. Parental leave, a relatively long period following the expiry of maternity leave, is available in some countries for both women and men. It can be a shared entitlement either parent can take (for example, Cuba, Estonia, Hungary and Viet Nam), or an individual, non-transferable entitlement (for example, Belgium, Iceland and Ireland), or a mixed entitlement, combining individual and family entitlements (Norway and Sweden). In Europe, the Council Directive on the framework agreement on parental leave[83] has been instrumental in increasing the number of countries providing for individual parental leave entitlements, thus encouraging both fathers' take-up of parental leave and greater gender equality.

315. Nonetheless, large proportions of working parents are denied these entitlements de jure, especially those in self-employment, or with temporary contracts, or working for small employers (United States), or depending on their prior employment history (Japan).

316. As for the take-up rate, data show that mothers everywhere continue to take more leave than fathers, although there are some encouraging changes in fathers' behaviour, for example in Iceland, where in three years the average number of days taken by men increased from 39 to 83, or in Portugal, where a quarter of eligible fathers took more than the five mandatory paternity leave days.[84] Everywhere the key factor encouraging the use of parental leave entitlements by both men and women is that such leave is paid and relatively well paid.[85]

317. In the Czech Republic, Hungary and Poland, during the 1990s women and men were given equal access to childcare benefits, thus breaking earlier rules that imposed stricter requirements on men or barred them altogether from using such entitlements. Anecdotal evidence shows, however, that up to now fathers' take-up of childcare benefits in these countries has been insignificant. The causes are low levels of benefits granted during child-rearing periods, cultural values that uphold women's role as the primary caregivers, and the gender wage gap, which discourages men from withdrawing from paid work for caring purposes.[86] An interesting development in the CEE countries has been the granting of care leave entitlements to a person other than the parents (e.g. grandmothers and/or grandparents or any other relative) who takes care of the child (Lithuania, Russian Federation and Republic of Moldova).

318. Many working mothers, however, seem not to avail themselves of their parental leave entitlements in these countries because they fear job losses or unfavourable reassignments.[87] But even if not or partially used, long parental leave provisions for women reinforce perceptions that they are "costly" and unreliable, contribute to skill depreciation which tends to affect women more than men,[88] and make it more difficult for mothers to shift back to employment.

319. The issue of whether parental leave should be shortened in order not to reinforce gender inequality in employment and in the household has been a matter of serious controversy in that region. To counter this trend, more consistent enactment of anti-discrimination legislation, coupled with a more balanced division of family responsibilities, would be in order.[89] It would also be useful to adopt measures to support parents returning from parental leave in re-entering employment.[90]

320. The nature, persistence and ramifications of discrimination call for integrated development strategies that rely on anti-discrimination measures targeting the workplace and the labour market, as well as other social arenas such as the community, the school or the family.

82. I. Öun and G. Pardo Trujillo: *Maternity at work: A review of national legislation – Findings from the ILO's Conditions of Work and Employment Database* (Geneva, ILO, 2005), pp. 37–38.
83. Council Directive 96/34/EC of 3 June 1996 on the framework agreement on parental leave concluded by UNICE, CEEP and the ETUC, *Official Journal* L145, 19 June 1996, pp. 4–9. According to this Directive, parental leave should be made available to both parents as an individual entitlement for a period of at least three months.
84. Iceland: I. Öun; G. Pardo Trujillo, op. cit., p. 38; Portugal: F. Deven; P. Moss (eds.): *Leave policies and research: Reviews and country notes*, CBGS Werkdocument 2005/3.
85. European Industrial Relations Observatory on-line (EIROnline): *Family-related leave and industrial relations*, Sep. 2004, at eurofound.europa.eu/eiro/2004/03/study/tn0403101s.html.
86. E. Fultz; S. Steinhilber: "The gender dimensions of social security reform in the Czech Republic, Hungary and Poland", in E. Fultz et al. (eds.): op. cit., p. 27.
87. ibid.
88. J. Rubery; D.P. Grimshaw; H. Figueiredo: *The gender pay gap and gender mainstreaming pay policy in EU Member States*, Synthesis Report for the Equal Opportunities Unit in the European Commission, 2002, p. 7.
89. UNECE, op. cit., p. 12.
90. C. Hein, op. cit., p. 118.

Recent developments
at the international level

321. While action by the State and workers' and employers' organizations is central to creating more inclusive workplaces, the international arena and its actors play an equally important role. Although discrimination existed long before globalization, it has transformed the scope and characteristics of discrimination. Therefore remedial action cannot focus only on country-level interventions; it must also target international and global frameworks in mutually reinforcing ways.

322. International institutions – both public and private – and processes of regional economic integration, among others, can determine whether globalization brings about equity and peace or fuels further inequalities and tensions. The scope and impact of several relevant initiatives are examined below.

Promoting good practices among borrowers through lending policies

323. Development finance institutions (DFIs) (which include international financial institutions (IFIs) – both global and regional – and national-based DFIs) have in recent years begun to examine the environmental and social impact of their lending, and in particular promotion of respect for the principles contained in international labour standards in the employment practices of their clients. The International Finance Corporation (IFC), the international development financial institution of the World Bank Group, has recently adopted Performance Standards (PS) and Guidance Notes on environmental and social standards which include a commitment by IFC to apply ILO core labour standards, as well as standards on safety and health and retrenchment. The PS establish requirements that the client has to meet in order to receive IFC support, including commitments to comply with applicable national law, with a reference to international standards as the baseline. The PS were developed in consultation with a broad range of actors, and in particular the ILO, and with the active participation of the International Confederation of Free Trade Unions (ICFTU).

324. Performance Standard 2 on labour and working conditions includes the following provisions on non-discrimination:

The Client will not make employment decisions on the basis of personal characteristics unrelated to inherent job requirements. The client will base the employment relationship on the principle of equal opportunity and fair treatment, and will not discriminate with respect to aspects of the employment relationship, including recruitment and hiring, compensation (including wages and benefits), working conditions and terms of employment, access to training, promotion, termination of employment or retirement, and discipline. In countries where national law provides for non-discrimination in employment, the client will comply with national law. When national laws are silent on non-discrimination in employment, the client will meet this Performance Standard. Special measures of protection or assistance to remedy past discrimination or selection for a particular job based on the inherent requirements of the job will not be deemed discrimination.

325. The IFC has also published a Good Practice Note on non-discrimination and equal opportunity, which presents a business case for diversity.[91] This was followed by the adoption of the "Equator Principles" by some 40 national development banks, representing about 85 per cent of global lending for development projects, which undertook to apply the IFC Performance Standards to project finance for projects of at least US$10 million.[92]

326. Similar encouraging developments have taken place in the regional development banks. In June 2006 the Inter-American Development Bank issued even more comprehensive requirements for applying international labour standards to infrastructure projects, while the European Investment Bank adopted a similar commitment in 2006, and in December 2006 the Asian Development Bank published a *Core labor standards handbook,* developed in close cooperation with the ILO.[93] In a similar vein, the President of the World Bank, in discussions with a high-level trade union delegation in December 2006, expressed his willingness to ensure that all infrastructure projects the Bank finances respect the ILO's core

---

91. The Performance Standards and Good Practice Note can be found on the IFC web site, at www.ifc.org.
92. The first set of Equator Principles was adopted by a small number of banks and the IFC in October 2002 and launched in Washington, DC, on 4 June 2003. A newly revised set of Equator Principles was released in July 2006, at www.equator-principles.com.
93. Inter-American Development Bank (IDB): *Managing labor issues in infrastructure projects,* at www.iadb.org; European Investment Bank (EIB): *The social assessment of projects outside the European Union: The approach of the European Investment Bank,* at www.eib.org; Asian Development Bank (ADB): *Core labor standards handbook* (Manila, 2006), at www.adb.org.

labour standards, including those on non-discrimination and equality. If implemented, this would mean that some US$8 billion worth of projects that the Bank funds each year will have to adhere to this new requirement.

Regional economic integration and free trade agreements: A mixed picture

327. Regional economic integration and the proliferation of free trade agreements have resulted in changing patterns of employment within and across countries. Efforts have been made on a number of fronts in the past years to minimize the negative social impacts of increased global trade. Up to now, however, discrimination, compared to the other principles and rights a work, has been only partially addressed.

328. Free trade agreements, defined as international agreements made between two or more nations that relate to common trade or service issues, differ from regional economic integration arrangements (such as the Southern Common Market (MERCOSUR) and the EU), which are broader in terms of the issues they cover, the depth of integration effects upon the region and/or geographic scope. As the two concepts and their resulting impacts are similar in nature, they will be examined together.

329. The approach to discrimination varies from one trade agreement to another. In North America, for instance, the North American Agreement on Labor Cooperation (NAALC), the Canada-Chile Agreement on Labour Cooperation (CCALC) and the Canada-Costa Rica Agreement on Labour Cooperation (CCRALC) explicitly cite non-discrimination and equal pay as principles and rights which the parties undertake to promote.[94]

330. On the other hand, in the United States bilateral free trade agreements, such as those with Jordan, Singapore and Chile, the parties reaffirm their "commitments under the ILO Declaration on Fundamental Principles and Rights at Work and its Follow-up",[95] thus endorsing the principle of non-discrimination and equality at work, but fail to include an explicit reference to that principle in the list of

principles and rights which the parties are requested to respect by ensuring compliance with the related national law. Nonetheless, these same agreements may include non-discrimination and equality as an item for technical cooperation (see below).

331. Other agreements currently under negotiation also appear to overlook the issue of discrimination. Failure to address workplace discrimination has been cited as a key shortcoming in the economic partnership agreements (EPAs) that are being negotiated between the EU and 77 African, Caribbean and Pacific (ACP) countries, and due to come into force in January 2008.[96]

332. The potential for supranational review in the event of labour rights violations is crucial to ensuring the observance of fundamental labour rights. Some analysts have noted that non-discrimination and equality are treated as a secondary right in regard to enforcement in the case of the NAALC and the CCALC. While these agreements provide for the option of dispute settlement and fines in the case of child labour, minimum wages and health and safety, the same system is not applicable in the case of non-discrimination and equal pay, as well as other fundamental principles and rights at work.[97]

333. Discrepancies in the treatment of discrimination across regions may arise as a result of differences in the national legal contexts and the power structures upon which regional agreements are built. This is evident in the treatment of gender issues under the EU, the North American Free Trade Agreement (NAFTA) and MERCOSUR: the EU has adopted comprehensive provisions relating to non-discrimination and equality, but MERCOSUR and NAFTA have yet to establish the same extensive provisions.[98]

334. In the context of the EU, its long-standing existence has allowed time for such legal principles to become well established. Moreover, under the strong influence of powerful women's groups, officials ensured that commonly held national legal standards were reflected in regional provisions.[99]

335. In the case of MERCOSUR, the women's rights agenda was not firmly established and women's groups lacked the regional representation to influence the provisions of the agreement.[100] Nevertheless, some

94. At www.naalc.org and www.hrsdc.gc.ca, respectively.
95. At www.ustr.gov.
96. K. Ulmer: "Are trade agreements with the EU beneficial to women in Africa, the Caribbean and the Pacific?", in *Gender and Development*, Vol. 12, No. 2 (July 2004).
97. S. Polaski: "Protecting labor rights through trade agreements: An analytical guide", in *Journal of International Law and Policy*, July 2004, at www.carnegieendowment.org/publications/index.cfm?fa=view&id=15796.
98. F. Duina: *The social construction of free trade: The European Union, NAFTA and MERCOSUR* (Princeton, N.J., Princeton University Press, 2006), p. 146.
99. ibid.
100. ibid.

progress has been made under the MERCOSUR agreement, with a supra-national tripartite commission being established to influence MERCOSUR working groups on gender issues. Moreover, tripartite national commissions operating in MERCOSUR countries are in the process of evaluating their capacity to gender mainstream through national labour ministries.

336. As for NAFTA, although the legislative environment was relatively well established, women's groups in the United States and Mexico appeared largely uninterested in shaping NAFTA and this is reflected in the lack of substantive provisions.[101] Thus, as agreements proliferate it may be worth exercising caution to avoid replicating existing national imbalances in regional agreements. Interest groups should take note of this trend and of the need to assert their influence in a supranational context.

337. Capacity building or sustained improvements in labour law enforcement are a further consideration. Several agreements (e.g. the NAALC, the US-Chile Free Trade Agreement (FTA) and the CCALC) include mechanisms providing for capacity building, and some benefits have been seen. In the case of the CCALC, the parties have agreed to meet each year to develop a programme of cooperative activities such as seminars, technical workshops, public conferences and site visits. Conferences have been held on topics related to discrimination in the workplace, such as addressing systemic discrimination and occupational segregation, as well as best practices in legislation, and policies, programming and enforcement.[102]

338. The NAALC has seen some improvements related to discriminatory practices. In one significant case, Mexican and US non-governmental organizations (NGOs) launched a complaint because female workers had been subject to mandatory testing and dismissal in the event of pregnancy. The complaints led to a series of cross-border workshops to discuss the problem and develop possible solutions. Subsequently, the Mexican Government discontinued this practice in the case of public sector employees.[103]

339. While the commitment to the Declaration and to technical cooperation is a notable demonstration of an intention to protect fundamental labour rights, it is also important to ensure explicit inclusion of non-discrimination and equality in all relevant areas of trade agreements, and within all enforcement provisions. It is similarly crucial to focus on technical assistance and capacity building, and the establishment of strong enforcement mechanisms and positive incentives. Together they can help ensure that fundamental labour rights are fully taken into account in the process of regional economic integration.

101. ibid.
102. Government of Canada: *Ministerial Council Report on the three-year review of the Canada-Chile Agreement on Labour Cooperation*, Dec. 2002, at www110.hrdc-drhc.gc.ca/psait_spila/aicdt_ialc/2003_2004/report_english.htm.
103. S. Polaski, op. cit.

2. The social partners on the move

340. *Time for equality at work* stressed that the achievement of equality at the workplace for all depends to a considerable extent on the genuine commitment and consistent action of employers' and workers' organizations. The potential impact of the social partners in fostering equality at the workplace and beyond is significant, given their involvement in the shaping of broader economic and social policies that have major implications for the structures of labour markets, as well as for social inclusion and poverty reduction.

341. Like any other social institution, the social partners also tend to mirror and perpetuate discriminatory practices prevailing around them. Acknowledging the existence of such practices and combating them from within their own structures, and through collective bargaining, is a first essential step in the right direction.

Employers' organizations

342. Employers, their associations and the human resources development and management policies and practices they pursue at the workplace are fundamental in overcoming discrimination at work.

343. Recruitment practices and policies that ensure that the best candidate for a job is selected are crucial for businesses' good performance. Moreover, where skills shortages are a problem these practices help reach out to an untapped pool of diverse talents. Job advertisements are one important component of recruitment practices, and getting them right is a first step towards attracting the best qualified applicants, while preventing costly discrimination cases. The Singapore National Employers Federation (SNEF) provides an interesting example of how these problems can be addressed through tripartite cooperation and awareness raising, as well as showing by doing. As part of a broader national campaign on responsible job advertisements, the SNEF disseminates tripartite guidelines on non-discriminatory job advertisements. The Federation invites members to post as reference models on its web page non-discriminatory advertisements pertaining to different occupational categories and different lengths of contract (part-time, temporary or full-time jobs).[104]

344. Employers' organizations can also help build job placement services free from gender, age or disability bias. In New Zealand, for example, the Equal Employment Opportunities (EEO) Trust, a joint initiative launched in 1992 by leading private and public sector employers to promote awareness of the business benefits of equal opportunities at the workplace, has developed jointly with the Recruitment and Consulting Services Association a publication targeting recruitment agencies and aimed at removing discriminatory practices.[105]

345. An increasing number of employers' organizations across the world are preparing guidelines and tools to help their member enterprises develop workplace plans and policies aimed at ensuring equal opportunities for different groups. An interesting example is the Disability Standard 2005 and 2007 launched by the Employers' Forum on Disability, an employers' association of about 400 members, employing around 20 per cent of the UK workforce.[106] The Disability Standard is a benchmarking tool that assesses the performance of employers and service providers in respect of disability: the aim is to help businesses know where they are, what they need to improve and how to get there. The benchmarking exercise lasts eight weeks, during which participants receive a detailed diagnostic report on their performance, which is compared to that of other participants. In 2005, 80 members participated; of these, 26 also assessed their performance on race and gender. The full results of this exercise were made public in a report that concludes that companies invest significantly less in disability than in promoting racial and gender equality.[107]

346. Gender equality, in particular issues such as sexual harassment, reconciling work and family responsibilities or promoting equal access and opportunities for career development for both women and men, has received growing attention by employers' organizations. In Sri Lanka, this concern is reflected in the Guidelines for Company Policy on Gender Equity/Equality developed by the Employers Federation of Ceylon (EFC) in cooperation with the ILO in 2006 (see Part IV, Chapter 1, section on promoting equal opportunities at the workplace). Similarly, in Kenya, the Federation of Kenya Employers (FKE), which presents itself and its member associations as affirmative employers, seeks to encourage a gender

---

104. See www.sgemployers.com.
105. Top Drawer Consultants: *Tools for tapping into talent: A training resource for recruitment consultants* (Auckland, EEO Trust).
106. See www.employers-forum.co.uk.
107. Employers' Forum on Disability: *The Disability Standard 2005: Benchmark report.*

balance in the composition of its Board of Management, although it recognizes the difficulty of such a task, given the small numbers of women chief executives. In respect of sexual harassment, FKE encourages its member organizations to adopt a policy on the subject and provides guidance on the main goals and elements of such a policy. This goes beyond what is required by the Public Officers Ethics Act, 2003, which makes sexual harassment a criminal offence but applies only to public officers.[108]

347. In the Philippines, the Employers' Confederation of the Philippines (ECOP) has taken an array of initiatives, including documenting and disseminating good practices on work-life measures, conducting cost-benefit analyses of these programmes, and networking with agencies such as the Personnel Management Association of the Philippines (PMAP). These initiatives are designed to persuade its member organizations of the benefits stemming from the adoption of work–family reconciliation measures for the workers concerned and their families, as well as for the companies and for customer satisfaction.[109] In New Zealand, the EEO Trust mentioned above promotes measures to ease work/family tensions by recognizing outstanding achievements by employers in this field through the annual EEO Trust Work and Life Awards.[110]

348. The International Organisation of Employers (IOE) is developing a broad body of knowledge in the area of gender equality and related ILO Conventions. In its publication *Approaches and policies to foster entrepreneurship: A guide for employers' organizations*, the IOE identifies the barriers limiting the potential of women entrepreneurs to develop and expand their businesses and explains how employers' organizations can provide better representation and support services.[111]

Trends in unionization

349. Increases in the representation of traditionally under-represented groups in trade union membership and leadership suggest the existence of more inclusive organizing strategies and more democratic structures. However, related data are patchy and often inaccurate, and tend to focus on gender inequalities in union membership and representation, rather than on inequalities along racial or disability lines.

350. The available information shows a continued tendency towards growth of female union membership in some countries and within specific sectors. An ILO study published in 2005, examining trade union membership and collective bargaining coverage in a number of countries, reveals that union density rates were higher for female workers than for males in about half of the countries examined across various regions (the figures for selected countries are shown in table 3.6).[112] Another recent study confirms this tendency in the industrialized world: while Canada, the United Kingdom and Ireland have approximately equal male/female unionization rates, in Sweden, Norway and Finland female unionization rates are even higher.[113]

351. This rapid advance of female union membership and density in particular countries and sectors reflects the increased attachment of women to paid work, higher female shares in public services in both developing and industrialized countries, and the adoption of equal opportunity policies. The expansion of union activity in the previously less unionized service sector, along with the decline of unionization rates in the male-dominated manufacturing sector, may have further contributed to progress in female union density rates.[114]

352. For trade unions to capitalize on gains in female union membership, it will become imperative that they address the specific circumstances of women workers, such as gender biases in wage structures and wage fixing systems, or the unequal treatment of contingent and part-time workers, among whom women predominate.[115] The five-year global campaign on pay equity launched by PSI in October 2002 shows that pay equity, by yielding pay gains for female members, can be used as an effective organizing strategy of female workers, with positive implications for the union as a whole.[116]

108. ILO: *Employers' organizations taking the lead on gender equality: Case studies from 10 countries* (Geneva, 2005), ACT/EMP No. 43, pp. 36–37.
109. ibid., pp. 62–66.
110. See www.eeotrust.org.nz.
111. IOE submission to the 2007 Annual Review under the Declaration follow-up; see also www.ioe-emp.org/en/policy-areas/gender/index.html.
112. S. Lawrence; J. Ishikawa: *Social dialogue indicators – Trade union membership and collective bargaining coverage: Statistical concepts, methods and findings*, Working Paper No. 59, Policy Integration Department, Bureau of Statistics and Social Dialogue, Labour Law and Labour Administration Department (Geneva, ILO, 2005).
113. J. Visser: "Union membership statistics in 24 countries", in *Monthly Labor Review*, Jan. 2006, table 4, p. 46.
114. Statistics Canada: "Study: The union movement in transition", in *The Daily*, 31 Aug. 2004, at www.statcan.ca/Daily/English/040831/d040831b.htm.
115. J. Visser, op. cit., p. 47.
116. See A. Hegewisch; S. Hammond; K. Valladares, op. cit.

Table 3.6. Union density by sex and by sector, selected countries (percentages)

Country	Year	Sex	Overall density (total membership/ paid employment) [1]	By sector (total membership/paid employment)			
				Agriculture	Manufacturing	Construction	Public services
Mauritius	2002	M	44.5	76.1	11.5	4.3	47.3
		F	26.6	68.9	7.3	0.2	18.2
		Total	**38.0**	**74.6**	**9.2**	**4.1**	**38.3**
Brazil	2001	M	30.0	n.a.	n.a.	n.a.	n.a.
		F	25.1	n.a.	n.a.	n.a.	n.a.
		Total	**27.9**	**n.a.**	**n.a.**	**n.a.**	**n.a.**
Canada	2003	M	30.5	15.8	33.9	36.5	16.8
		F	30.0	5.3	19.2	5.2	12.0
		Total	**30.3**	**13.1**	**29.7**	**32.9**	**14.4**
Egypt	2003	M	45.2	n.a.	n.a.	n.a.	n.a.
		F	32.5	n.a.	n.a.	n.a.	n.a.
		Total	**42.8**	**n.a.**	**n.a.**	**n.a.**	**n.a.**
Hungary	2003	M	12.2	6.0	13.4	2.4	10.3
		F	16.3	7.7	14.0	7.6	9.2
		Total	**14.1**	**6.4**	**13.6**	**2.8**	**9.8**
Ireland	2003	M	39.0	11.0	42.7	34.4	71.0
		F	36.0	5.0	36.3	14.3	27.1
		Total	**37.6**	**10.0**	**40.7**	**33.3**	**41.6**
Philippines	2003	M	3.6	n.a.	n.a.	n.a.	n.a.
		F	2.7	n.a.	n.a.	n.a.	n.a.
		Total	**3.2**	**n.a.**	**n.a.**	**n.a.**	**n.a.**

[1] Employment denominator is paid employment, except in the case of Hungary, where only reported employment is available for density by sector; in the case of overall density, total employment has been used as the denominator. n. a.: not available.

Source: S. Lawrence; J. Ishikawa: *Social dialogue indicators – Trade union membership and collective bargaining coverage: Statistical concepts, methods and findings*, Working Paper No. 59, Policy Integration Department, Bureau of Statistics and Social Dialogue, Labour Law and Labour Administration Department (Geneva, ILO, 2005).

353. The drive within the national and international labour movement to accommodate, through non-traditional organization strategies and forms, unorganized workers who are especially vulnerable to discrimination, such as informal workers, is another encouraging development, exemplified by the recent affiliation of the Self Employed Women's Association (SEWA) to the ICFTU in 2006.[117] SEWA is now a member of the new International Trade Union Confederation (ITUC).

354. Racial and ethnic minorities appear to be better represented by unions in some industrialized countries. In the United Kingdom, for instance, over the last decade blacks have had the highest unionization rates (33 per cent) among all groups, including whites (29 per cent).[118] Given the 32 per cent pay differential

117. Self Employed Women's Association (SEWA): "SEWA Joins the ICFTU", electronic newsletter, No. 8, July 2006, at www.sewa.org/newsletter/enews8.htm.
118. H. Grainger: *Trade union membership 2005* (London, Department of Trade and Industry, 2006); H. Grainger; H. Holt: *Trade union membership 2004* (London, Department of Trade and Industry, 2005), both at www.dti.gov.uk.

Box 3.13.
Family care provisions in collective agreements

Finland

Some sectoral agreements increase workers' entitlement to short temporary absences from work in the event of illness of children aged under ten years.

Greece

The national occupational collective agreement of 1999, covering 4,000 workers in all notary offices, grants working mothers two paid hours of time off per day for the first two years after birth and one paid hour off for the following two years; the father may take the leave if the mother chooses not to. Cosmote, a mobile telephone provider, allows 32 hours of annual leave for employees to monitor children's progress in school.

Italy

Company-level collective agreements provide employees with time off to care for sick family members and disabled or drug-addicted children.

Canada

Leave provisions for employees to accompany family members to health-care appointments, graduations or court hearings have appeared in collective agreements in both the public and the private sector.

Sources: Finland, Greece, Italy – European Foundation for the Improvement of Living and Working Conditions: "Reconciliation of work and family and collective bargaining in the EU" (Dublin, 2006), at www.eiro.eurofound.eu.int; Canada – K. Bentham: "Labour's collective bargaining record on women and family issues", in G. Hunt; D. Rayside (eds.): *Equalizing labour: Union response to equity in Canada* (University of Toronto Press, forthcoming).

---

between unionized and non-unionized black workers, there is a significant impetus to provide representation for minority workers.[119] In the United States, in 2003, unionization rates of African Americans – both men (18 per cent) and women (15 per cent) – were among the highest (compared to 14 per cent for white men and 11 per cent for white women).[120]

355. In France, in response to the social unrest in the urban *banlieues* of the end of 2005, trade unions are working to raise the representation of ethnic minorities within their internal structures in order to strengthen the labour movement's ability to address their plight in the workplace. The General Confederation of Labour (CGT) has taken steps to increase the number of immigrants on its Executive Board, the French Democratic Confederation of Labour (CFDT) has carried out a study on the extent of racial discrimination in the workplace to raise awareness among their members and start changing their mindsets, and the National Union of Autonomous Trade Unions (UNSA) has amended its by-laws and

provided training to its representatives on non-discrimination and equality issues.[121]

356. In São Paulo, Brazil, the union representing workers in commerce signed a collective agreement with one of the city's largest enterprises in the commerce sector whereby 20 per cent of positions are allocated to black workers.

Collective bargaining: What's new?

Work and family

357. A growing number of trade unions, especially in industrialized countries, are placing the issue of work–family reconciliation measures on their bargaining agenda, regarding it as an effective device to increase membership (box 3.13). In Latin America, progress is beginning to be seen, with clauses in collective agreements that go beyond what is required by national legislation (box 3.14)

---

119. See Commission for Racial Equality (CRE): "TUC Black Workers Conference – Trevor Phillips' speech", 12 Apr. 2003, at www.cre.gov.uk/Default.aspx.LocID-0hgnew04y.RefLocID-0hg00900c002.Lang-EN.htm.

120. American Federation of Labor and Congress of Industrial Organizations (AFL-CIO): "The union difference: Unions are important for minorities", at www.aflcio.org/joinaunion/why/uniondifference/uniondiff12.cfm.

121. Novethic.fr: *Les syndicats cherchent à mieux representer les minorités ethniques*, at www.novethic.fr/novethic/site/dossier/index.jsp?id=99341.

> **Box 3.14.**
> **Clauses on work–family reconciliation measures in collective agreements,**
> **selected Latin American countries, 1996–2001**
>
> *Pregnancy*
>
> - Extension of the time during which pregnant women are protected from dismissal (Brazil).
> - Reduction in hours of work for pregnant women (Brazil).
> - Leave for prenatal checkups (Brazil).
> - Leave and protection against dismissal in the event of spontaneous abortion (Brazil).
>
> *Maternity leave*
>
> - Payment of a wage supplement (Paraguay) and guarantee of full wages during maternity leave (Uruguay).
> - Extension of maternity leave by up to 36 days beyond the statutory entitlement (Paraguay).
> - Maternity leave in cases of "unborn children" (Argentina).
> - Extension of leave in the event of multiple births and children with disabilities (Argentina).
>
> *Breastfeeding*
>
> - Extension of daily breaks for breastfeeding (Argentina, Paraguay, Uruguay).
> - Extension of the period during which daily breastfeeding breaks are allowed (Brazil, Uruguay).
>
> *Childcare*
>
> - Leave to accompany children for health or educational reasons (Brazil).
> - Up to four hours per day of leave in the event of illness of a child aged under one year (Chile).
> - Extension of the period of entitlement to childcare (Brazil and Paraguay).
>
> *Paternity leave*
>
> - Introduction of paternity leave (Uruguay and the Bolivarian Republic of Venezuela).
> - Extension of the length of paternity leave (Brazil, Chile, Paraguay).
> - Protection of the father against dismissal in the event of birth of a child (Brazil).
> - Extension of childcare entitlement to the father (Brazil).
>
> *Adoption*
>
> - Extension of entitlements for adoptive fathers and mothers (Brazil, Paraguay).
>
> *Care-giving leave*
>
> - Leave in the event of serious illness of a close relative (Chile, Paraguay).
>
> Source: L. Abramo; M. Rangel: *Negociação coletiva e igualdade de gênero na América Latina* (Brasilia, ILO, 2005), p. 49.

358. In many other countries, however, including the new Member States of the EU, such as Cyprus, the Czech Republic, Estonia and Romania, these issues are absent from collective bargaining agendas.[122]

359. Funding or on-site provision of day-care services is a growing trend across countries with institutionalized collective bargaining systems, and such provisions are beginning to extend beyond the requirements laid down by law, including in Latin America (box 3.14). However, Brazil has seen crèche benefits increase only in large enterprises, where trade unions are more active. In the EU, an enterprise-level collective agreement covering 18,500 telecommunications workers in Greece covers the cost of day care.[123] A study of collective agreements in Italy found numerous company day-care facilities, especially in large organizations with high proportions of women workers, such as hospitals, call centres and insurance companies.[124] A 2003 study from the Netherlands reported a marked increase in the

---

122. European Foundation for the Improvement of Living and Working Conditions (Eurofound): "Reconciliation of work and family and collective bargaining in the European Union" (Dublin, 2006), at www.eiro.eurofound.eu.int.
123. ibid., p. 23.
124. ibid., p. 37.

number of collective agreements containing child-care provisions, with 85 per cent of collective agreements covering large enterprises likely to contain such provisions and 40 per cent of those covering smaller enterprises, representing a fourfold increase since the 1990s.[125]

360. In Italy, several company-level agreements provided maternity and paternity counsellors to maintain contact with absent employees or organize tutoring or refresher courses for employees returning after maternity leave or long spells of parental leave.[126]

361. Part-time and contingent work, telework and other flexible arrangements are proliferating throughout the industrialized nations, carrying both the benefits of balancing work/family life and potential drawbacks as regards job security and trade union organization. In Canada progress has been made in extending health-care benefits, sick leave, vacation coverage and holiday pay to part-time workers, while advances have been more limited in regard to pensions, job security and pay.[127]

362. Telework has emerged as a collective bargaining issue for the social partners in numerous EU countries, including Norway, Spain and the United Kingdom. In Ireland and Portugal, trade unions are cautious with regard to teleworking and flexible work arrangements, fearing that they will result in more precarious employment. Although teleworking arrangements are rare in Ireland, a number of trade unions have developed guidelines for negotiating teleworking arrangements with employers.[128]

363. On the maternity or parental leave front, there has been a recent move to extend family care provisions such as family care leave, parental leave benefits and paternity leave beyond what is required by law. In Canada, for instance, while the law provides for replacement of up to 55 per cent of the worker's salary, many collective agreements raise this to 93 per cent.[129] Forms of leave allowing employees to care for children or elders are also becoming increasingly common. This is particularly important for the "sandwiched generation" who need to care for both their ageing parents and their children.[130]

364. The extension of leave provisions for fathers is another discernable trend. In Brazil, Chile and Paraguay, collective agreements provide for paternity leave beyond legal requirements. As noted earlier, fathers have not made as much use of such provisions as mothers because the gender pay gap often compels the latter to take the leave as a more economically viable choice for the family.[131] The absence of well-developed parental leave provisions for fathers can reinforce perceptions of the primary role of women in child-rearing, thus increasing occupational segregation by sex, as observed in Ireland.[132]

365. Further strengthening of the leave provisions for fathers, encouraging the use of these provisions, and addressing the gender pay gap as well as occupational segregation are all necessary to ensure that parental leave provisions achieve their aims.

Pay equity

366. As mentioned above, there is a clear tendency, especially in industrialized countries, to incorporate pay equity concerns in collective agreements (box 3.15).

367. The inclusion of pay equity requirements in such agreements reflects an important recognition of the fact that the elimination of sex discrimination in remuneration is central to the achievement of gender equality at the workplace. Nonetheless, leaving pay equity entirely to the bargaining context runs the risk of allowing it to become subordinated to other concerns. A 2004 review of the pay equity system in Canada pointed out that the union or the employer might compromise on or even abandon pay equity objectives because of the emphasis on reaching a "deal".[133] A more recent study notes the scarcity in Canada of guarantees of gender-neutral pay systems in collective agreements.[134]

---

125. ibid., pp. 43–44.
126. ibid., p. 37.
127. See Manitoba Federation of Labour: Brief to the House of Commons Federal Labour Standards Review Commission (Sep. 2005), at www.fls-ntf.gc.ca/en/sub_fb_25.asp.
128. See European Foundation for the Improvement of Living and Working Conditions: op. cit., pp. 28 and 47.
129. See Government of Canada: "Work and family provisions in Canadian collective agreements", Ch. II, A. Maternity leave, at www.hrsdc.gc.ca/asp/gateway.asp?hr=/en/lp/spila/wlb/wfp/11Maternity_Leave.shtml&hs=.
130. K. Bentham: "Labour's collective bargaining record on women and family issues", in G. Hunt; D. Rayside (eds.): *Equalizing labour: Union response to equity in Canada* (University of Toronto Press, forthcoming).
131. ibid.
132. European Foundation for the Improvement of Living and Working Conditions: op. cit., p. 29.
133. Pay Equity Task Force, op. cit.
134. K. Bentham, op. cit.

> **Box 3.15.**
> **Bargaining for pay equity: Recent developments**
>
> In **Cyprus**, the Ministry of Labour and Social Insurance sent a circular to all the social partners requesting the examination and amendment of collective agreement provisions found to be contrary to the Equal Pay Act of 2002.
>
> In **France**, Act No. 2006-340 of 23 March 2006 on equality of remuneration between women and men sets a five-year target date (31 December 2010) for eliminating the remuneration gap. It strengthens the current obligation of employers to conduct negotiations on occupational equality by introducing measures that, for example, authorize the Labour Minister to intervene and initiate bargaining where it has not taken place, as well as make such negotiations a requirement before a collective agreement becomes enforceable. The law also seeks to reconcile work and family responsibilities and improve women's access to vocational training as means to promote equal pay.
>
> In **Singapore**, the Tripartite Declaration on Equal Remuneration for Men and Women Performing Work of Equal Value affirms the commitment of the Government and the social partners to the principle embodied in Convention No. 100. The tripartite partners also agreed to insert an appropriate clause in collective agreements to ensure that employers adhere to the principle of equal remuneration for work of equal value.

368. Another factor that has been shown to have an impact on the size of the gender pay gap is the level at which collective agreements are negotiated – at enterprise or sectoral level – and the degree of coordination among different levels of bargaining. The more collective bargaining is decentralized, the wider the wage disparities and hence the gender pay gap.[135]

369. As the commitment to equal pay for equal work continues to advance, the social partners will need to keep exploring new modalities to best give effect to this right both inside and outside the collective bargaining context. The PSI Pay Equity Campaign launched in 2002, which has been recently evaluated,[136] provides some useful guidance in this regard (box 3.16).

Disability

370. In most European countries, some collective agreements at the sector or company level have included provisions on disability. In the United Kingdom disability issues are often dealt with in a consultative format at the workplace level, with equal opportunity policies developed jointly. At the national level, in the public sector, most agreements contain an equal opportunities clause that refers to disability. In Norway many agreements have specific clauses on the adaptation of work for older employees and those with impaired health, and in the Netherlands one-third of agreements include regulations dealing with issues related to reintegration and selection of people with disabilities.[137]

371. In Belgium four national sectoral agreements contain provisions on disability matters, and in Ireland the social partners have demonstrated a keen commitment to addressing the needs of individuals with disabilities in collective agreements (box 3.17).[138]

Black, ethnic minority and migrant workers

372. In the United Kingdom, progress is evident in respect of provisions concerning black, ethnic minority and migrant workers, with 50 per cent of unions covered by the Trades Union Congress (TUC) Equality Audit 2005 reporting some negotiated improvements in this area: 35 per cent of unions surveyed mentioned provisions ensuring equal access to promotion, training and career progression, while 31 per cent reported agreements tackling racism in the workplace. Smaller, but significant percentages of unions succeeded in negotiating provisions allowing members to reorganize leave time to accommodate travel to visit overseas family members (27 per cent), providing for

---

135. J. Plantenga; C. Remery: "The gender pay gap. Origins and policy responses", coordinators' synthesis report prepared for the Equality Unit, European Commission (EU Expert Group on Gender, Social Inclusion and Employment, July 2006), at www.retepariopportunita.it/Rete_Pari_Opportunita/UserFiles/news/report_pay_gap_economic_experts.pdf.

136. A. Hegewisch; S. Hammond; K. Valladares: op. cit.

137. EIROnline: "Workers with disabilities: Law, bargaining and the social partners", 2001, at www.eiro.eurofound.eu.int/2001/02/study/tn0102201s.html.

138. ibid.

Box 3.16.
PSI Pay Equity Campaign

Launched by Public Services International in 2002 to promote pay equity among PSI affiliates, the Pay Equity Campaign provided extensive support in the form of resource packs, training, expert guidance, the facilitation of local pay equity campaigns and a specialized newsletter on the matter. The recommendations of the recent evaluation of the Campaign are as follows:

- continue training and capacity building for national affiliates, strengthening the "train-the-trainer" component;
- strengthen capacity on job evaluation by preparing a database of materials, developing materials to help unions in screening consultants hired to assist job-evaluation programmes and provide a recommended list of consultants with expertise in a variety of languages;
- broaden the pay equity agenda to focus on performance-related pay and appraisal, skill development and monitoring of recruitment, selection and promotion decisions and provide support for the establishment of bipartite and tripartite committees;
- increase awareness of the gender pay gap through educational campaigns, negotiating guidelines regarding collection and sharing of information, continued cooperation with the ILO and support of research initiatives with external bodies;
- continued emphasis on knowledge sharing, for example through newsletters, online discussion forums and strategic discussions at global and regional levels;
- sharing of expertise through twinning arrangements between developing countries and experienced PSI affiliates with pay equity experience (for example in Australia, Canada, New Zealand, Sweden and the United Kingdom);
- continued cooperation with the ILO to increase mechanisms for cooperation at the national level, support technical consultation on job evaluation methods free from gender bias, in order to assist unions wanting to submit comments under ILO monitoring arrangements, and increase training opportunities supported by the ILO;
- demonstrate the link between pay equity and the anti-poverty agenda, particularly in regard to the MDGs, by developing guidelines, campaigning and encouraging affiliates to campaign based on countries' MDGs.

Source: A. Hegewisch; S. Hammond; K. Valladares: *Report of the evaluation of the PSI Pay Equity Campaign*, Oct. 2006, at www.world-psi.org.

Box 3.17.
Programme for Prosperity and Fairness – Irish social partners
in action to assist people with disabilities

The Programme for Prosperity and Fairness is a three-year tripartite national agreement signed in March 2000. It provides for assisting people with disabilities by:

- a working group to address relevant workplace issues, including contractual status and remuneration;
- legislative reform: a Disabilities Bill to be prepared and published;
- public service accessibility improvements: government commitment to take steps to improve access to services;
- improved statistics;
- improved vocational training programmes;
- a commitment to achieve 3 per cent employment target for people with disabilities in the public service;
- funding to social partners for joint initiatives to stimulate awareness and promote employment;
- funding to employers to implement workplace accommodations;
- grants for disability-awareness training programmes;
- grants to train/retrain people who become disabled at work.

Source: EIROnline: "Workers with disabilities: Law, bargaining and the social partners", 2001, at www.eiro.eurofound.eu.int/2001/02/study/tn0102201s.html.

language training (13 per cent) and for the recognition of foreign qualifications (10 per cent) – all provisions of great importance to migrant workers.[139]

373. In the United States, UNITE HERE, which represents mainly textile, catering and hotel workers, has fought for collective agreements to include a provision whereby employers notify the union as soon as they hear of a visit by the Immigration and Naturalization Service.[140] While issues pertaining to migrant workers are beginning to feature more prominently on bargaining agendas, the prevalence of subcontracting among migrants makes it difficult to assist them through collective bargaining.

374. As labour migration intensifies, it is likely that provisions such as those highlighted above will become increasingly important. However, migrant workers may be perceived as a threat to national workers' jobs or as a source of social disruption. The International Federation of Building and Wood Workers (IFBWW) has identified a list of strategies and actions to address these challenges.[141]

Corporate social responsibility: Potential to promote equality

375. Corporate social responsibility (CSR) programmes have emerged in response to expanding global labour markets as "a way in which enterprises give consideration to the impact of their operations on society and affirm their principles and values both in their own internal methods and processes and in their interaction with other actors. CSR is a voluntary, enterprise-driven initiative and refers to activities that are considered to exceed compliance with the law."[142]

376. To date CSR initiatives have acquired varying forms, ranging from corporate codes of conduct, certification and audit procedures to management frameworks or intergovernmental initiatives which occur independently or in conjunction with busi-ness associations, NGOs, governments and/or international organizations.

377. As the prevalence of CSR programmes has grown, so has the debate regarding CSR and the role of enterprises in society. While CSR cannot substitute for the role of government,[143] it has the potential to enhance compliance with labour standards and to advance the non-discrimination and equality agenda. Through the ILO Tripartite Declaration of Principles concerning Multinational Enterprises and Social Policy, the UN Global Compact and other initiatives, CSR seems to have raised awareness among enterprises of the importance of non-discrimination in their operations. According to a recent survey, many of the world's 500 largest companies state that they are partially addressing non-discrimination and equality matters through their management policies and practices. Such a survey result would have been unlikely a mere five years ago.[144]

378. A World Bank review[145] of the codes of conduct of about 100 multinational enterprises (MNEs) reveals that in four of the five sectors examined (apparel/footwear/light manufacturing, agribusiness, oil/gas and mining)[146] virtually every code had some form of non-discrimination and equality guarantee, although its scope varied by industry and company. In some instances, this guarantee covered only hiring and recruitment practices, while in others it also encompassed career advancement policies. Codes may also address issues not covered by Convention No. 111 or by national law. For instance, several companies in the mining and oil/gas sector reviewed by the World Bank ban discrimination on the basis of sexual orientation or on grounds such as weight and physical condition.

379. However, ILO Conventions Nos. 100 and 111 are only occasionally mentioned, and greater reference to them would prove useful, especially in the face of a proliferation of different codes that may lead to increased confusion in firms about which standards they should apply.

139. Trades Union Congress (TUC): *TUC Equality Audit 2005* (London, TUC, 2005), at www.tuc.org.uk, pp. 32–33.
140. N. David: "Migrants get unions back to basics", in *Labour Education* (Geneva, ILO), 2002/4, No. 129, at www.ilo.org/public/english/dialogue/actrav/publ/129/12.pdf.
141. International Federation of Building and Wood Workers (IFBWW): *Trade Union Responses for a better management of migrant and cross-border work* (Geneva, 2004), at www.ifbww.org /files/migrantwork.pdf.
142. ILO: *InFocus Initiative on Corporate Social Responsibility (CSR)*, Governing Body doc. GB.295/MNE/2/1 (Mar. 2006), para. 1.
143. ibid., para. 2.
144. J. Ruggie: *Human rights policies and management practices of Fortune Global 500 firms: Results of a survey*, Corporate Social Responsibility Initiative Working Paper No. 28 (Harvard University, John F. Kennedy School of Government, 2006), at www.ksg.harvard.edu/m-rcbg/CSRI/publications/workingpaper_28_ruggie.pdf.
145. The World Bank Group, Corporate Social Responsibility Practice: "Company codes of conduct and international standards: An analytical comparison", Parts I and II (Washington, DC, 2003 and 2004).
146. The tourism industry appears to be still at the early stages of developing principles and formal codes of conduct. This would explain the low profile of non-discrimination and equality issues in the codes of conduct of this sector.

380. A recent impact assessment study of the Ethical Trading Initiative (ETI),[147] an alliance of companies, NGOs and trade unions, which monitors progress through an annual reporting and review process, shows that the impact on discrimination has been less than that in other areas such as health and safety issues, child labour, working hours and minimum wages.

381. Some advances have been noted in five of 25 worksites examined. These include enhanced efforts to provide better working conditions for pregnant women in Costa Rica, the development of an equal employment opportunity policy on one farm in South Africa and the removal of age limitations on job advertisements in Viet Nam. The study notes that the progress to date tends to be based on practical gender needs, such as payment of maternity leave and postnatal entitlements; however, efforts are lagging behind in relation to influencing strategic gender needs, such as equal opportunities in relation to employment status, promotion or training. The study notes little impact on eliminating racial or religious biases in recruitment and selection policies in South Africa and India, and voices concern about discrimination against local workers in favour of migrant labourers in the United Kingdom. The study also points out that employers, auditors, workers and unions often fail to notice non-discrimination and equality matters in the implementation of codes, and provides a number of practical measures to remedy this situation.

147. S. Barrientos; S. Smith: *The ETI code of labour practice: Do workers really benefit?* (Institute of Development Studies, University of Sussex, 2006), at www.ethicaltrade.org; the report assessed cases in India (garment sector), Viet Nam (garments and footwear), South Africa (fruit), United Kingdom (horticulture) and Costa Rica (banana industry). The ETI Base Code requires that there be no discrimination in hiring, compensation, access to training, promotion, termination or retirement based on race, caste, national origin, religion, age, disability, gender, marital status, sexual orientation, union membership or political affiliation.

PART IV

ILO action, past and future

382. This part of the Global Report begins by reviewing the ILO's work on non-discrimination and equality since 2003 and goes on to recommend follow-up action for the next four years.

1. The ILO's achievements and challenges

Action plan regarding the elimination of discrimination in employment and occupation

383. While emphasizing the need to maintain and consolidate the Office's ongoing action in respect of HIV/AIDS and disability, the follow-up action plan adopted by the Governing Body in 2003 identified two thematic priorities for 2004–07: the gender pay gap and racial/ethnic equality and its gender dimensions.[1] The rationale for this choice was the persistence and universal nature of the gender pay gap, and the resilience of racial and ethnic discrimination and their link to poverty. Pay and wages, as well as wage-fixing mechanisms, are central to the ILO's mandate and this is an area in which the ILO has recognized expertise. Similarly, the elimination of poverty, including chronic poverty associated with discriminatory practices, through the promotion of decent work features as a high priority in the ILO's current agenda. Last but not least, although these themes are long-standing ILO concerns, the related action has not always been consistent.

Narrowing the gender pay gap

384. As shown earlier, gender differentials in labour earnings are a persistent feature of labour markets everywhere and a growing concern for public policy. Several factors, including sex discrimination in remuneration, account for this situation. Convention No. 100, one of the most widely ratified ILO instruments, seeks to address this problem by ensuring that equal pay is received for jobs that differ in content but are of equal value.

Promoting pay equity

385. The notion of "equal pay for work of equal value" is perhaps one of the least understood concepts in the field of action to combat discrimination. As noted earlier, in some countries this is a reflection of laws and regulations that continue to give a narrow interpretation to the equal pay principle, as they refer only to "identical" or "similar" work. In

1. ILO: *Follow-up to the ILO Declaration on Fundamental Principles and Rights at Work: Priorities and action plans for technical cooperation*, Governing Body document GB.288/TC/4 (Nov. 2003), paras. 15–22.

many countries, the lack of reliable sex-disaggregated data on wages conceals the existence of a gender pay gap, thus making it difficult to monitor trends in the size and underlying causes of the gender pay gap over time.

386. The social partners may have difficulties in understanding both the notion of work of "equal value" and how wage structures and remuneration practices may lead to the undervaluation of women's jobs. Alternatively, while recognizing the problem, they may consider that family-friendly measures or the mentoring of female managers with a view to breaking through the "glass ceiling" are more urgent and relevant to improving women's status in the workplace. In all instances, the cost implications of pay equity are a matter of significant concern, especially for SMEs, as is the perception that it would not lead to any tangible benefits for labour productivity.

387. This component of the action plan has therefore focused on: (a) generating knowledge on the costs and benefits of promoting pay equity, trends in the gender pay gap and its underlying causes; (b) networking and cooperating with global union federations; and (c) providing technical assistance at the country level.

388. Country fact sheets covering Africa, Europe and Latin America have been prepared to provide an overview of: (i) trends in the gender pay gap over the past 15 years by sector and occupation, and the associated causes and processes; (ii) relevant national institutional and regulatory frameworks; and (iii) the related comments of the CEACR over the past 15 years. Similar work has also recently been commenced for East Asia. A paper assessing the costs and benefits of pay equity has been produced (box 4.1), with a guide on how to carry out a job evaluation free from gender biases.[2]

389. In Portugal, the ILO has provided technical assistance to an EQUAL project financed by the European Commission for the development of a job evaluation method free from gender biases for the restaurant and beverage sectors. The project involves the General Confederation of Portuguese Workers (CGTP-IN), the Portuguese Trade Union Federation of Agriculture, Food, Beverages, Hotels and Tourism (FESAHT), the Association of Restaurants and Allied Trades of Portugal (ARESP), the Committee for Equal Opportunities in Employment (CITE) and the General Directorate for Labour Inspection.

390. The catering sector in Portugal is dominated by small enterprises and low earnings levels, and is characterized by low productivity and high turnover and absenteeism, particularly among women workers. The "ageing" of the female workforce of the sector has attracted young, mainly undocumented, migrant female workers from Brazil and Cape Verde, lowering wages still further. Both employers' and workers' organizations are worried about this situation, but they hold different views about the appropriate course of action. The project seeks to redress the undervaluation of particular professions through the development of job evaluation methods free from gender bias, modernize the sector's occupational classification systems that date back to the early 1970s and establish remuneration systems based on transparent and gender-neutral criteria and procedures. While the process may not always be smooth, the involvement of the social partners is key to ensuring that the concerns and priorities of both parties are taken into account and the outcomes accepted by all.

391. Since 2000, Public Services International (PSI) and other global union federations (GUFs), together with the ILO, have participated every year in one-day Pay Equity Discussion Forums. These forums aim to: (a) facilitate the sharing of up-dates on the work of the GUFs in relation to pay equity and of the ILO in its follow up to the Global Report *Time for equality at work* (2003) and the resolution concerning the promotion of gender equality, pay equity and maternity protection adopted by the International Labour Conference in 2004; (b) plan strategies to build capacity and ownership of pay equity issues among the GUFs and trade union membership; and (c) discuss how the ILO could best assist in this process.

Engendering employment policies

392. As discussed earlier, reducing the gender pay gap means implementing a host of policy measures including pay equity interventions, promoting equal opportunities in access to job counselling and vocational training and adopting measures to reconcile work and family. Employment policies and programmes are often gender-blind, in the sense that they do not take into account the specific circumstances and needs of women and men, thus leading to unequal opportunities and outcomes and reduced policy effectiveness. Targeted programmes for particular categories of women may sometimes be based on stereotyped views of the jobs that women can do best or which it might be more "convenient" for them to do, with the

---

2. M.-T. Chicha: *A comparative analysis of promoting pay equity: Models and impacts*, DECLARATION/WP/49/2006 (Geneva, ILO, 2006); ILO: *Promoting pay equity through job evaluation methods: A step-by-step guide* (forthcoming).

**Box 4.1.
What are the pay-offs of pay equity?**

Very few studies have examined the costs and benefits of pay equity, and most of those that have concern Canada and Sweden. The scarcity of studies reflects the double difficulty of obtaining long-series wage data and isolating the effect of pay equity or other measures on labour productivity or other variables. The ILO study identifies benefits in relation to human resources management (better knowledge of job requirements, thus better targeted firm-level training, and greater efficiency in remuneration, as well as in recruitment and selection practices), employee motivation and loyalty, labour management relations, avoidance of litigation costs, and enhanced company reputation. The costs include increases in the wage bill, administrative costs (associated with job evaluation process) and a decline in the morale of employees not benefiting directly from pay equity. The study emphasizes that, while increases in the wage bill and in administrative costs are easily and immediately quantified, the benefits, and especially indirect benefits, are more difficult to measure and materialize only in the medium and long term. The limited data available seem to show that wage adjustment costs are not especially significant, e.g. the wage bill increased between 0.5 and 2.2 per cent in the Province of Ontario and 1.5 per cent in Quebec. The study proposes a useful set of indicators and related characteristics (direct/indirect, frequency of occurrence, quantifiable) for each cost and benefit, and identifies a number of good practices to reduce the costs and maximize the positive effects.

Source: M.-T. Chicha: *A comparative analysis of promoting pay equity: Models and impacts*, DECLARATION/WP/49/2006 (Geneva, ILO, 2006).

---

end result that they are pushed into dead-end jobs where there is an over-supply of labourers.

393.   To redress this situation, the ILO has sought to engender its advice to Ministries of Labour in the design and implementation of national employment policies. An example is the project financed by the Government of Belgium entitled "Promoting Equal Opportunities for Women and Men in the Country Employment Reviews of Stability Pact Countries". This complements ILO technical support to follow up on the Declaration adopted by the South-East European Ministerial Conference on Employment (Bucharest, October 2003). In this Declaration, the Ministers of Labour of the Stability Pact countries undertake to cooperate at the regional level to address employment challenges and call upon the ILO and the Council of Europe to provide technical assistance throughout the process of assessing the employment situation of the countries concerned. This involves developing recommendations in the form of Country Reports on Employment Policy (CREPs). Drafted on the model of the Joint Assessment Papers (JAPs) on employment policies of the European Commission,[3] CREPs are intended to contribute to the preparation of Stability Pact countries for future integration in the EU. The project, financed by the Government of Belgium, was designed to draw attention to and offer possible remedies for the problem of gender inequalities in the labour markets in the countries covered. The employment situation of women has declined

sharply over the past 15 years in all South East European countries. Fewer women than men even register as unemployed, and once unemployed, women take longer than men to find paid work, even though on average women have similar levels of education and training to men. They face discrimination in relation to hiring and firing decisions and discrimination is even expressed occasionally in formal job advertisements and job specifications. There are accounts of widespread gender discrimination at national employment offices. As a result, there are a vast number of inactive women who would be happy to work if suitable opportunities and support mechanisms were available. For women with paid work in the formal economy, job segregation contributes to a sizeable wage gap in all four countries where CREPs have already been completed (Albania, Croatia, Republic of Moldova and Serbia). Women tend to work in occupations and in sectors that are valued and paid less than male-dominated ones.

394.   The project has organized gender seminars (for example in Serbia and the Republic of Moldova), where the social partners, officials of national employment agencies and representatives of national equality institutions discuss the causes and possible policy remedies to the most pressing gender and employment issues. A different set of problems have emerged in each country. In Serbia, for example, the gender seminar discussed ways in which women's entrepreneurship could be encouraged, including credit opportunities,

---

3.   JAPs are prepared by the European Commission and countries preparing for accession.

training and the formation of cooperatives. In the Republic of Moldova, the key area of discussion was maternity leave policies and their impact on women's labour market participation. The most important issues raised at the gender seminars were presented at the tripartite meetings which endorsed the CREPs and were taken into consideration in the final revision of the documents.

395.   Gender sessions have also been systematically included in all high-level meetings associated with the "Bucharest process". A project spin-off has been the launch, with funding from the Government of Switzerland, of a project in Serbia to equip the national employment service with the know-how required to increase women's access to paid work through the promotion of active labour market policies and gender mainstreaming in the general functioning of employment services.

396.   The project has managed to engender the CREPs and engage policy-makers in the related discussions. However, gender inequality is still perceived as a marginal concern, owing in large part to a backlash against emancipation policies under the former communist system. Women themselves, exhausted by the double burden of household work and paid employment, are often disappointed with the political call for gender equality, as it often involves additional responsibilities compared to the past. For all these reasons, the introduction of policies and regulations addressing gender equality in the labour market is often the lowest of political priorities.

397.   In Peru, the employment programmes of the Ministry of Labour were examined from a gender viewpoint in 2005, at the request of the Commission for Equality of Opportunity, established in 2004. The findings and recommendations of the gender assessment were shared and discussed with the members of the Committee, and possible follow-up action plans were examined. A workshop was organized to review experiences of gender mainstreaming in employment programmes developed in neighbouring countries (Bolivia, Colombia and Ecuador). But the frequent changes in the direction of the Ministry between 2004 and 2006, resulting in shifting priorities, affected the composition of the Committee and its operations. This weakened the legitimacy and sustainability of the Committee's work. Similar experiences in other countries serve to show the many challenges associated with institution-building in countries where governments are unstable and subject to frequent change.

Fighting racism and poverty

398.   Technical assistance has been provided to governments which have indicated their interest in developing employment and social policies to promote racial equality and inclusion. In Brazil, for example, the National Policy for Racial Equality Project, financed by the Government of the Netherlands, assisted the Special Secretariat for Policies to Promote Racial Equality (SEPPIR) and the Ministry of Labour in this domain in 2004–06. One of the main achievements of the project has been to foster the institutional link between SEPPIR and the Ministry of Labour, showing the central importance of combating racism at the workplace in freeing society from discrimination. The project has helped to streamline the Ministry's Federal programme "Brazil, Gender and Race" and its Units for promoting equal opportunities and fighting discrimination by developing a new methodology of work for these units based on a common set of goals, impact indicators and standardized procedures and practices (see box 3.4 in Part III, Chapter 1). The project has also been actively involved in a series of workshops convened by the Ministry of Labour in various regions of the country to develop a common understanding of the mission and modus operandi of the units.

399.   Through the project, the ILO contributed both financially and substantially to the "International Dialogue on Advancing Equity and Racial Inclusion", promoted jointly by the ILO, the Inter-American Development Bank (IDB), UNDP Brazil and DFID Brazil in Brasilia in April 2005. The joint meeting brought together 150 government representatives, mainly from ministries of planning, together with racial equality practitioners, academics and representatives of black or African-descendent groups from all over the Americas to address racial discrimination in access to justice, education and health, housing, economic assets and the world of work. The ILO's participation was crucial in weaving work-related matters and industrial relations issues into the programme and making a persuasive case for racially and gender-inclusive labour market and workplace interventions as central components of development strategies to promote racial equality and reduce poverty in the region.

400.   In a similar vein, the ILO's follow-up action plan has promoted the differentiated treatment of indigenous and tribal peoples within the framework of Poverty Reduction Strategy (PRS) processes. An ethnic audit was undertaken of World Bank and IMF-driven Poverty Reduction Strategy Papers (PRSPs) in 14 countries around the world (box 4.2).

> **Box 4.2.**
> **PRSPs and indigenous and tribal peoples**
>
> Since 1999, the Poverty Reduction Strategy Papers (PRSPs), under the aegis of the World Bank and the IMF, have provided the overall framework for lending, debt relief and development cooperation in low-income countries. They are intended to be open and participatory and to reach out to traditionally marginalized groups. As indigenous and tribal peoples are commonly found at the bottom of all conventional socio-economic indicators, the ILO carried out an audit to assess whether and how the needs and aspirations of these peoples had been taken into account and whether they had been involved in the consultations leading to the PRSPs. The audit, covering 14 countries in Africa, Asia and Latin America, shows significant variations between and within regions. Nonetheless, countries where the PRSPs were more likely to address the structural causes of the pauperization of these peoples were those where:
>
> - legal frameworks recognize indigenous and tribal peoples' group rights;
> - institutions and policies respect and accommodate cultural diversity;
> - indigenous and tribal peoples have organized and mobilized for political change.
>
> The audit concludes that the recognition – in legal, administrative and policy terms – of the rights of indigenous and tribal peoples, as articulated in ILO Convention No. 169, is an essential requirement to address their poverty and social exclusion. It recommends the identification and testing of poverty indicators that are relevant to the circumstances of indigenous and tribal peoples, including their employment patterns, and capacity building for indigenous organizations and local government authorities so that they can plan, implement and monitor inclusive local development plans.
>
> Source: M. Tomei: *Indigenous and tribal peoples. An ethnic audit of selected Poverty Reduction Strategy Papers*, DECLARATION (Geneva, ILO, 2005).

401. The dissemination and discussion of the ethnic audit at the United Nations Permanent Forum on Indigenous Issues in May 2005, and at the technical donor meeting convened by the ILO in October 2005, contributed to a growing common understanding of the conditions required for indigenous peoples to benefit from development and poverty-reduction policies. At the Conference on Poverty and Indigenous Peoples, hosted by the World Bank and attended by the ILO in May 2006, the World Bank committed itself to addressing indigenous peoples' concerns and rights in future PRSPs.

402. The ethnic audit has attracted extra-budgetary funding from the Government of Sweden for follow-up activities in Bolivia, Peru and Paraguay to address forced labour and labour market discrimination issues that affect indigenous peoples. There is a clear added value in addressing discrimination and forced labour issues together, especially where groups such as indigenous and tribal peoples are concerned. Forced labour in their case can indeed be considered as the worst form of ethnic discrimination.[4] Recognizing and addressing this nexus can result in better informed and more cost-effective policy interventions addressing both the root causes

and the symptoms of forced labour, as shown by the preliminary results of the project.

403. An important contribution to the consolidation of a human-rights based approach to the alleviation of the poverty faced by indigenous and tribal peoples has been made by the ILO's Project to Promote ILO Policy on Indigenous and Tribal Peoples (PRO 169), which has been in operation since 1996. The strategy of PRO 169 is to promote, protect and monitor respect for the rights of these peoples, as enshrined in ILO Convention No. 169, while ensuring that they participate in and benefit from broader efforts to achieve decent work and respect for international labour standards. PRO 169 is implemented in liaison with other international organizations, donors and actors, including the United Nations Permanent Forum on Indigenous Issues. In the context of this project, the ILO has developed capacity-building activities for indigenous, government and development partners and supported regional and country-specific initiatives. Over the past four years, activities have included: research in tandem with the African Commission on Human and Peoples' Rights on the legal protection of indigenous communities in Africa; the promotion of indigenous and tribal peoples' rights

---

4. ILO: *A global alliance against forced labour*, Global Report under the follow-up to the ILO Declaration on Fundamental Principles and Rights at Work, Report I(B), International Labour Conference, 93rd Session, Geneva, 2005.

in South Asia; capacity building and development of national legislation (for example, in Cambodia, Cameroon and Congo); and technical assistance for the implementation of Convention No. 169 (Latin America).[5]

Ongoing ILO commitments

404. As already noted, the need was recognized in the follow-up action plan to consolidate traditional ILO areas, such as the supervision and the application of Conventions Nos. 100 and 111 and other relevant labour standards, and assistance in the development of enabling regulatory frameworks, while maintaining action in more recent areas of concern, such as HIV/AIDS and disability and the promotion of gender equality.

Contributing to the shaping of effective laws

405. If it is to be eliminated, discrimination needs to be prohibited, which requires specific legislative provisions. At the same time, national law, to be truly effective, must be enforced, and the adequate handling of discrimination cases by lawyers and magistrates is a step in the right direction.

Developing enabling legislative frameworks

406. Monitoring the application of ILO's labour standards, including Conventions Nos. 100 and 111, and providing technical assistance to member States to ensure that national law and practice comply with ratified ILO Conventions are central aspects of the ILO's work. The assistance provided can take many forms: it can range from providing legal advice on the content and scope of a draft labour law, helping to develop a strategy for law implementation or supplying capacity building to law drafters or labour judges and magistrates, or a combination of these elements. In Bosnia and Herzegovina, for instance, further to the discussion at the Conference Committee on the Application of Standards in 2005 of the country's failure

to provide reports on ratified Conventions, the ILO assisted in the formulation in 2006 of a strategy outlining the priorities of the public authorities and the social partners for the effective implementation of the Gender Equality Law. This helped the different institutions involved to learn more about their respective competencies and responsibilities, which was key to bringing about the desired changes in law and practice.

407. In Mauritius, following the ratification of Conventions Nos. 100 and 111 in 2002, a joint ILO/UNDP project entitled "Capacity building for Gender Equality and Empowerment of Women" was launched in 2005 to develop measures and strategies to redress existing gender inequalities in employment, access to vocational training and remuneration within the framework of the National Gender Policy and National Gender Action Plan (2005–15). To this end, the project seeks to assist in harmonizing national law with these Conventions and to remove discriminatory practices in remuneration against women.

408. The ILO's assistance in this field also consists of developing and disseminating guidelines to assist law-makers in the drafting process. For instance, in the case of labour or discrimination laws that seek to include AIDS-related provisions, the ILO recommends that national law cover the ten principles enshrined in the ILO's code of practice on HIV/AIDS and the world of work and reflect the outcomes of multi-stakeholder consultations at national or regional level.[6] The ILO has also recently developed guidelines on HIV/AIDS for labour judges and magistrates.[7]

409. Similarly, the ILO has produced guidelines on how to promote equal employment opportunities for people with disabilities through legislation[8] and has conducted impact studies of legislation in selected countries in Asia and the Pacific and Southern Africa. These studies shed light on the variety of forms and objectives of legislation aimed at regulating discrimination on grounds of disability (table 4.1).

410. One indicator to measure the effectiveness of law is the number of discrimination cases that are brought before the courts or other competent authorities and are adequately handled, for which the training of judges and lawyers is key.

---

5. See the ILO Indigenous and Tribal Peoples web site: www.ilo.org/public/english/indigenous.
6. See: J. Hodges: *Guidelines on addressing HIV/AIDS in the workplace through employment and labour laws* (Geneva, ILO, 2004); M.-C. Chartier: *Legal initiatives to address HIV/AIDS in the world of work* (Geneva, ILO, 2005).
7. ILO: *Using the ILO code of practice and training manual: Guidelines for labour judges and magistrates* (Geneva, ILO, 2005). Several training sessions based on these Guidelines have been held at the ILO Turin Centre and in Southern, East and West Africa and South-east Asia.
8. ILO: *Achieving equal employment opportunities for people with disabilities through legislation: Guidelines* (Geneva, 2004).

Table 4.1. Location of disability provisions in selected countries

	Countries or areas	Provisions
Constitutional law	Brazil, Cambodia, Canada, China, Fiji, Germany, Ghana, Seychelles, Slovenia, South Africa, Tanzania, Uganda	Provisions on human rights, fundamental freedoms prohibiting discrimination on different grounds, including disability
Criminal law	Finland, France, Spain	Fines and imprisonment
Specific legislation on people with disabilities	China, India, Cambodia, Ethiopia, Ghana, Mauritius, Mongolia, Sri Lanka, United Republic of Tanzania	Provisions on different aspects (medical, social life, welfare) as well as the rights of disabled people, including employment
General laws	Australia, Fiji, Seychelles, Zanzibar (United Republic of Tanzania)	Employment Act (Seychelles), Equal Employment Opportunity Acts (Australia)
Quotas	China, France, Germany, India, Italy, Japan, Mauritius, Mongolia, Poland, Tanzania, Thailand	Provisions requiring enterprises or a category of companies (e.g. enterprises with more than a certain number of employees) to hire a certain percentage of disabled. Law may also impose a compensatory payment for non-compliance (Mauritius)
Employment promotion measures	Australia, Canada, India, Japan, Mauritius, Nordic countries, South Africa, United Kingdom, United States	Workplace accommodation and accessibility
	Cambodia, Ethiopia, India, Japan, Sri Lanka, Thailand	Employment services (job placement agencies)
	China, France, Japan, Singapore, Sri Lanka, Thailand	Financial incentives to compensate employers for any financial burden due to the employment of disabled workers: start-up loans for business (China), financial assistance to disabled persons' self-employment and microfinance services for ex-combatants (Sri Lanka), financial support for training (Japan, Thailand), and tax reduction (China, Singapore)

Enhancing the capacity of judges and lawyers to handle discrimination cases

411.   The judiciary can play a proactive role in improving the enforcement of anti-discrimination legislation. Since 1999, the International Training Centre of the ILO (the Turin Centre) has organized training activities for judges, lawyers and law professors on international labour law, including non-discrimination and equality in employment and occupation. While courts are required to apply national laws and regulation, they can rely on the legal principles, concepts and definitions of relevant ILO instruments to guide their interpretation and application of national legislation. This training therefore enables legal practitioners to use international labour standards when settling labour disputes. These training sessions include detailed analysis of key legal concepts, such as direct and indirect discrimination, discrimination based on the various grounds, including the newly recognized ones, equal pay for work of equal value and appropriate remedies to eliminate discriminatory situations.

412.   To maximize impact, cooperative relations have been developed with judicial training centres and law faculties, with the objective of ensuring that national partner agencies include international labour law and equality law in their training curricula. Long-term cooperation is now in place with judicial training centres and universities in Albania, Argentina, Brazil, Madagascar, Morocco and Senegal.

Box 4.3.
Impact of training activities for judges and lawyers on Madagascar case law related to equality

Since 2002, there has been a long-term cooperation arrangement between the ILO Turin Centre and the Madagascar school of magistrates. In 2003, the Supreme Court of Madagascar used ILO Convention No. 111 to argue that the earlier retirement age applied to women by a company collective agreement constituted sex discrimination. The Court found that the difference of treatment, causing an important economic loss to women workers, was not justified by objective reasons related to the inherent requirements of women's jobs. A recent labour tribunal decision applied this jurisprudence in another case.

In 2004, the Antsirabé Labour Tribunal applied ILO Convention No. 111 to make the case that the dismissal of an employee by a religious institution was discriminatory. The worker, employed as a statistician, was terminated for changing his religion after marrying a woman from another confession. The tribunal based its ruling on Article 1, paragraph 2, of ILO Convention No. 111 to determine that religion was not an inherent requirement to perform the job of statistician. The dismissal was therefore declared discriminatory.

Source: Antananarivo Labour Tribunal, Judgement No. 529 of 2 June 2006, Antsirabé Labour Tribunal, *Ramiaranjatovo Jean-Louis* vs *Fitsaboana Maso*, 7 June 2004, reported in International Training Centre of the ILO: *Use of international law by domestic courts: Compendium of court decisions* (Turin, ILO, 2006).

---

413. An independent impact assessment study of the training activities carried out between 1999 and 2003[9] revealed that 68 per cent of respondents had explicitly referred to international labour standards in legal cases, thereby influencing their country's case law (box 4.3), while 64 per cent reported changes in the curriculum of national law faculties and judiciary schools.

Gender mainstreaming for achieving gender equality in the world of work

414. As already noted by *Time for equality at work*, the ILO relies on a two-pronged strategy to promote equality for women and men in the world of work. This strategy combines: (1) the integration of a gender perspective in the design and implementation of all ILO programmes and projects; and (2) targeted interventions aimed at either women or men to close gender gaps. The experience acquired up to now by the ILO and other institutions (see box 3.7 in Part III) confirms the relevance and importance of maintaining this two-pronged approach. Gender mainstreaming offers added value, as it enriches understanding of the structures and functioning of the labour market and workplaces, thereby enhancing policy design and implementation. But it risks becoming ineffective if it is not supplemented by measures explicitly addressing significant and persistent gender gaps in "voice" and representation, labour market outcomes and social protection.

415. The ILO Gender Network, connecting gender specialists and gender focal points from the field and headquarters, has helped in the cross-fertilization of experience and practices on how to implement gender equality. It has also encouraged gender specialists to act more strategically and start building a common global agenda, while addressing specific regional and programmatic concerns.[10]

416. Another way that has been used to promote organizational learning on how to ensure that ILO policies, programmes and structures address gender issues is office-wide participatory gender audits. Between 2001 and 2005, 25 units/offices underwent a gender audit (ten units at headquarters and 15 field offices in South and South Asia, the Middle East, Europe, Africa and Latin America).[11] ILO constituents, such as the ICFTU, also approached the ILO for assistance in this field. While this experience, the first of its kind to be introduced in the UN system, has helped raise awareness about the need to integrate gender into technical areas, it has also shown that follow-up to the recommendations of gender audits is problematic and that accountability is loose because of the lack of monitoring mechanisms.[12] This in turn reflects the difficulty of moving on from gender as an "add-on" to its more thorough integration into the ILO's Decent Work Agenda, which is instrumental to the success of the Agenda.

---

9. See International Training Centre of the ILO: *Evaluation d'impact des cours sur les normes internationales du travail pour juges, juristes et professeurs de droit (1999–2003)* (Turin, 2005), at training.itcilo.org/ils/ILS_Judges/training_materials/francais/RapportFR.pdf.
10. ILO: *Sharing knowledge: Gender equality in the world of work*, Bureau for Gender Equality, at www.ilo.org/gender.
11. ILO: *ILO participatory gender audit: A tool for organizational change*, at www.ilo.org/gender.
12. ibid.

Box 4.4.
The ILO Gender Equality Partnership Fund

Under the auspices of the ILO Gender Equality Partnership Fund, 13 projects are being undertaken in 25 countries. All the projects are carried out in response to requests for assistance by labour ministries, workers' and employers' organizations or groups of women working in the informal economy. While the range of issues supported by the Fund is broad, all projects rely on a common and multi-staged strategy that includes needs assessment, capacity building, knowledge management and sharing, and partnership development. In Morocco, the fund helped to devise practical solutions to women's special protection needs and to address their concerns in the context of the restructuring of the textile and clothing industries. In Yemen, the social partners received training on how to ensure that social dialogue recognizes and addresses the different opportunities and risks of men and women and the project promoted gender equality not only during tripartite discussions, but also in national policy planning. In the Russian Federation, four action plans envisaging gender-sensitive measures in the field of employment and social protection were developed for the Central, Far Eastern, Siberian and Volga federal okrugs (districts). Fifty journalists working in these fields were sensitized to the gender dimensions of such policies, and over 100 publications and radio/TV programmes were released in the framework of an all-Russian Federation competition by the end of 2003. In China, ILO constituents and the All-China Women's Federation (ACWF) received training on gender-mainstreaming strategies, mechanisms and tools, and carried out research and impact assessments with a gender perspective.

Source: ILO, Bureau for Gender Equality: *ILO Gender Equality Partnership Fund: What it is and what it does*, at www.ilo.org/dyn/gender/docs.

Gender mainstreaming in technical cooperation

417. The ILO Gender Equality Partnership Fund launched in 2003 and gender mainstreaming in technical cooperation are further means through which the ILO has sought to give practical effect to gender equality at work in various sectors and socio-economic and cultural contexts.

418. In March 2005, the Governing Body adopted a decision requiring due consideration to be given in all ILO technical cooperation to the promotion of gender equality. The framework agreements recently signed by the ILO with Denmark, France, the Netherlands, Norway, Sweden and the United Kingdom explicitly refer to the importance of mainstreaming gender equality in programme implementation. The agreements with Denmark, the Netherlands, Norway and Sweden go a step further in setting aside a specific supplementary contribution to the ILO Gender Equality Partnership Fund. Launched in 2003 with funding from the ILO regular budget, the Fund seeks to enhance the capacity of the ILO's constituents to take positive steps to promote equal opportunities between men and women in the world of work (box 4.4).

419. Since early 2006, a key criterion in the technical screening of new ILO technical cooperation proposals is whether and how the proposals under review include a strategy to mainstream gender equality. This is proving critical in assisting the Bureau for Gender Equality and field gender specialists in implementing a growing share of gender-specific or gender-relevant technical cooperation activities. However, gender analysis and gender planning skills among ILO programming and technical staff are still limited.

420. In the context of the present development aid paradigm, which calls for country ownership and full coordination of donor assistance, the ILO, through the Turin Centre, has assisted the European Commission to place gender equality at the core of its aid delivery agenda (box 4.5).

Gender mainstreaming in social dialogue

421. Over the past 15 years, national social dialogue institutions have emerged or been consolidated in all regions as a strategy to address the challenges of labour markets in a rapidly changing environment. Strengthening social dialogue institutions is closely linked to strengthening participation and democracy, as it implies giving a voice in the decision-making process to those directly affected. In 2006, the ILO's Social Dialogue, Labour Law and Labour Administration Sector (DIALOGUE) undertook a research initiative to establish baseline data on the participation of women in social dialogue institutions. The picture is rather bleak, as shown by the low average proportion of women participating in such institutions (box 4.6). Raising the proportion of women in managerial positions, through training, quotas or

Box 4.5.
Mainstreaming gender equality in European Union development aid: A capacity-building project

The European Union (EU) is one of the largest donors in the world for development aid, and EU-funded aid represents over 50 per cent of overall development assistance. Gender equality features in the EU development agenda as both a goal and a precondition for socially sustainable development. As part of its Programme of Action for the mainstreaming of gender equality at all levels and in all sectors of EU-funded development cooperation, the European Commission (EC) asked the Turin Centre to help bridge the gap between policy and practice by reinforcing the EC's own capacity to mainstream gender equality from upstream policy dialogue with recipient countries to aid delivery and project implementation. Since January 2004, for over 36 months, the project has sought to facilitate a process of organizational change and institutional learning, focusing on three closely related areas of action:

(1) *Tools and procedures:* Development of a user-friendly and standardized set of gender mainstreaming tools, guidelines and information resources, such as a *Toolkit on mainstreaming gender equality in EU development cooperation* in four languages, and country- and sector-specific gender-related information briefs.

(2) *Sensitizing decision-makers and training operational staff on "how to" mainstream gender in their everyday work and engaging in dialogue at all levels and in all sectors of EU assistance*: 1,200 EC staff, government representatives from third countries and representatives of donor institutions, international organizations and women's NGOs were involved in 50 workshops and sensitization activities in Brussels, in 24 EU delegations in Africa, Asia, Latin America and Europe. Internet-based learning was also used to expand outreach and stimulate the exchange of ideas.

(3) *Offering tailor-made technical assistance, facilitating institutional learning, gender networking and exchange of information*: Gender Help Desk, staffed by three full-time gender specialists, provided ad hoc consultancy on specific current programmes and projects and future cooperation strategies between the EU and third countries, particularly from Africa, the Caribbean and the Pacific. A quarterly newsletter and Intranet-based information facilities are also made available.

Sources: *GENRE 2003/076514 E950135 Preliminary summary assessment of the results achieved over the period 1 January 2004–31 March 2006*, 20 April 2006, ITC/ILO, at ec.europa.eu/comm/europeaid/projects/gender/toolkit_2006; and www.itcilo.org/ec (for online learning).

Box 4.6.
Women's participation in national social dialogue institutions

Through the use of questionnaires, data were gathered from 48 bipartite, tripartite and tripartite-plus bodies – approximately half of the social dialogue institutions currently operational at the national level in the socio-economic field. Data showed that the average proportion of women participants for all regions stood at 14.68 per cent. By region, the highest share was found in Europe, with 16.76 per cent of women participants, followed by Latin America and the Caribbean (14.16 per cent), Africa (12.34 per cent) and Asia (11.21 per cent). Substantial differences arose within the regions: while Latin America showed an average of 11.46 per cent of women participants, women occupy 34.57 per cent of all seats in the social dialogue institutions in the Caribbean. By group, women made up 18.93 per cent of government representatives, 12.95 of workers and 10 per cent of employers across all regions. No women represented the social partners or the government in social dialogue institutions in Ecuador and Romania. Initiatives to promote a more balanced representation have been undertaken in Belgium, Haiti and Peru.

A review of the procedures for the appointment of representatives in all countries indicated that, while the government officially appointed the members of social dialogue bodies, responsibility for electing representatives lay solely with workers and employers' organizations and governments themselves. Strategies to improve gender balance in social dialogue institutions should therefore aim to promote women in managerial positions in the organizations of the social partners, the public administration and the government.

Data also showed that 48 per cent of the bodies had included gender in the dialogue agenda, although not in a systematic way. No link seemed to exist between placing gender on the agenda of the institution and the percentage of women participants in social dialogue bodies. The enactment of EU gender-related legislation has contributed to the fact that 64 per cent of the social dialogue bodies surveyed in the European Union have placed gender on the dialogue agenda.

Source: ILO: *Women's participation in social dialogue institutions* (forthcoming).

Box 4.7.
ILO resource materials to improve maternity protection and to promote work-life balance

Reconciling work and family responsibilities – Practical ideas from global experience: Presents concrete examples of what is being done around the world to help workers reconcile more effectively work and family responsibilities, such as caring for children and the elderly. The examples provide useful ideas for action by governments, employers' and workers' organizations and civil society organizations. Working papers assessing trends, issues, policies and programmes to reconcile work and family responsibilities in three countries, Brazil, Japan and the Republic of Korea, have recently been prepared and research is under way in a number of developing countries.

Maternity at work – A review of national legislation: is a comprehensive review of the main legal provisions in maternity protection legislation of 166 countries. The publication analyses national provisions on maternity leave (duration of leave, cash benefits, source of payment and scope); other types of leave (paternity leave, parental leave and adoption leave); provisions regarding protection from dismissal and discrimination; and health protection for pregnant and nursing workers. The Online Maternity Protection Database, which compiles information on national maternity protection legislation for 160 countries, has been recently updated. A series of eight fact sheets on work and family responsibilities were also prepared as a guide entitled *Healthy beginnings: Guidance on safe maternity at work*, containing information on the basic principles of the Maternity Protection Convention, 2000 (No. 183), and practical workplace tools for identifying risks and hazards, and improving maternity protection and health at work. *How are workers with family responsibilities faring in the workplace?* is a short publication showing concrete examples of how family responsibilities affect men's and women's ability to obtain and keep jobs.

---

measures to reconcile work and the family, would help to ensure a balanced participation of women and men in decision-making processes. But the most important element for change will probably be the full recognition of the democratic deficit implied by imbalanced participation.

422. This concern prompted DIALOGUE to focus on enhancing the ability of the social partners to comprehend and address issues of gender inequality in consultations for the preparation of PRSPs led by the World Bank and the IMF (see box 4.2 above).

Promoting maternity protection and work–life balance

423. Family responsibilities affect the ability of women and men to obtain and keep jobs and to earn a decent living, while pregnancy across the world is still a major cause of dismissal or denial of employment. As discussed earlier, the changes in working time and work organization brought about by globalization have widened inequalities in employment patterns and working conditions by gender and class and have also affected the manner in which women and men can care for their families.

424. To address these challenges, over the past few years the ILO has focused on strengthening its

knowledge base on these issues and as a result has developed a range of publications and practical information tools (box 4.7).

425. Advocacy and training were also undertaken to assist ILO constituents in the promotion and implementation of the Maternity Protection Convention, 2000 (No. 183), and the Workers with Family Responsibilities Convention, 1981 (No. 156). For instance, in 2005, training on workers with family responsibilities was provided to representatives women's networks of the ICFTU and WCL from 20 Central and Eastern European countries and Newly Independent States at the Sixth International Women's Trade Union School, held in Ohrid in The former Yugoslav Republic of Macedonia in September–October 2005. At the conclusion, the participants adopted a resolution calling on their unions and governments to create workplace conditions friendly to women workers and all workers with family responsibilities.[13]

Tackling multiple discrimination against domestic workers

426. Domestic work provides millions of jobs throughout the world, mostly for women, but also men. These workers are in high demand in all countries, regardless of their level of development. In Latin

---

13. ICFTU-WCL, Central and Eastern Europe and Newly Independent States Women's Network: "Declaration on globalization and fair transition for working families", Ohrid, 1 October 2005.

America, for example, domestic work is the main source of non-agricultural employment for women and in 2003 absorbed 15 per cent of all economically active women.[14]

427. The lack of affordable and reliable care services for children and other dependent family members, coupled with the need for both men and women to engage in paid work to make ends meet, explains why demand for domestic work services is on the rise. Demand does not decline much, even in situations of economic downturn, in view of the essential nature of the care services provided by domestic workers. Interestingly enough, in times of economic revitalization following a period of economic crisis, demand for domestic workers rises very rapidly, while earnings levels take significantly longer to recover.[15]

428. On the other hand, domestic work remains one of the few sources of income and jobs for many young and older women with little, if any, education. But domestic work is often "invisible", undervalued and unprotected. It is carried out in homes, which are not considered to be workplaces, for private persons who are not considered to be employers, and by workers who are not considered to be employees. Regarded as an extension of women's traditional unpaid domestic duties and family responsibilities, it is given little monetary value. This explains why national law usually grants this category of workers different and inferior treatment to that afforded to other employees. Moreover, very often, the applicable law is not enforced.

429. It is increasingly widely recognized that direct and indirect discrimination based on sex and age, often combined with migrant status or ethnicity, is at the root of the situation of disadvantage of domestic workers. This has prompted the ILO's offices to develop several regional and subregional initiatives targeted at these workers. While the common goal is to address discriminatory treatment against them, the rationale varies according to the regional context. In the Middle East, Asia and Africa, action in support of domestic workers has been framed within the broader concern of contributing to a better regulation of international migration for labour. The provision of advice to governments on how to ensure that recruitment practices by private employment agencies do not result in the abuse of migrant domestic workers features prominently in this part of the world. In South Asia, measures aimed at these workers form part of initiatives geared towards the elimination of the worst forms of child labour and forced labour. In Latin America, efforts have been made to address the nexus between feminization of poverty and gender inequalities in employment outcomes.

430. In all regions, however, the strategy has centred on: (a) documenting the scale of the phenomenon and the specific circumstances of domestic workers; (b) revealing and redressing their lower legal rights and entitlements; (c) encouraging dialogue on these issues between governments and employers' and workers' organizations; and (d) promoting the organization of domestic workers. In Lebanon, for instance, a National Steering Committee bringing together representatives of the Government, employers' organizations, embassy representatives and NGOs has been established to develop a national action plan to promote decent work for domestic migrant workers. The Committee has three working groups covering: legal reform (labour law in Lebanon does not cover domestic workers), producing a workers' rights booklet and developing a standardized labour contract. In Uruguay, the ILO supplied legal advice on the drafting of a law on domestic work that was submitted to Parliament with the Government's endorsement in April 2006. Efforts have also been made to develop links between domestic workers' associations, such as the Latin American and Caribbean Domestic Workers' Confederation (CONLACTRAHO) and its national associations, with regional and national trade unions, including the Inter-American Regional Organization of Workers (ORIT). A Joint Declaration was adopted in Montevideo in December 2005 asking the ILO, among other action, to adopt further standards for the protection of domestic workers.[16]

431. Though fruitful, these initiatives have tended to be small-scale and partial in scope. For example, regulating only the domestic work of minors or migrant workers, or focusing on the worst cases, excludes millions of young and older domestic workers who have often migrated from rural to urban areas in search of jobs. There is a need to develop a coherent global ILO approach and action on this subject.

14. L. Abramo; M.E. Valenzuela: "Inserción laboral y brechas de equidad de género en América Latina", in L. Abramo (ed.): *Trabajo decente y equidad de género en América Latina* (Santiago, ILO, 2006), pp. 29–62.

15. R. Cortés: "Salarios y marco regulatorio del trabajo en el servicio doméstico", Serie Documentos de Trabajo No. 9 (Buenos Aires, ILO, 2004).

16. Available at www.oitchile.cl/especial.php?id=193.

Promoting equal employment opportunities at the workplace

432. The workplace is a strategic locus for tackling discrimination in employment and creating a more diverse and equal workforce. Employers' and workers' organizations, as well as management and trade unions, are central players in this respect. The ILO has provided technical support to government-led and employer-driven initiatives aimed at developing equal employment opportunity policies at the enterprise level. Of special relevance is the ILO code of practice on HIV/AIDS in the world of work, which has generated very encouraging results. Experience shows that the content and scope of such policies are as important as the process through which they are produced: the broader the consultations, the greater the likelihood that such policies will eventually be endorsed.

433. In Indonesia, for instance, the Department of Manpower and Transmigration, through a consultative process with the trade unions and employers' organizations, and with the technical assistance of the ILO, between 2003 and 2005 developed a set of Guidelines on Equal Employment Opportunity (EEO) for the private sector.[17] While initially the tripartite task force established by the Department focused on gender discrimination, as women are the largest group vulnerable to discrimination and disadvantage, it eventually addressed broader concerns, such as unlawful practices based on race, ethnicity and disability. The EEO Guidelines are intended to provide direction to companies on how to give effect to the relevant national legislation. They explain the meaning of EEO and the benefits stemming from it for enterprises. They describe the conditions necessary for the success of EEO programmes, while outlining practices, from recruitment and placement to wages and working conditions, that translate into greater equality at the workplace. The three partners adopted the Guidelines in late 2005 and have since engaged in their dissemination.

434. In Chile, the ILO provided technical support for the development of the Code of good labour practices on non-discrimination for the State Central Administration, adopted by a Presidential Instruction of 15 June 2006. The Code is compulsory in the public sector, and private enterprises are encouraged to implement it on a voluntary basis. The Code is intended to strengthen the principles of non-discrimination, equal opportunities and treatment, while helping men and women to reconcile work and family responsibilities, taking into account constantly evolving societal and family patterns. It covers all aspects of the employment relationship from recruitment to working conditions. The Code insists on transparent advancement and promotion processes based on merit, as well as equal access to training and qualifications. Appropriate measures are encouraged to allow persons with disabilities to compete on an equal footing with other candidates. Better access of women to responsibility and managerial posts is strongly encouraged. The Code also recalls the importance of maternity protection and the need for specific measures to accommodate pregnant women and breast-feeding. Equally notable are the recognition of paternity rights and measures to reconcile work and family responsibilities, such as flexible working schedules and the attention paid to the prevention of harassment at work, especially sexual harassment, in accordance with Act No. 20,005 of March 2005 (Part III, Chapter 1, section on discrimination and law reforms). The National Directorate of the Public Service is to prepare a plan of good practices and every service or department will have to report annually on the measures taken to implement it.

435. In Sri Lanka, the Employers' Federation of Ceylon (EFC) and the ILO undertook a joint research study in 2003 to assess the relative situation of women workers and managers in the workplace, identify barriers to women's career progression and come up with a set of possible remedial measures. The study was based on a survey of 100 private companies in various sectors, including the plantation and garment sectors.[18] It revealed widespread scepticism among managers about the necessity for an equal opportunities policy in their organizations. Most felt that such a policy would be discriminatory and would be relevant only in workplaces where large numbers of women were employed, such as factories. A workshop was organized to discuss the findings and recommendations of the study and this led, eventually, to the formulation and adoption in 2005 of the *Guidelines for company policy on gender equity/equality*. These seek to make workplaces more aware of and responsive to the distinct needs and constraints of men and women by providing suggestions on how to change work organization, workplace structures, human resources policy, the mental attitudes of managers and how to monitor the change process. Table 4.2 provides a checklist of issues on which management should focus when developing a gender policy.

---

17. Ministry of Manpower and Transmigration: Guidelines: *Equal employment opportunity in Indonesia* (Jakarta, ILO, 2005), at www.ilo.org/public/english/region/asro/jakarta/download/eeoguidelines.pdf.
18. M. Wickramasinghe; W. Jayatilaka: *Beyond glass ceilings and brick walls: Gender at the workplace* (Colombo, ILO, 2005).

Table 4.2. Checklist of gender issues

Advertising campaigns	Lighting	Rest rooms
Allowances and bonuses	Maternity space	Restructuring
Career mobility/advancement	Medical and health care	Retirement
Communication facilities	Meetings	Segregation
Compensation	Night work	Sexual harassment
Day care	Nursing time	Staff development
Decision-making	Language usage	Supervision
Dress code	Office layout and design	Termination
Exit interviews	Office memos	Training and scholarships
Functions and ceremonies	Office romances	Transfers
Furnishing	Organizational philosophy	Transport
Gender stereotyping	Parenting and family responsibilities	Transport facilities
Grievance redress	Productivity motivation	Use of equipment and reagents
Harassment	Promotion	Vacations
Health and safety	Recreation	Vision
Image	Recruitment	Work time
Instructing	Redundancies	Work environment
Insurance	Remuneration	Working from home
Leave		

Source: ILO and Employers' Federation of Ceylon: *Guidelines for company policy on gender equity/equality* (Colombo, ILO, 2005).

436. To respond to the growing demand for technical assistance in this field, the Bureau for Employers' Activities, in close collaboration with the Conditions of Work and Employment Programme (TRAVAIL), the International Labour Standards Department (NORMES) and the Skills and Employability Department (EMP/SKILLS), has developed a training package for employers' organizations on key gender equality and diversity issues, such as work–family balance, sexual harassment, maternity protection, disability and ageing. For each theme, the package includes information sheets, activity sheets for use in training courses, practical action sheets, case studies, examples of good practice and notes for trainers.

437. *Better Factories Cambodia*, a unique ILO programme, is an example of how tripartism, together with an integrated strategy promoted initially through ILO technical cooperation, has the potential to improve the governance of private self-regulation and of global production systems.[19] *Better Factories Cambodia* was established in 2001 and combines monitoring, remediation and training in a virtuous cycle of improvement. It benefits workers, employers and their organizations, as well as consumers in Western countries, and helps reduce poverty in one of the poorest nations of the world. It does this by monitoring and reporting on working conditions in Cambodian garment factories, based on core international labour standards and national law, by helping factories to improve working conditions and productivity through workplace cooperation on remediation and training, and by working with the Government, national producers and international buyers to ensure a rigorous, transparent and continuous cycle of improvement (box 4.8).

438. The programme has contributed to enhanced compliance with labour law, an increase in exports and the growth of relatively well paid jobs in the garment industry. International garment buyers have indicated a strong desire to continue or to increase the sourcing of their products from Cambodia, as they perceive that labour standards in this industry meet their international requirements.[20]

19. S. Polaski: *Cambodia blazes a new path to economic growth and job creation*, Carnegie Paper No. 51 (Carnegie Endowment for International Peace, October 2004), at www.CarnegieEndowment.org/publications.
20. Foreign Investment Advisory Service: *Cambodia: Corporate social responsibility and the apparel sector buyer survey results* (Washington, DC, World Bank Group, Dec. 2004).

> **Box 4.8.**
> **Monitoring discriminatory practices through *Better Factories Cambodia***
>
> On issues of discrimination, a recent *Better Factories Cambodia* report indicates that 11 per cent of the factories monitored between 1 May and 31 October 2006 engaged in discriminatory practices. These practices typically take the form of the dismissal of pregnant workers and changes in the seniority of working mothers after they return from maternity leave. The experience of *Better Factories Cambodia* shows that men also suffer from discrimination during hiring. The report further indicates that problems with anti-union discrimination were found in 6 per cent of the factories monitored.
>
> To further explore gender and workplace issues that are difficult to monitor and cross check key monitoring results, *Better Factories Cambodia* commissioned CARE International in Cambodia to conduct a survey of 1,000 garment factory workers and 80 human resources and administrative managers (the Gender Survey). Preliminary results from the Gender Survey suggest that verbal and sexual harassment, including rape on the way to and from the factory, may be more common than the monitoring process had indicated, possibly due to differing interpretations of the term "sexual harassment". The results of the study were shared with trade union and employer representatives, international organizations, NGOs and the Government with a view to developing extensive recommendations to address these and other issues.
>
> Source: *Better Factories Cambodia*, ILO: *Seventeenth synthesis report on working conditions in Cambodia's garment sector*, at www.betterfactories.org/ilo.

Implementation of the ILO code of practice on HIV/AIDS and the world of work

439. The right not to suffer discrimination on the grounds of real or perceived HIV/AIDS status is one of the cornerstones of the ILO policy in this field. The Declaration of Commitment on HIV/AIDS by the United Nations General Assembly Special Session (UNGASS) in June 2001 set the target of developing national legal and policy frameworks by 2003 that protect the rights and dignity of persons living with HIV/AIDS or at high risk of HIV/AIDS in the workplace. The Declaration called for relevant international guidelines to be taken into account in achieving this objective. Five years later, UNGASS reaffirmed this commitment in its Political Declaration on HIV/AIDS of June 2006, thereby re-emphasizing the relevance of the ILO code of practice on HIV/AIDS and the world of work (box 4.9).[21] The code is being used to provide practical guidance in around 40 countries[22] and as a reference tool by policy-makers and the social partners in over 60 countries.

440. ILO technical cooperation activities have been a major vehicle for disseminating the code and assisting the social partners to give practical effect to it. An effective workplace plan requires six elements: a sound policy; an HIV/AIDS workplace committee with a fully representative membership, adequate strategy, work plan and resources; a behaviour change programme; a network of focal points and peer educators; access to confidential testing and treatment; and an effective performance monitoring plan.

441. Strategic HIV/AIDS Responses by Enterprises (SHARE), an ILO programme that that has reached out to 300,000 formal and informal workers in 23 countries, has been instrumental in fostering the implementation of the code and the adoption of enabling legislative frameworks.[23] Since its inception in 2000, SHARE has trained over 2,500 people, including employers and workers, government officials, labour inspectors, labour judges and NGO representatives. Toolkits for the workplace have also been produced, showing how to avoid language that perpetuates stigma and discrimination and other discriminatory practices.[24]

---

21. See also the related education and training manual: *Implementing the ILO code of practice on HIV/AIDS and the world of work*, at www.ilo.org/public/english/protection/trav/aids/publ/manual.htm.

22. To date: Argentina, Azerbaijan, Bahamas, Barbados, Benin, Botswana, Brazil, Cameroon, Chile, China, Côte d'Ivoire, Ethiopia, Ghana, India, Japan, Kenya, Kyrgyzstan, Malawi, Malaysia, Mauritius, Mexico, Mozambique, Namibia, Netherlands, Philippines, Russian Federation, Senegal, Seychelles, Saint Lucia, South Africa, Sri Lanka, Swaziland, Thailand, Timor-Leste, Togo, Trinidad and Tobago, Uganda, Uzbekistan, Zambia; as well as the Southern African Development Community (SADC) and the United Kingdom's Foreign Service.

23. See ILO: *Saving lives, protecting jobs*, International HIV/AIDS Workplace Education Programme, SHARE: Strategic HIV/AIDS Responses by Enterprises, Interim Report (Geneva, 2006).

24. See the ILO-FHI *HIV/AIDS behaviour change communication toolkit for the workplace*, at www.ilo.org/public/english/protection/trav/aids/publ/bcctoolkit.htm.

> **Box 4.9.**
> **The ILO code of practice on HIV/AIDS and the world of work**
>
> "In the spirit of decent work and respect for the human rights and dignity of persons infected or affected by HIV/AIDS, there should be no discrimination against workers on the basis of real or perceived HIV status. Discrimination and stigmatization of people living with HIV/AIDS inhibit efforts aimed at promoting HIV/AIDS prevention" (paragraph 4.2).
>
> "HIV infection is not a cause for termination of employment" (paragraph 4.8) or for being deprived of social benefits (paragraph 4.10).
>
> Employers should not allow personnel policies or practices that discriminate against workers infected with or affected by HIV/AIDS; they should not require HIV/AIDS screening or testing for job applicants or employees (paragraph 4.6) and the confidentiality of personal data should be ensured (paragraph 4.7).
>
> Employers should also encourage persons with HIV to work as long as medically possible. Employers should have procedures that can be used against any employee who discriminates on the grounds of real or perceived HIV status or who violates the workplace policy on HIV/AIDS. Employers should take measures to reasonably accommodate workers with AIDS-related illness, including the rearrangement of working time, special equipment, opportunities for rest breaks, time off for medical appointments, flexible sick-leave, part-time work and return-to-work arrangements (paragraph 5.2).

442. A sectoral approach has also proven effective in addressing discrimination based on HIV/AIDS status. In sub-Saharan African countries, the ILO has contributed to national and regional efforts aimed at HIV/AIDS prevention in the transport sector, where workers are particularly at risk of contracting the disease. The ILO's main input has consisted of assisting in the harmonization of regional transport and border-crossing regulations, in line with the ILO's *Guidelines for the transport sector.*[25]

Enhancing the employability of people with disabilities

443. With a view to enhancing the employability of people with disabilities, the ILO has centred its action on three areas: knowledge development on disability issues in the field of training and employment, including the integration of disabled trainees into general vocational training programmes; advocacy and policy advice to governments and the social partners; and the provision of support services through technical cooperation activities. The action carried out has included projects to enhance the skills of workers with disabilities, such as the projects on developing entrepreneurship among women with disabilities in Ethiopia and those on skills development and work for youth with disabilities in Africa and Asia.

444. The ILO's disability programme AbilityAP, operating in Asia and the Pacific, has recently created the most comprehensive database on laws and policies pertaining to people with disabilities in the region to meet recurring requests from constituents for information about what other countries are doing to promote their rights and welfare.[26] The ILO is working with the United Nations Economic and Social Commission for Asia and the Pacific (UNESCAP), the Asia Pacific Development Center on Disability, the Global Applied Disability Research and Information Network on Employment and Training (GLADNET) and the World Bank to further develop this database. This joint initiative is particularly timely as more requests for assistance are expected in view of the proposed United Nations Convention on the Rights of Persons with Disabilities.

445. Based on the ILO code of practice on managing disability at the workplace, AbilityAP has also provided advice to employers' organizations, individual companies and multinational organizations on how to develop policies and programmes that accommodate the employment needs of disabled persons, while meeting the demands and expectations of employers. These efforts include the holding of a joint ILO/ESCAP meeting in 2005 bringing together multinational corporations, governments, NGOs and representatives of persons with disabilities to start a stakeholder dialogue on the business case for hiring

---

25. See ILO: *Using the ILO code of practice on HIV/AIDS and the world of work: Guidelines for the transport sector* (Geneva, 2005).
26. The bulk of the data concern countries in Asia and the Pacific, but data for countries outside the region are also available. See www.ilo.org/public/english/region/asro/bangkok/ability/laws.htm.

> ## Box 4.10.
> ## ILO Multilateral Framework on Labour Migration: Non-discrimination provisions
>
> Governments should adopt and enforce policies and legislation that "eliminate all forms of discrimination in employment and occupation" (paragraph 8.4.4).
>
> Migrant workers should benefit from remedies for violation of their rights and be given the opportunity to "lodge complaints and seek remedy without discrimination, intimidation or retaliation" (paragraph 10.5).
>
> Governments and social partners should "promote social integration and inclusion, while respecting cultural diversity, preventing discrimination against migrant workers and taking measures to combat racism and xenophobia" (paragraph 14).
>
> There is a need for "promoting and implementing anti-discrimination legislation and policies, establishing or strengthening specialized bodies on equality and non-discrimination for migrant workers and conducting periodic gender-sensitive data collection and analysis on these issues" (paragraph 14.1), and the relevant recommendations in the Programme of Action adopted in 2001 in Durban by the World Conference Against Racism, Racial Discrimination, Xenophobia and Related Intolerance should be taken into account (paragraph 14.2).

workers with disabilities. The following year similar roundtables were organized in China, Hong Kong (China) and Viet Nam, and several multinational enterprises have reported initiatives to improve their records in recruiting people with disabilities.[27]

Towards a fairer deal for migrant workers

446.   The Office's report for the general discussion on migrant workers held during the 92nd Session of the International Labour Conference in June 2004 highlighted issues of discrimination and xenophobia in the workplace.[28] Migrant workers are frequently subject to unequal treatment and unequal job opportunities, while temporary (and undocumented) migrant workers are often excluded from wage protection and social security. The Conference decided on a plan of action for migrant workers, including the development of a non-binding multilateral framework for a rights-based approach to labour migration.

ILO Multilateral Framework on Labour Migration

447.   A Tripartite Meeting of Experts held in Geneva on 31 October–2 November 2005 adopted the "ILO Multilateral Framework on Labour Migration: Non-binding principles and guidelines for a rights-based

approach to labour migration", which was endorsed by the Governing Body in March 2006 (box 4.10). The Framework places special emphasis on the multiple disadvantages and discrimination often faced by migrant workers on the basis of gender, race and migrant status and insists on the fact that "the human rights of all migrant workers, regardless of their status, should be promoted and protected". In particular, they should "benefit from the principles and rights in the 1998 ILO Declaration on Fundamental Principles and Rights at Work and its Follow-up" (chapter V, paragraph 8).[29]

448.   The ILO also contributed, in cooperation with the OSCE and the IOM, to the *Handbook on establishing effective labour migration policies in countries of origin and destination*.[30] In the field of technical cooperation, the ILO project DOMWORK in Indonesia and the Philippines has assisted those countries in addressing the issue of domestic work and developing a better position to negotiate with other countries to improve protection of their own migrant domestic workers.[31]

Carrying out discrimination testing surveys

449.   The ILO has continued to carry out discrimination testing projects in several European countries to capture and show the extent of discrimination against migrant workers in access to employment on the basis

---

27. See www.ilo.org/public/english/region/asro/bangkok/ability/.
28. ILO: *Towards a fair deal for migrant workers in the global economy*, Report VI, International Labour Conference, 92nd Session, Geneva, 2004.
29. Available at www.ilo.org/public/english/protection/migrant/new/index.htm.
30. At www.osce.org/item/19187.html.
31. See R. R. Casco: "Lighting a torch for empowerment: 'We matter' say Filipino domestic workers", in *World of Work*, No. 58, Dec. 2006.

Box 4.11.
Documenting good practices in fighting racial discrimination

The Colruyt Group in Belgium has developed a "Diversity in practice" approach as an integral part of its personnel policy, including an important non-discrimination policy based on "zero tolerance" regarding racism and discrimination. No distinction is allowed based on religion, sex, colour or age in recruitment and selection. Vocational training and languages courses are organized for the human resources staff and in cooperation with Turkish and Moroccan federations.

With European Union support and in the context of the Decade of Roma Inclusion 2005–15, the Bulgarian Ministry of Labour and Social Policy is currently implementing a project to foster the employment of Roma workers, which includes the provision of training courses in professions that mainly require specific production skills and a low level of literacy. It is expected that 1,000 people from minorities will be provided with business training and consultancies for business start-up and that 2,000 long-term unemployed from minority groups will benefit from vocational training in marketable craft and agricultural skills to help them find jobs or become self-employed.

At the initiative of the social partners, codes of conduct against racial discrimination, sexual harassment and all forms of discrimination have been integrated into general labour agreements in the Netherlands. They are non-voluntary agreements: organizations have to develop such a code, but they are free to adjust it to their own needs. Codes have been adopted in the corporate and non-profit world. In 2001, the Government of the Netherlands also issued a model code of conduct to be developed by all departments.

Source: www.wisdom.at/ilo/index.aspx.

---

of name. Studies were conducted in Italy in 2004,[32] where they concentrated on Moroccan jobseekers, and in France and Sweden, in 2005–06, where the focus was on young second-generation migrant job applicants (aged 20–25). Previous testing studies carried out by the ILO have had a significant impact in the countries concerned: for example, the study carried out earlier in Belgium was used to improve the content of the legislation adopted in 2003 by the Belgian Parliament with a view to implementing the EU Directive on racial equality (Council Directive 2000/43/EC of 29 June 2000 implementing the principle of equal treatment between persons irrespective of racial or ethnic origin). Moreover, both private and public employers in Flanders have been encouraged to develop positive action plans and anti-discrimination activities. In the Brussels region, awareness-raising campaigns have been conducted and employees in the regional employment office benefited from training courses on non-discrimination. Jobseekers now have the opportunity to lodge a complaint if they encounter discriminatory practices.[33]

Documenting good practices in promoting the integration of migrant workers

450. Another area of action has been the expansion and consolidation of an ILO European database, which contains around 150 profiles of good practices (box 4.11). Through the programme "Promoting equality in diversity: Integration in Europe", supported by the EU, further studies have been conducted on relevant national experiences, good practices have been identified and disseminated and a methodology and tools have been developed to assess the effectiveness of workplace anti-discrimination practices.

451. In 2004, the ILO, with EU support, launched in East, North and West Africa a programme entitled "Labour Migration for Integration and Development in Africa" to strengthen the capacities of governments and the social partners to manage labour migration, while promoting labour standards through social dialogue. An ILO/UNIFEM/ EC project "Asian Programme on the Governance of Labour Migration", begun in 2006 is pursuing similar objectives.

---

32. E. Allasino; E. Reyneri; A. Venturini; G. Zincone: *Labour market discrimination against migrant workers in Italy*, ILO International Migration Papers, No. 67, 2004, at www.ilo.org/public/english/protection/migrant.
33. Act of 20 January 2003 to strengthen legislation against racism.

Box 4.12.
Gender equality as part of regional agendas for decent work in Asia and the Americas

The tripartite constituents concluded the 14th Asian Regional Meeting by launching an Asian Decent Work Decade, with the commitment to "the achievement of specific decent work outcomes in accordance with their respective national circumstances and priorities, and to cooperate on specific initiatives at the regional level where joint action and sharing of knowledge and expertise will contribute to making decent work a reality by 2015". The conclusions of the Meeting emphasized the importance of "promoting gender equality by, inter alia, empowering women by promoting equality of opportunity to decent and productive work" and also of giving special attention to the needs of vulnerable groups of workers, a large proportion of whom are women and girls.

To implement the Asian Decent Work Decade, the DWCPs have to identify gender-sensitive strategies to contribute to the achievement of decent work outcomes. Templates that have been developed for regular monitoring and reporting on progress in the DWCPs include a section on how gender concerns are being mainstreamed. A number of initiatives have also been proposed to promote gender equality at the regional level during the Decade, including maternity protection, equal pay for work of equal value and the improvement of the rights and protection of female migrant workers, in particular domestic workers.

In the Americas, the Agenda for the Hemisphere (2006–15) adopted by the Ministers of Labour in Brasilia in May 2006 sets a number of objectives, targets and timelines, as well as the corresponding strategies and policies, to make decent work a reality in the region. Echoing the Heads of State of the Americas in Mar del Plata in November 2005, they declared that the promotion of decent work is key to strengthening democracy, curbing poverty and reducing inequalities and social exclusion. Respect for and the achievement of fundamental principles and rights at work, including non-discrimination and equality, is central to this agenda, as is the promotion of gender equality. In particular, the Ministers undertook to increase the female labour participation rate by 10 per cent and to raise female employment rates proportionately, and to reduce by half the gender gap in labour earnings and the incidence of informality over the next ten years. To this end, action will focus, inter alia, on promoting equal pay policies, such as the development and promotion of job evaluation methods free from gender bias and the inclusion of relevant clauses in collective agreements; promoting active labour market policies that combat occupational segregation by sex, with attention to female youth; and improving the situation of domestic workers.

Source: GB.297/5, op.cit.

Decent Work Country Programmes and Poverty Reduction Strategies

452. The ILO's programming in the field is increasingly focused on Decent Work Country Programmes (DWCPs), which form the ILO's distinct contribution to the United Nations Development Assistance Framework (UNDAF) and other national development frameworks. To ensure that non-discrimination and equality issues are effectively addressed at the national level, it is essential that DWCPs fully reflect these concerns. This can represent a challenge, as ILO constituents often tend to seek ILO assistance more readily in addressing, for example, employment creation or social protection, rather than the more controversial and challenging issues of fundamental rights at work. This underlines the need for a process of dialogue and progressive action over time, both within the ILO (between headquarters and the field) and with constituents, so as to build consensus on how best to address persistent and entrenched problems of discrimination.

453. The ILO's experience in trying to enhance the participation of its constituents in PRSP processes, while helping to develop a coherent approach linking poverty reduction with the Decent Work Agenda, provides certain insights in this regard. In some countries, special efforts were made to ensure that constituents were aware of and addressed the specific circumstances of low-income women and people with disabilities, who experience poverty in distinct ways and are vulnerable to discrimination.[34] These countries include Ghana, where the focus was on the inclusion of people with disabilities in the labour market; the United Republic of Tanzania, where a baseline analysis was developed on the interlinkages between gender, poverty and employment; and Indonesia, where gender equality issues were raised through policy briefs. In overall terms, however, issues of non-discrimination and equality, with the

---

34. ILO: *Decent Work and Poverty Reduction Strategies: A reference manual for ILO staff and constituents* (Geneva, ILO, 2005).

exception of gender equality, have been dealt with in a rather uneven and limited manner. Training materials have been developed for representatives of ministries of labour and the social partners,[35] and training sessions were conducted to show the added value of a gender perspective when examining the causes and processes of poverty and in seeking remedial action through decent work.

454. Recent developments provide grounds for hope. The representatives of governments and employers' and workers' organizations gathered in Brasilia in May 2006 for the Sixteenth American Regional Meeting to launch a Decade for Promoting Decent Work in the Americas.[36] A few months later, the Fourteenth Asian Regional Meeting (Busan, August/September 2006) declared an Asian Decent Work Decade up to 2015.[37] In both regions, specific commitments and targets have been set to curb the decent work gaps between mainstream groups and groups vulnerable to discrimination (box 4.12).

35. ILO: *Social dialogue and poverty reduction strategies: A guide to the integration of gender equality*, InFocus Programme on Social Dialogue, Labour Law and Labour Administration (Geneva, 2004). See www.ilo.org/public/english/dialogue/ifpdial/downloads/papers/gender.pdf.

36. See ILO: *Report and conclusions of the Sixteenth American Regional Meeting (Brasilia, 2–5 May 2006)*, Governing Body document GB.297/5 (Nov. 2006).

37. See ILO: *Report and conclusions of the Fourteenth Asian Regional Meeting (Busan, 29 August–1 September 2006)*, Governing Body document GB.297/6 (Nov. 2006).

2. The next steps

455. The first Global Report on discrimination in employment and occupation emphasized the need to build on and consolidate existing activities, such as the ILO's work to combat discrimination based on disability, actual or perceived HIV/AIDS status or migrant status, and to strengthen ILO action in areas where it identified particularly important needs and gaps. These included the achievement of pay equity and addressing more effectively the link between poverty and systemic discrimination stemming from the intersection of race or ethnic origin and gender. It also argued that, as discrimination at work permeates the functioning and structure of labour markets, labour market institutions and ILO constituents, any action plan geared towards its elimination had to be aligned with the strategic objectives of the Organization and the promotion of decent work. It also highlighted the need to strengthen knowledge, advocacy and services pertaining to the elimination of discrimination and the promotion of equality in the workplace.

456. The recommendations of this second Global Report for follow-up action in the next four years echo those of the first Report, although they are more focused as they draw upon the experience gained in the process and take into account the orientations of the ILO's strategic planning and operations. These include, in particular, the introduction of DWCPs as the main framework for ILO work at the country level, supplemented by research and services at the regional and global levels.[38] This means that, at the national level, the forms of discrimination warranting priority attention and the policy areas for action have to be determined on a case-by-case basis bearing in mind both the needs and demands of the ILO's constituents and, whenever relevant, the comments of the standards supervisory bodies. In all cases, gender equality is to be pursued with determination as an ILO strategic goal. A number of outcomes to be attained over the next four years, and a set of activities to achieve them, are outlined below.

Promoting gender equality in the world of work

457. A review of the ILO's work over the past four years in the field of non-discrimination and equality shows that, as in the past, gender equality remains a prominent concern. Nonetheless, the approach adopted to pursue gender equality has been changing gradually. There is a discernable trend towards the mainstreaming of a gender perspective into the ILO's means of action, and more specifically into ILO technical cooperation activities and policy areas, such as employment policy, social dialogue and poverty reduction processes. Although the scope, depth and impact of gender mainstreaming in these different fields vary considerably, this trend proves that the commitment made to gender equality at the highest level in both programmatic and policy terms has started to bear some tangible results.

458. However, this has not been matched by sufficiently vigorous action to narrow gender deficits in relation to a number of crucial labour market indicators, such as employment rates, the incidence of informal work, labour earnings and the division of paid and unpaid work between women and men. This, in turn, increases the risk of diluting the impact of gender mainstreaming, which is based on a combination of efforts aimed at introducing a gender perspective into all ILO programmes and projects together with gender specific measures aimed at advancing equality between men and women.

459. There is therefore a need for more integrated, better coordinated and more focused ILO global action geared towards the reduction of these inequalities. The need to balance work and family demands reduces women's options as to whether to work, where and in what kind of jobs, thereby undermining their work experience, training, seniority and career prospects. This contributes to keeping their earnings down. Moreover, even when women with family responsibilities manage to remain and advance in the labour market and occupy high-status jobs, they continue to earn less than their male peers. This shows that the promotion of gender equality in the world of work requires a set of short- and long-term policies that understand and address these interlinkages.

460. In line with the resolution concerning the promotion of gender equality, pay equity and maternity

---

38. ILO: *The Director-General's Programme and Budget proposals for the biennium 2006–07*, Governing Body document GB.292/PFA/8 (Rev.) (Mar. 2005).

protection, adopted by the International Labour Conference in 2004, the follow-up action plan will collect and make available information and good practices in the areas of gender discrimination in the labour market, the promotion of women's entrepreneurship, recruitment and job evaluation procedures, pay differences based on gender and reconciling work and family life. Together with the observations of the supervisory bodies concerning ratified Conventions relating to gender equality, this information will be used to organize a series of tripartite and bipartite dialogues to identify measures for the advancement of gender equality. This global action will be designed in the light of the goals and requirements of the ILO's four key gender equality Conventions with a view to improving their application and promoting their ratification.

Mainstreaming non-discrimination and equality in Decent Work Country Programmes

461. The commitment to decent work and employment generation is firmly established in national and international policies, as well as in the global development agenda, as reflected for instance in the Ministerial Declaration adopted by the ECOSOC High-level Segment in 2006. This Declaration emphasizes the importance of mainstreaming the goals of full and productive employment and decent work in the policies, programmes and activities of United Nations agencies, funds and programmes, and of financial institutions.

462. The elimination of discrimination is at the heart of decent work for all women and men, which "is founded on the notion of equal opportunities for all those who work or seek work and a living, whether as labourers, employers or self-employed, in the formal or the informal economy".[39] Hence mainstreaming non-discrimination and equality in Decent Work Country Programmes (DWCP) is instrumental in ensuring that they achieve their intended goals.

463. Placing the promotion of decent work firmly on the agendas of the UN system and of financial institutions lays the ground for integrated and coherent international and national action against discrimination within and beyond the workplace. While discrimination at the workplace can be tackled more readily and effectively, its elimination depends on consistent and parallel action that is also geared to eradicating it in the household, at school and in the community. The International Dialogue on

Advancing Equity and Racial Inclusion, convened jointly by the ILO, the Inter-American Development Bank (IDB), UNDP Brazil and DFID Brazil (Brasilia, April 2005) offers an example of an inter-agency, integrated development approach for racial equality, which combines equal access to education, health and housing with equal treatment and opportunities in the world of work (see section on fighting racism and poverty in Part IV, Chapter 1 of this Part). Increased awareness of the importance of action in the world of work in achieving progress on non-discrimination and equality issues will also contribute to catalyzing system-wide action in support of the Decent Work Agenda at the country and global levels.

464. This report has shown that there is a close correlation between being poor and being vulnerable to discrimination, and between being subject to multiple and persistent forms of discrimination at work and being vulnerable to forced labour or child labour. For the effective integration of a non-discrimination and equality perspective into the DWCPs and the broader Decent Work Agenda, a number of conditions have to be met.

465. First, all the components and related activities of DWCPs need to take into account the specific needs and circumstances of different groups based on their gender, race, religion and abilities so that all can benefit equally from emerging opportunities. This requires the ILO and its constituents to be able to plan, implement, monitor and assess DWCPs in a way that leads to more equal outcomes. Such an approach involves the ILO's tripartite constituency working with equality commissions and other specialized bodies, as well as associations representing the interests of groups that are vulnerable to discrimination. Interacting with a range of institutions will strengthen the ILO's capacity to catalyse system-wide action in pursuit of decent work for everyone.

466. Second, an enabling set of laws and institutions, enforcement mechanisms and public policies must be in place and properly resourced to bring about equality at work. Such an enabling framework pertains to the functioning of labour markets, as well as working conditions and broader social protection issues. It should also encompass macroeconomic policies, trade and fiscal policies, so that adequate safeguards can be included against any potentially discriminatory impact of these policies on particular groups. In this regard, inter-agency cooperation between UN agencies is of critical importance.

467. Workplace initiatives driven by employers' and workers' organizations individually or together

---

39. ILO: *Time for equality at work*, op. cit., p. 1.

are essential. At the same time, while a sound regulatory framework, backed up by a well-qualified and resourced labour inspectorate, is an essential step in eliminating discrimination, non-regulatory initiatives can complement and enhance the impact of both national and international laws.

Better laws and better enforcement

468. This review has shown that the prohibition of discrimination by law is an essential step in its elimination, and that regulatory frameworks must be coherent and comprehensive. Despite the significant legal advances over recent years in many countries around the world, problems persist in respect of both the content and scope of laws aimed at combating discrimination in employment and occupation, as well as their application. The problem of the application of the laws that seek to give effect to the principle of equal remuneration for work of equal value is a case in point. Depending on the ground involved, laws may provide partial protection against discrimination, as they may cover only certain aspects of the employment relationship. Or laws may provide for differential and inferior treatment to particular categories of workers, especially where certain vulnerable groups are disproportionately represented. The ILO therefore needs to produce and disseminate a set of user-friendly multi-media materials, including guides or briefs on the legal requirements of Conventions Nos. 100 and 111 and other relevant Conventions, providing concrete examples of how different countries have given effect to these provisions in national law and practice, and responding to the most common questions and concerns on particular aspects of such labour standards. Dissemination will involve not only the identification of non-conventional distribution channels, but also the establishment of closer ties with other international agencies within the UN system, the regional development banks and the EU.

469. Even after putting in place the right sets of laws, their enforcement is often problematic. As shown in this review, labour inspectors have an important role to play in giving practical effect to anti-discrimination legal provisions. Strong and effective labour inspection systems and sound labour administration and labour relations based on modern labour laws are essential for the good governance of labour markets. Documenting good practices, producing checklists or guidelines on how to trace and prevent discrimination in employment, including through broad prevention campaigns, and providing capacity building for labour inspectors to enhance the enforcement of anti-

discrimination law are all important components of the follow-up action plan. Broader national and international networking needs to be encouraged with a view to improving the professional competence and experience of labour inspectors.

More effective non-regulatory initiatives

470. This Global Report has shown that businesses may also be persuaded to modify their human resource management practices and policies with a view to achieving greater diversity in their workforces through a number of non-regulatory measures. These may range from government purchasing policies and practices to lending and investment policies by international or national banks, trade policies that affect firms through market access at the country and regional levels or voluntary private initiatives (CSR) that motivate firms through peer pressure and learning. Such initiatives, such as voluntary codes of conduct for subcontractors, regularly refer to fundamental principles and rights at work, including non-discrimination.

471. Understanding what needs to be changed and how, and identifying the most cost-effective means of doing so is of utmost importance. Learning from the experiences of other enterprises and countries is also equally useful. The follow-up action plan for 2004–08 envisages documenting promising practices, producing checklists and policy briefs and developing knowledge-sharing forums at the national or regional levels, with a sectoral or cross-sectoral focus on a range of issues. The main goal of these initiatives is to identify the conditions under which and ways in which public procurement policies, lending policies or CSR initiatives can best contribute to the achievement of non-discrimination and equality goals.

Social partners better equipped to make equality a reality at the workplace

472. The social partners, as shown by this review, are key actors in the elimination of discrimination and the promotion of equality at work. They can contribute to the achievement of this goal by removing discriminatory practices within their own structures and in the type of services that they supply to their members. Collective bargaining is a crucial means through which workers' and employers' organizations can bring about concrete changes in the living and working conditions and prospects of workers who are vulnerable to discrimination. While a wealth of information exists on anti-discrimination and equality clauses that have been incorporated in collective agreements in industrialized countries, very little is known about such clauses in developing countries and transition economies. This knowledge gap must be filled so as to be able to determine the best course of action to ensure that collective bargaining pays greater attention to discrimination issues in these countries. This is of special relevance in view of the interlinkages between equality and productivity, on the one hand, and equality and freedom of association, on the other. In cooperation with the institutions concerned, it is proposed to carry out an audit of collective agreements in a number of countries per region.

473. Employers' and workers' organizations can also develop workplace initiatives individually or through tripartite cooperation. The follow-up action plan will compile information on these experiences, includes their scope, content and impact by sector and by beneficiary group, and will develop model codes of conduct or guidelines to promote equal treatment and opportunities for all. Capacity building could also be provided in selected countries in which initiatives of this type have been launched and need to be consolidated.

474. Through their involvement in the formulation of employment and social policies, the social partners can help find ways of levelling the playing field so that everyone, regardless of sex, race or disability, among other grounds, enjoys equality of opportunity to succeed in the workplace. To this end, the social partners have to be aware of the differential impact of employment and social policies on the various social groups, so that they can identify ways of minimizing their adverse impact on particular groups and ensure a more equitable distribution of opportunities. The ILO's work in enhancing the ability of the social partners to comprehend and address issues of gender inequality in the framework of nation-wide consultations for the preparation of PRSPs is a good example of such an approach.

475. Over the next four-year cycle, similar work should be carried out in relation to gender equality and equality in other areas, such as racial or ethnic equality. The work should build on and customize the tools developed up to now and referred to in this Report. The identification of the forms of inequalities to be addressed will depend to a large extent on specific national circumstances.

476. "Discrimination in the world of work not only constitutes an abuse of fundamental principles and rights at work, but is of huge cost to society (…) . If no remedial action is taken, disadvantages tend to accumulate and intensify over time, with negative repercussions on life after work – and on society more generally".[40] Together, nationally and internationally, with political will and technical know-how, the ILO and its constituents can make equality a reality.

---

40. ILO: *Changing patterns in the world of work* (Geneva, 2006), pp. 31–33.

Appendix

Methodological note

In compiling the tables and figures in Part II, priority was given to as many countries or areas with complete information for the period 1995–2004 as possible; when data on every year between 1995 and 2004 were not available, information on the closest year was used. Thus, the data for 1995 (or closest year) as well as the data for 2004 (or closest year) were identified. The absolute percentage increase between 1995 and 2004 was calculated for each country or area with available information. Countries or areas that only provided data for one or two years between 1995 and 2004 were excluded from the sample, as were those that only reported data on one decade (either the 1990s or the 2000s).

Once all of the data were calculated and odd results revised, the countries and areas were arranged in two tables: one according to regional classification, and the other by income level (see below for definitions and a list of classifications). In each of the columns, the average (median) value for each of the previously identified categories was calculated following the formula: Σ values in Column A/number of countries and areas belonging to that category (i.e. by income and region).

Definitions[1] and data sources of variables used

Female labour force participation rates (table 2.1)

The labour force is defined as all persons of either sex who furnish or are available to furnish labour for the production of goods and services, during a specific reference period; it comprises all persons aged between 15 and 64 who were either employed or unemployed during that time. The labour force participation rate is calculated by dividing the labour force by the working-age population, expressed as a percentage.

Source: *KILM, Fourth edition*, table 1a.

Employment-to-population ratios by sex and by region (table 2.2)

Employment refers to people above a certain age who worked, or held a job, during a reference period. Employment data include both full-time and part-time workers whose remuneration is determined on the basis of hours worked or number of items produced and is independent of profits or expectation of profits.

The employment-to-population ratio provides information on the ability of an economy to create employment. It is defined as the proportion of a country's working-age population that is employed. A high ratio means that a large proportion of a country's population is employed, while a low ratio means

---

1. Definitions from ILO database on labour statistics (LABORSTA), at laborsta.ilo.org, and ILO: *Key Indicators of the Labour Market (KILM), Fourth edition* (Geneva, 2006), at www.ilo.org/public/english/employment/strat/kilm/indicators.htm#kilm1.

that a large share of the population is not involved directly in market-related activities, because they are either unemployed or (more likely) out of the labour force altogether. The employment-to-population ratio is calculated by dividing employment by the working-age population, expressed as a percentage.

Source: Individual country data: *KILM, Fourth edition*, table 2. Aggregates: ILO: Global Employment Trends Model 2005.

Unemployment rates by sex and by region (table 2.3)

Unemployment refers to all persons above a specified age who during the reference period were: (a) without work; (b) available for work; and (c) seeking work (i.e. had taken specific steps in a specified reference period to seek paid employment or self-employment). The unemployment rate is calculated by dividing unemployment by the labour force, expressed as a percentage.

Source: Individual country data: *KILM, Fourth edition*, table 8. Aggregates: ILO: Global Employment Trends Model 2005.

Female shares in non-agricultural paid employment (table 2.4)

The share of women in wage employment (paid employment) in the non-agricultural sector is the proportion of female workers in the non-agricultural sector expressed as a percentage of total employment in the sector. It is one of the indicators under Millennium Development Goal (MDG) 3 (promote gender equality and empower women).

It was calculated by dividing the total number of women in paid employment (employees) in the non-agricultural sector by the total number of people in paid employment (employees) in that same sector, expressed as a percentage.

The non-agricultural sector comprises industry and services. Under the International Standard Industrial Classification of all Economic Activities (ISIC), industry includes mining and quarrying (including oil production), manufacturing, construction and electricity, gas and water supply. Services include wholesale and retail trade; restaurants and hotels; transport, storage and communications; financial, insurance, real estate and business services; and community, social and personal services.

Source: United Nations Statistics Division: United Nations Common Database, at unstats. un.org/unsd/cdb.

Female shares in total paid employment (table 2.4)

The share of women in wage (or paid) employment is the proportion of female workers as a percentage of total wage employment. People in wage employment are those working as wage earners or salaried employees. The rest of the employed workers are self-employed, whether as own-account workers, cooperative members or contributing family workers (unpaid work).

The female share of total paid employment is calculated by dividing the total number of women in paid employment (employees) by the total number of employees in the economy, expressed as a percentage.

Source: ILO database on labour statistics (LABORSTA), table 2D, at laborsta.ilo.org.

These data are updated annually by LABORSTA and provided to the United Nations Statistics Division.

Percentage distribution of women workers by status in total female employment (figure 2.1)

This variable refers to female employment by status (unpaid, self-employed and employees) and shows how these trends have evolved in the last ten years.

Source: LABORSTA, table 2D.

Female shares in legislative and managerial positions (table 2.5)

According to the International Standard Classification of Occupations (ISCO-68), Major Group 2, Administrative and managerial workers, includes legislative officials and government administrators and managers, while ISCO-88 Major Group 1, Legislators, senior officials and managers, comprises legislators and senior officials, corporate managers and general managers. The share of women working in this top occupational group is calculated by dividing the absolute number of women employed in legislative and managerial positions by total employment of both sexes in that category, expressed as a percentage.

Source: Calculated on the basis of occupational data from LABORSTA, table 2C.

Gender pay gaps in manufacturing (figure 2.3)

This is calculated using the following equation: gender wage gap = 1 – (female wages/male wages) × 100.

Source: *KILM, Fourth edition*, table 15.

Country and area classifications

The information on the different variables defined above has been organized and analysed by grouping countries and areas according to the following categories:

(a) by region, based on geographical and political similarities;

(b) by income level, according to the World Bank income group classification.

(a) Regional classification

East Asia and Pacific (28): Australia; Brunei Darussalam; Cambodia; China; Fiji; Hong Kong (China); Indonesia; Japan; Democratic People's Republic of Korea; Republic of Korea; Lao People's Democratic Republic; Macau (China); Malaysia; Marshall Islands; Mongolia; Myanmar; Netherlands Antilles; New Zealand; Papua New Guinea; Philippines; Samoa; Singapore; Solomon Islands; Taiwan (China); Thailand; Timor-Leste; Tonga; Viet Nam.

Europe (non-EU) and Central Asia (23): Albania; Armenia; Azerbaijan; Belarus; Bosnia and Herzegovina; Bulgaria; Croatia; Georgia; Iceland; Kazakhstan; Kyrgyzstan; Republic of Moldova; Norway; Romania; Russian Federation; Serbia and Montenegro; Switzerland; Tajikistan; The former Yugoslav Republic of Macedonia; Turkey; Turkmenistan; Ukraine; Uzbekistan.

EU (25): Austria; Belgium; Cyprus; Czech Republic; Denmark; Estonia; Finland; France; Germany; Greece; Hungary; Ireland; Italy; Latvia; Lithuania; Luxembourg; Malta; Netherlands; Poland; Portugal; Slovakia; Slovenia; Spain; Sweden; United Kingdom.

Latin America and the Caribbean (30): Argentina; Aruba (Netherlands); Bahamas; Barbados; Belize; Bolivia; Brazil; Chile; Colombia; Costa Rica; Cuba; Dominica; Dominican Republic; Ecuador; El Salvador; Guatemala; Guyana; Haiti; Honduras; Jamaica; Mexico; Nicaragua; Panama; Paraguay; Peru; Puerto Rico (United States); Suriname; Trinidad and Tobago; Uruguay; Bolivarian Republic of Venezuela.

Middle East and North Africa (20): Algeria; Bahrain; Djibouti; Egypt; Islamic Republic of Iran; Iraq; Israel; Jordan; Kuwait; Lebanon; Libyan Arab Jamahiriya; Morocco; Oman; Qatar; Saudi Arabia; Syrian Arab Republic; Tunisia; United Arab Emirates; West Bank and Gaza Strip; Yemen.

North America (2): Canada; United States.

South Asia (8): Afghanistan; Bangladesh; Bhutan; India; Maldives; Nepal; Pakistan; Sri Lanka.

Sub-Saharan Africa (46): Angola; Benin; Botswana; Burkina Faso; Burundi; Cameroon; Cape Verde; Central African Republic; Chad; Comoros; Congo; Côte d'Ivoire; Democratic Republic of the Congo; Equatorial Guinea; Eritrea; Ethiopia; Gabon; Gambia; Ghana; Guinea; Guinea-Bissau; Kenya; Lesotho; Liberia; Madagascar; Malawi; Mali; Mauritania; Mauritius; Mozambique; Namibia; Niger; Nigeria; Rwanda; Sao Tome and Principe; Senegal; Sierra Leone; Somalia; South Africa; Sudan; Swaziland; United Republic of Tanzania; Togo; Uganda; Zambia; Zimbabwe.

(b) Income level classification

Low-income economies (59): Afghanistan; Bangladesh; Benin; Bhutan; Burkina Faso; Burundi; Cambodia; Cameroon; Central African Republic; Chad; Comoros; Congo; Côte d'Ivoire; Democratic Republic of the Congo; Eritrea; Ethiopia; Gambia; Ghana; Guinea; Guinea-Bissau; Haiti; India; Kenya; Democratic People's Republic of Korea; Kyrgyzstan; Lao People's Democratic Republic; Lesotho; Liberia; Madagascar; Malawi; Mali; Mauritania; Republic of Moldova; Mongolia; Mozambique; Myanmar; Nepal; Nicaragua; Niger; Nigeria; Pakistan; Papua New Guinea; Rwanda; Sao Tome and Principe; Senegal; Sierra Leone; Solomon Islands; Somalia; Sudan; Tajikistan; United Republic of Tanzania; Timor-Leste; Togo; Uganda; Uzbekistan; Viet Nam; Yemen; Zambia; Zimbabwe.

Lower middle-income economies (51): Albania; Algeria; Angola; Armenia; Azerbaijan; Belarus; Bolivia; Bosnia and Herzegovina; Brazil; Bulgaria; Cape Verde; China; Colombia; Cuba; Djibouti; Dominican Republic; Ecuador; Egypt; El Salvador; Fiji; Georgia; Guatemala; Guyana; Honduras; Indonesia; Islamic Republic of Iran; Iraq; Jamaica; Jordan; Kazakhstan; Maldives; Marshall Islands; Morocco; Namibia; Paraguay; Peru; Philippines; Romania; Samoa; Serbia and Montenegro; Sri Lanka; Suriname; Swaziland; Syrian Arab Republic; Thailand; The former Yugoslav Republic of Macedonia; Tonga; Tunisia; Turkmenistan; Ukraine; West Bank and Gaza.

Upper middle-income economies (30): Argentina; Barbados; Belize; Botswana; Chile; Costa Rica; Croatia; Czech Republic; Dominica; Equatorial Guinea; Estonia; Gabon; Hungary; Latvia; Lebanon; Libyan Arab Jamahiriya; Lithuania; Malaysia; Mauritius; Mexico; Oman; Panama; Poland; Russian Federation; Slovakia; South Africa; Trinidad and Tobago; Turkey; Uruguay; Bolivarian Republic of Venezuela.

High-income economies (42): Aruba (Netherlands); Australia; Austria; Bahamas; Bahrain; Belgium; Brunei Darussalam; Canada; Cyprus; Denmark; Finland; France; Germany; Greece; Hong Kong (China); Iceland; Ireland; Israel; Italy; Japan; Republic of Korea; Kuwait; Luxembourg; Macau (China); Malta; Netherlands; Netherlands Antilles; New Zealand; Norway; Portugal; Puerto Rico (United States); Qatar; Saudi Arabia; Singapore; Slovenia; Spain; Sweden; Switzerland; Taiwan (China); United Arab Emirates; United Kingdom; United States.

Countries and areas with available information by table

Tables 2.1, 2.2 and 2.3.
Female labour force participation rates and female-to-male ratios, employment-to-population ratio and unemployment rate by sex

List of countries and areas (173): Afghanistan; Albania; Algeria; Angola; Argentina; Armenia; Australia; Austria; Azerbaijan; Bahamas; Bahrain; Bangladesh; Barbados; Belarus; Belgium; Belize; Benin; Bhutan; Bolivia; Bosnia and Herzegovina; Botswana; Brazil; Brunei Darussalam; Bulgaria; Burkina Faso; Burundi; Cambodia; Cameroon; Canada; Cape Verde; Central African Republic; Chad; Chile; China; Colombia; Comoros; Congo; Costa Rica; Côte d'Ivoire; Croatia; Cuba; Cyprus; Czech Republic; Democratic Republic of the Congo; Denmark; Dominican Republic; Ecuador; Egypt; El Salvador; Equatorial Guinea; Eritrea; Estonia; Ethiopia; Fiji; Finland; France; Gabon; Gambia; Georgia; Germany; Ghana; Greece; Guatemala; Guinea; Guinea-Bissau; Guyana; Haiti; Honduras; Hong Kong (China); Hungary; Iceland; India; Indonesia; Islamic Republic of Iran; Iraq; Ireland; Israel; Italy; Jamaica; Japan; Jordan; Kazakhstan; Kenya; Democratic People's Republic of Korea; Republic of Korea; Kuwait; Kyrgyzstan; Lao People's Democratic Republic; Latvia; Lebanon; Liberia; Libyan Arab Jamahiriya; Lithuania; Luxembourg; Macau (China); Madagascar; Malawi; Malaysia; Maldives; Mali; Malta; Mauritania; Mauritius;

Mexico; Mongolia; Morocco; Mozambique; Myanmar; Namibia; Nepal; Netherlands; Netherlands Antilles; New Zealand; Nicaragua; Niger; Nigeria; Norway; Oman; Pakistan; Panama; Papua New Guinea; Paraguay; Peru; Philippines; Poland; Portugal; Puerto Rico (United States); Qatar; Republic of Moldova; Romania; Russian Federation; Rwanda; Saudi Arabia; Senegal; Serbia and Montenegro; Sierra Leone; Singapore; Slovakia; Slovenia; Solomon Islands; Somalia; South Africa; Spain; Sri Lanka; Sudan; Suriname; Swaziland; Sweden; Switzerland; Syrian Arab Republic; Tajikistan; United Republic of Tanzania; Thailand; The former Yugoslav Republic of Macedonia; Timor-Leste; Togo; Trinidad and Tobago; Tunisia; Turkey; Turkmenistan; Uganda; Ukraine; United Arab Emirates; United Kingdom; United States; Uruguay; Uzbekistan; Bolivarian Republic of Venezuela; Viet Nam; West Bank and Gaza Strip; Yemen; Zambia; Zimbabwe.

Table 2.4. Female shares in non-agricultural paid employment (MDG 3) and in total paid employment, 1995–2004

List of countries and areas (79): Argentina; Australia; Austria; Bahamas; Bangladesh; Barbados; Bolivia; Botswana; Brazil; Canada; Chile; Colombia; Costa Rica; Croatia; Cyprus; Czech Republic; Denmark; Dominican Republic; Ecuador; Egypt; El Salvador; Estonia; Finland; France; Georgia; Germany; Greece; Guatemala; Honduras; Hong Kong (China); Hungary; Iceland; Ireland; Israel; Italy; Jamaica; Japan; Republic of Korea; Latvia; Lithuania; Macau (China); Malaysia; Mauritius; Mexico; Namibia; Netherlands; Netherlands Antilles; New Zealand; Norway; Oman; Pakistan; Panama; Paraguay; Peru; Poland; Portugal; Puerto Rico; Republic of Moldova; Romania; Russian Federation; San Marino; Singapore; Slovakia; Slovenia; Spain; Sweden; Switzerland; Thailand; The former Yugoslav Republic of Macedonia; Trinidad and Tobago; Turkey; Ukraine; United Kingdom; United States; Uruguay; Bolivarian Republic of Venezuela; Viet Nam; West Bank and Gaza Strip; Zimbabwe.

Figure 2.1. Percentage distribution of women workers by status in total female employment by region, 1995 and 2004

List of countries and areas (68): Argentina; Australia; Austria; Bahamas; Bangladesh; Barbados; Bolivia; Botswana; Cameroon; Canada; Chile; Colombia; Costa Rica; Croatia; Czech Republic; Denmark;

Dominica; Ecuador; Egypt; El Salvador; Estonia; Finland; Georgia; Germany; Greece; Honduras; Hong Kong (China); Hungary; Ireland; Israel; Italy; Jamaica; Japan; Republic of Korea; Latvia; Lithuania; Macau (China); Malaysia; Mexico; Namibia; Netherlands; Netherlands Antilles; New Zealand; Norway; Pakistan; Panama; Peru; Poland; Portugal; Puerto Rico; Republic of Moldova; Romania; Russian Federation; Singapore; Slovenia; Spain; Switzerland; Thailand; The former Yugoslav Republic of Macedonia; Trinidad and Tobago; Turkey; Ukraine; United Kingdom; Uruguay; Bolivarian Republic of Venezuela; Viet Nam; West Bank and Gaza Strip; Zimbabwe.

Figure 2.2. Female-to-male gross enrolment ratios in primary, secondary and tertiary education

List of countries and areas (133): Albania; Argentina; Armenia; Aruba (Netherlands); Australia; Austria; Azerbaijan; Bahrain; Bangladesh; Barbados; Belarus; Belgium; Belize; Botswana; Brazil; Brunei Darussalam; Bulgaria; Burkina Faso; Burundi; Cambodia; Cameroon; Canada; Cape Verde; Chile; China; Colombia; Comoros; Congo; Costa Rica; Croatia; Cuba; Cyprus; Czech Republic; Denmark; Djibouti; Dominican Republic; El Salvador; Eritrea; Estonia; Ethiopia; Finland; France; Georgia; Germany; Ghana; Greece; Guatemala; Guyana; Hungary; Iceland; India; Indonesia; Islamic Republic of Iran; Iraq; Ireland; Israel; Italy; Jamaica; Japan; Jordan; Kazakhstan; Kenya; Republic of Korea; Kyrgyzstan; Lao People's Democratic Republic; Latvia; Lebanon; Lesotho; Libyan Arab Jamahiriya; Lithuania; Luxembourg; Macau (China); Madagascar; Malawi; Malaysia; Malta; Marshall Islands; Mauritania; Mauritius; Mexico; Mongolia; Morocco; Namibia; Nepal; Netherlands; Netherlands Antilles; Nicaragua; Niger; Nigeria; Norway; Oman; Pakistan; Panama; Paraguay; Peru; Philippines; Poland; Portugal; Qatar; Republic of Moldova; Romania; Rwanda; Samoa; Sao Tome and Principe; Saudi Arabia; Serbia and Montenegro; Sierra Leone;

Slovakia; Slovenia; South Africa; Spain; Suriname; Swaziland; Sweden; Switzerland; Tajikistan; Thailand; The former Yugoslav Republic of Macedonia; Tonga; Trinidad and Tobago; Tunisia; Turkey; Uganda; Ukraine; United Arab Emirates; United Kingdom; United States; Uruguay; Uzbekistan; Bolivarian Republic of Venezuela; Viet Nam; West Bank and Gaza Strip; Zambia; Zimbabwe.

Table 2.5. Female shares in legislative and managerial positions

List of countries and areas (73): Argentina; Australia; Austria; Bahamas; Bangladesh; Barbados; Belgium; Bolivia; Botswana; Canada; Chile; Colombia; Costa Rica; Croatia; Cyprus; Czech Republic; Denmark; Dominica; Egypt; El Salvador; Estonia; Ethiopia; Finland; Georgia; Germany; Greece; Hong Kong (China); Hungary; Iceland; Ireland; Israel; Italy; Japan; Republic of Korea; Latvia; Lithuania; Macau (China); Malaysia; Mauritius; Mexico; Netherlands; Netherlands Antilles; New Zealand; Norway; Oman; Pakistan; Panama; Peru; Philippines; Poland; Portugal; Puerto Rico; Republic of Moldova; Romania; Russian Federation; Saint Lucia; Saudi Arabia; Singapore; Slovakia; Slovenia; Spain; Sweden; Switzerland; Thailand; Trinidad and Tobago; Turkey; Ukraine; United Arab Emirates; United Kingdom; United States; Bolivarian Republic of Venezuela; Viet Nam; West Bank and Gaza Strip.

Figure 2.3. Gender pay gaps in manufacturing

List of countries and areas (37): Australia; Austria; Bahrain; Botswana; Brazil; Bulgaria; Costa Rica; Cyprus; Czech Republic; Denmark; Egypt; El Salvador; Finland; Georgia; Germany; Hong Kong (China); Hungary; Iceland; Islamic Republic of Iran; Ireland; Japan; Jordan; Kazakhstan; Republic of Korea; Latvia; Lithuania; Luxembourg; Netherlands; New Zealand; Norway; Singapore; Sri Lanka; Sweden; Switzerland; Taiwan (China); United Kingdom; West Bank and Gaza Strip.